A PRACTICAL GUIDE TO
FORENSIC PSYCHOLOGY

A PRACTICAL GUIDE TO FORENSIC PSYCHOLOGY

PAUL L. DEYOUB, PH.D.

with

GRETCHEN V. K. DOUTHIT, M.S.

JASON ARONSON INC.
Northvale, New Jersey
London

Production Editor: Elaine Lindenblatt

This book was set in 10 pt. Goudy Oldstyle by Alpha Graphics of Pittsfield, New Hampshire and printed and bound by Book-mart Press of North Bergen, New Jersey.

Library of Congress Cataloging-in-Publication Data

Deyoub, Paul L.
    A practical guide to forensic psychology / by Paul L. Deyoub with
Gretchen V. K. Douthit.
      p. cm.
    Includes bibliographical references and index.
    ISBN 1-56821-668-8 (hardcover : alk. paper)
    1. Psychology, Forensic—Practice. 2. Psychology, Forensic—
Vocational guidance. I. Douthit, Gretchen V. K. II. Title.
RA1148.D49 1996
614'1—dc20   96-12668

Manufactured in the United States of America. Jason Aronson Inc. offers books and cassettes. For information and catalog write to Jason Aronson Inc., 230 Livingston Street, Northvale, New Jersey 07647.

Dedicated to
our spouses,
Nancy
and
Scotty,
who have supported us
in this work.

CONTENTS

FOREWORD

The field of forensic psychology, the interface of psychology and the law, is an area where potential remains largely untapped by clinical practitioners. While the rapid growth of doctoral level psychologists has resulted in an overabundance of clinicians in many parts of the country, the forensic population is still underserved. At one time there were legal constraints to forensic work, which was felt to be the province of the forensic psychiatrist. However, the status of clinical psychology in the courtroom gained judicial recognition in 1962 with the landmark case of Jenkins v. United States.[1] In this decision the United States Court of Appeals reversed a trial court verdict and confirmed that psychologists could offer expert testimony on the question of mental disease or defect. Since psychologists are now readily accepted in almost all courts as expert witnesses, the major reason that many psychologists tend to avoid the forensic arena appears to be twofold: (1) many psychologists are intimidated by the prospect of going to court and having their expertise challenged and possibly even attacked, and (2) even many of the most well-trained psychologists are limited in their knowledge of how to apply their clinical training to the legal system.

In this volume, Dr. Deyoub addresses both of these issues in depth. He advocates a forensic psychology practice that emphasizes objectivity, integrity, and the search for the "truth." He stresses that psychologists should not accept referrals from private parties, lest they fall into the trap of becoming a "hired gun." By accepting only referrals that come directly through the court or some other third party or agency (e.g., Social Security Disability Determination) the psychologist will much more likely be viewed as an unbiased evaluator providing the system with information, rather than an advocate for one side or the other. In this type of forensic practice it is difficult for either side to portray the psychologist as an adversary, and so the likelihood of being vigorously attacked on cross examination is greatly diminished. Thus the psychologist who does objective, unbiased forensic evaluations has little to fear.

With regard to the second issue, this volume presents a straightforward, no-nonsense approach to forensic assessment and evaluation. It is clearly a "how to"

---

1. Jenkins v. United States, 113 U.S. App. D.C. 300, 307, F2nd 637 (1962).

manual that provides a great deal of information in a concise, easy-to-read format. It is replete with case examples and sample reports that deal with most of the major issues faced by the forensic evaluator. These are helpful in demonstrating that the psychologist will be able to incorporate most of the skills he is already using on a daily basis, if he chooses to move into forensic work. The reader is assured that being a legal expert is not a prerequisite for beginning a forensic practice, although familiarizing yourself with the law is certainly important. It is also made clear that there is a lot more to forensic psychology than just the high profile criminal cases that get most of the attention. Doing forensic work certainly does not mean having to place yourself in the limelight.

Dr. Deyoub shares a wealth of personal experience gained from eighteen years in forensic work. The information presented will certainly be of value to the psychologist who is already working in the forensic area. However, it will be especially useful to the psychologist who is contemplating beginning a forensic practice but has been reluctant to do so because of the factors discussed above.

Michael J. Simon, Ph.D.
Supervising Forensic Psychologist
Arkansas State Hospital

1

THE BASICS
OF FORENSIC PRACTICE

This book is a practice manual in forensic psychology. Forensic psychology includes all areas where psychology and law interface. It includes psychological evaluations for the courts, administrative or governmental agencies, and other decision makers or fact finders. I also consider assessments of handicapped children under the requirements of Public Law 94–142 to be in the realm of forensic assessment.

This book is quite different from other published forensic books. It is not a referenced or academic work. It is not a survey on law and psychology. Academic sources are excellent as reference books and I use them as such in my practice. This book, however, is intended to be a manual about the day-to-day practice of forensic psychology. It grows out of eighteen years—the last twelve in private practice—during which I have been primarily involved in forensic work. I practice in a metropolitan area of approximately 350,000 people and also serve several rural areas within an eighty-mile radius of the city. It is the private practice of psychology by doctoral-level psychologists that I will be describing in this book, although I hope the guidelines in the book will also be helpful to other mental health professionals.

ADVANTAGES OF FORENSIC PRACTICE

There are several distinct advantages to a forensic practice. The psychologist is not dependent on the whims of health maintenance organizations, managed care companies, or insurance companies, all of which are increasingly trying to restrict patients' access to mental health services or to impose their own requirements for inclusion on preferred provider lists. Forensic psychology is not dependent on insurance reimbursement and, in fact, insurance will not cover evaluations done for the courts. If clients wish to file insurance claims for psychological evaluations, that is their responsibility. The forensic psychologist must be paid at the time of the evaluation. The client cannot owe money on an evaluation that may well be unfavorable.

There are usually few, if any, practitioners in a given community doing forensic work. Having an assessment-only practice, following the guidelines outlined below, will allow you to stand out from other providers, especially in communities that are saturated with therapists competing for the psychotherapy dollar. In most communities there is a tremendous need for psychologists who can do high-quality evaluations.

In a forensic practice a psychologist can be more productive through the use of technicians, since several evaluations can take place at the same time. Clients can take paper-and-pencil tests, while others are taking intelligence tests from a technician, and still another client is interviewed by the psychologist, all at the same time. This is not possible in a psychotherapeutic practice, since there is no way to do therapy except to devote that hour and one's full attention to that patient.

And last, a forensic practice, especially an assessment-only practice, avoids the actual practice of psychotherapy. It avoids dependent patients, after-hours responsibility, and sometimes a great deal of effort and work for an hourly fee. Unlike much psychotherapy, forensic work is rewarding because it is time-limited, it results in a finished product, and it impacts on very important decisions affecting the lives of clients.

GUIDELINES FOR A SUCCESSFUL PRACTICE

These are the guidelines I consider essential for having a successful forensic practice.

1) *Stay independent—do not become a "hired gun."* I consider this probably the most important factor in establishing a forensic practice. *Do not* do evaluations for either the defense or prosecution in a criminal case. Do not do child custody evaluations for either parent's attorney. Do not do disability evaluations for private attorneys. Once you start doing evaluations for private parties, you can forget about having the kind of forensic practice I will be describing in this book. You may be successful, but it will be as a hired expert and you will be disregarded and irrelevant to most judges and attorneys in the long run. The purpose of defense psychologists is to influence juries, but in all other settings without a jury, their testimony is disregarded.

All of my evaluations—forty or more each week—are done for the courts or other third parties. Around the country, state departments of mental health are contracting with individual providers to perform forensic criminal evaluations. I perform these evaluations in the jails, or in my office if a defendant is out on bond. If a defense attorney calls and wants his client evaluated, I tell him to submit a request for a forensic evaluation to the court, putting at issue his or her client's mental state. The court can then order an evaluation and the results can be introduced by either the defense or the prosecution, depending on the findings. (In most cases, defense attorneys do not want to do this, since they know the issues of competency and responsibility are not germane to their case. They are usually looking for extenuating or mitigating circumstances or some type of exotic psychiatric or psychological defense that a traditional forensic evaluation will not provide.)

This law of objectivity applies to every area of forensic work. For juvenile delinquents, I take referrals only from the Department of Human Services or the juvenile court. For child abuse cases, I only do evaluations when the court orders the evaluation of the parent and, possibly, the abused child. In custody cases, I take referrals only from the juvenile or chancery court. If an attorney for one parent calls requesting an evaluation, I tell the attorney I will be happy to do the evaluation, *if* it comes through the court and *all* parties are evaluated—both parents and the child or children in dispute. In Social Security disability cases that have been denied, I will not do evaluations for claimants. I do them on an appeal, only when ordered to do so by an administrative law judge.

In forensic psychology, as opposed to psychotherapy, the goal is not to help individual clients, although they may benefit indirectly from this work. The forensic psychologist should strive to provide the truth. In the beginning there will be referrals you will not get because of this approach, but ultimately you will be respected by judges and other agencies and third parties who wish to receive objective evaluations. After one or two appearances in a particular court, the judge and lawyers will see that you are "a straight shooter" and the court will start making referrals to you to assist them in making decisions.

2) *Give recommendations—say what you think and what you have found.* This advice is directly in contrast to that contained in most of the more academic works written about forensic psychology. Following an established psychological tradition, those books urge the psychologist to hedge and never state a direct opinion. They recommend more ambiguous reports, giving different possibilities for disposition without taking a direct position. This is contrary to how I have built my practice. I give conclusions, recommendations, and suggestions for disposition in almost every evaluation I do. I write reports in plain language, rather than in "psychobabble." This is what the courts and most other decision-making bodies want. In child custody cases, for example, judges are very frustrated when an expert will not say what should happen to the child or who the most capable custodial parent is. In abuse and neglect cases, judges want to hear what recommendations you have, that is, whether the child should be returned to the parent and/or whether the parent is a danger to the child.

In most forensic books, predicting dangerousness is approached with great caution. The basic message is that dangerousness cannot be accurately predicted by psychologists. I consider this view to be academic. If I am evaluating a mother who has a pattern of abuse and the evaluation reveals low intelligence, poor coping ability, substance abuse, marital instability, and other factors, then it is my responsibility to give my best clinical judgment about what will happen to that child if the child is returned. On the other hand, parents who have more positive traits deserve a chance to try again with their child. None of this is without risk, because you can make the wrong decision. The court understands, however, that you are giving your best professional opinion. The judge or jury is still responsible for the final decision.

Despite this advice to make specific recommendations, it is important to know situations in which a recommendation or opinion is inappropriate. In Social Security evaluations, the deciding agency does not want the psychologist to state whether or not the person is disabled. In criminal cases, the psychologist should never comment on the person's guilt, innocence, or intent, but should stick to issues of responsibility and competency.

3) *Provide timely services.* This means being available to see clients within a reasonable period of time, having quick turnaround time on reports, and being available to appear in court. Reports should be prepared within a few days. Having a quick turnaround time is essential and will make you valued and unique among other providers. In fact, most of the third parties for whom I work require that evaluations be received on a timely basis. Psychologists who are busy with psychotherapy are often not able to see clients for evaluation quickly and or to prepare reports in a timely fashion.

4) *Provide services at a low cost.* In my practice, I do the majority of evaluations for a two- or three-hour charge. Appearing in court is extra, and more complicated evaluations might take longer and require additional charges. Staying with these fee guidelines, which I have done for the past twelve years, will differentiate you from others in the community who are charging huge fees for psychological evaluations.

5) *Have no fear of appearing in court.* Most practitioners have some trepidation about appearing in court and these fears are fueled by some of the more academic forensic works. These books say that you had better be prepared for court, or the other side will tear you apart. This basic assumption about the adversarial court system comes from the approach of being a hired expert. In those cases, each side must try to discredit the testimony of the expert hired by the other side and you may indeed have something to fear.

In the evaluations I do, I end up testifying on one side or another, since I make specific recommendations in my reports. However, I have come to those conclusions as the result of an objective examination of the facts of the case. In my experience, it is extremely difficult for the losing side to vigorously attack you on cross-examination, knowing that you were not a biased expert but that you were appointed by the court to perform the evaluation. In fact, over 90 percent of the evaluations I do are submitted to the judge or fact-finder and are accepted by both sides, without my having to appear to testify.

6) *Be available to all parties.* If you are a neutral party doing assessments, attorneys from both sides will refer to you, social service agencies involved in the case will be contacting you, or the attorney *ad litem* will want to talk to you. You should maintain good relationships with all parties, since each one of them will probably refer to you in the future. A losing attorney will ask for you in another case, knowing that he lost as the result of objective court-appointed testimony.

7) *Deal respectfully with clients being evaluated.* People coming in for assessment are often angry and hostile, as opposed to therapy clients who come in wanting your help. They realize that your evaluation can hurt them. This is especially true in custody cases or in cases of parents referred for evaluation in abuse and neglect cases. Even Social Security claimants come in angry, in pain, and feeling that they have been cheated by the system. Juvenile delinquents brought in by detention officers or their parents are angry, hostile, and rebellious.

It is important that all of these people, no matter how angry or hostile, are treated with respect and dignity by all members of your staff. In my office, testing rooms are provided that are private and comfortable, so that clients can take MMPIs and other tests. They are offered something to drink, they are offered frequent breaks when they are taking long paper-and-pencil tests, and they may even break the sessions up into two or three visits, if necessary. (However, I never allow them to take test data home, which I have seen some practitioners do.)

Every client being assessed should receive informed consent. You should tell them that this is not therapy, that nothing is confidential, and that everything they say will or could be in your report. Never tell clients, or anyone else involved in the case, your impressions or conclusions until you finish the evaluation. This is another example of how you have to think differently from a psychotherapist, who might legitimately share impressions with a client. If you tell a client that you have a certain impression during the evaluation, it will come back to haunt you, especially if you write a report that does not state exactly what you said in person. You may even be accused of prejudice by the other side.

Do not give clients copies of your evaluations, even if requested to do so. The evaluations are sent to the judge or agency requesting the evaluation, and usually to the lawyers, if the clients are represented. Individual clients or other interested parties may request copies from the court or other third parties which ordered the report, with appropriate signed releases.

8) *Don't allow yourself to be crippled by ethical dilemmas or fears of being sued.* The job of a forensic psychologist is to get to the truth of a situation. You must be as ethical as you can possibly be, but it is impossible to have a busy forensic practice if you are crippled by doubt and rumination. The issue is reasonableness. Are

you doing evaluations and reaching conclusions which are reasonable, based on sound judgment according to professional standards?

In each case, you must evaluate all parties, realizing that often no one will be happy with your conclusions. For example, if I recommend in a child custody case that one parent have custody and the other parent have only supervised visitation, then that parent is the aggrieved party. Nothing will prevent that parent from suing. I have been lucky enough over the last eighteen years not to be sued, but I realize it could happen at any time. The only obligation I have is to reach my conclusions based on reasonable data from the test results, background information, clinical interview, and my overall clinical judgment.

Clearly, one should not be involved in forensic psychology if one does not fundamentally believe that psychologists, psychiatrists, and other mental health professionals have something to offer. Those who believe that psychologists and psychiatrists should stay out of the courtroom are entitled to their views, but this is certainly not the majority opinion. All the courts and administrative bodies for which I have done work value psychological testimony. This work is worthwhile, and psychological testimony is superior to lay opinion.

SOURCES OF FORENSIC WORK

Following is a list of third parties who request forensic evaluations and are responsible for payment.

Type of Evaluation	*Responsible Party*
Juvenile delinquency	Juvenile Court or State Division of Youth Services responsible for detention, assessment, and referral
Abuse and neglect— evaluation of child victims and offending parents	State Department of Human Services, the Juvenile Court, or the County
Social Security determination	State Social Security Disability Determination Office
Criminal forensic evaluation	State Department of Human Services, State Mental Health Division, or the forensic State Hospital
Child custody	Litigants ordered to pay for a court-ordered evaluation of both parents and children

Children and adolescents evaluated for a PL 94–142 handicapping condition	School district or regional educational cooperative
Hospitalized adults and juveniles	Psychiatric hospital

As can be seen, I am recommending a private forensic assessment practice put together by contracts with many different payment sources. All the state agencies mentioned above, the state hospitals, school districts, and private psychiatric hospitals sign contracts for evaluations. This approach to building a forensic practice may seem logical and obvious, but actually it is atypical. The typical forensic psychologist is hired by clients and involved in the adversarial system. This means both sides parade their experts in front of the court, especially in custody cases or personal injury cases. Forensic psychologists working for mental health centers and forensic inpatient units are probably closer to the model of objectivity and freedom from influence that I am recommending for psychologists in private practice.

In signing contracts for forensic evaluations, it is vital to arrange the contracts on a fee-for-service basis: the contract should pay a flat rate for each evaluation done. This not only encourages speed and efficiency in your practice, but it allows you to be independent rather than being "owned" for a certain number of hours. If you are paid by the evaluation, you can hire as many technicians or other psychologists as you need to get the job done, and you are rewarded for efficiency.

A psychologist with these kinds of contracts will not receive the high fees that are sometimes charged in private practice, since these agencies are usually under severe financial pressures, but the volume of work available will result in a financially successful practice. With so many sources of payment, losing any particular contract will not be a threat to your practice. In this business, contracts will run out and personnel in contracting agencies will change, but if you have earned a solid reputation as an honest, objective, not-for-hire forensic evaluator, there will be no shortage of work. You also will have the satisfaction of knowing that you are independent and do not have to sacrifice any of your integrity or objectivity to do this work.

2

COURT TESTIMONY

Psychologists and mental health professionals probably fear court testimony more than anything else. Other forensic books and seminars on these subjects seem to perpetuate the fear and anxiety about testifying. Much of this is based on the tradition of adversarial testimony and reflects the problem of psychologists as expert witnesses for one side or the other. When a mental health professional is hired by one side, the expert is seen as an enemy by the other side and cross-examination can be intense, even hostile. The expert will be asked questions about who hired him and how much he is being paid. In general, every attempt will be made to discredit him and render his testimony irrelevant.

Mental health professionals are sometimes offended by these attacks, since they consider their results truthful and in the interest of their client. However, it is easy to see why psychological results in this adversarial system are open to question. If the defense secures evaluations on its own, rather than having the court order the evaluations, the experts will only end up testifying if the reports are favorable to the defense. Even if the experts think they found the truth, it will not be perceived that way by the court, the prosecution, or a jury. Being attacked on the stand is then just a natural consequence of the system they are working in and the way they were hired to do evaluations.

On the other hand, if you stick with the policy of doing evaluations only for neutral fact-finders, it will not take long before lawyers and judges recognize you as a psychologist who is objective and professional, thereby ensuring a pleasant and professional court appearance. In the vast majority of cases, testimony will not be necessary, since the parties will reach an agreement out of court. On occasion, however, the side receiving unfavorable results will want to question you on the stand. In those cases, you will be challenged not on the basis of your motivation or who paid you, but on the validity of the results. If you performed the evaluation for the court, the state or federal government, or an agency appointed by the court, or if you did an evaluation both parties agreed to, then hostile, discrediting tactics will not be used against you. After appearing in court hundreds of times, I can say that there have been few instances when there has been vigorous or heated cross-examination. Court appearances are usually very civilized and respectful. The typical testimony will go something like this:

First, you will be sworn in and asked your name and address. You will be asked to state your qualifications. As the lawyer asks for your qualifications, the other side may stipulate, that is, accept your qualifications as an expert, especially if they are familiar with your work. If they do not stipulate, state briefly what your qualifications are. Include your education, the years you graduated, the type of license you hold, any national organizations to which you belong, a brief history of positions you have held since graduation, and your current position and the nature of your practice. You will also be asked how many times you have testified in court and you can state what your court involvement is on the average per year. If the opposing lawyers ask for more information, you can give additional details.

When talking about your qualifications, it is important not to exaggerate your background, experience, or qualifications. You will sometimes be asked if you are a medical doctor. If you are a psychologist doing evaluations, the answer, of course, is, "No, I am not." The testimony of doctoral level psychologists is highly accepted around the country. There have been a few challenges to neurological testimony involving neuropsychological testing, but, for the most part, doctoral level psychologists will not have a problem being accepted as experts in assessment. Psychiatrists will naturally be experts on questions involving medication, but psychologists who administer psychological tests and perform comprehensive evaluations have parity with psychiatrists, if not superiority over them, in their role as experts before the court. (The same is not true of master's level mental health professionals. Although such persons are often qualified, I have heard lawyers refer to them as "just a social worker" or "just a counselor.")

At times you may be asked to explain your qualifications in the particular area for which you are testifying. For example, in a forensic criminal case, you may be asked to explain your background in forensic psychology or in criminal evaluation. State your training in this area and the nature of your practice. If you are asked whether you are an expert in the area of sexual abuse, if that is what the case involves, state approximately how many sexual abuse cases you see per year, the fact that you have attended workshops in this area, and that you have testified in court before on this subject matter. The court is not looking for an expert with a Ph.D. in sexual abuse, since that doesn't exist, but a psychologist who has experience, knowledge, and some training in that particular area. If you are not an expert in a particular area, it is important to admit it.

Once you have stated your qualifications on direct examination, the other lawyer may ask additional questions, or, if it is hostile cross-exmination, he or she may try to diminish your experience in the area for which you are testifying. Unless you are grossly underqualified for some reason, the judge will almost always indicate that you are an expert. For the sake of a possible appeal, the opposing lawyer may object to your qualifications as an expert, but that should not worry you.

After you have been qualified as an expert by the judge, direct examination will proceed. Direct examination is very easy, because you are providing information that is presumably beneficial to the party that put you on the stand, even though you originally performed the evaluation as an objective expert. The most common direct examination follows the written report that you generated for the court. The lawyer will first ask you how the case was referred, under what circumstances, when you saw the client or family members, and what you did. For example, if it is a custody case, you would say that you were asked by the court to evaluate the children and the disputing divorced parents. If they were referred in some other way, you would simply state how they came to you. State the dates you saw the parties, the tests you administered, the nature of the interviews, the time you spent, and anything else you believe is relevant. If you read reports or talked to other professionals, state that. Although you want to include all the facts, keep your answers brief and then wait for the next question.

After being asked what you did, do not go into your findings until you are asked about them. The lawyer questioning you may go in a different direction from what you anticipate. Some lawyers will want you to go over the test results and the interview data for each person. Others may just ask for a summary of your findings. Your role at this point is to answer specific questions, not to provide information that is not asked for. If you wish to elaborate on an answer, ask if you may explain.

When you are asked for your conclusions, listen carefully to the question and answer it as specifically as you can. The lawyer will ask for your conclusions in a way that he or she wants to ask the question. Remember, the lawyers already have your written report. The lawyer questioning you is choosing what he or she wants the judge or jury to hear. For example, in a custody case you may be asked where you recommend that the child be placed. You may be asked very specifically what type of visitation you recommend and how the parties can handle certain conflicts. Other times you may be asked to state your conclusions in a more general way.

In criminal cases, it is particularly important to respond only to the question asked. If you are asked the question, "Is the defendant able to appreciate the charges against him?" you are able to answer directly. After all, determining that fact was the point of the forensic criminal evaluation you did. In most criminal cases you will also be asked, "Did the defendant understand right from wrong?" and "Was the defendant able to conform his behavior to the requirements of the law at the time of the alleged offense?" Those questions should be answered with a straightforward yes or no. Do not elaborate or add details unless asked to do so.

If you do not wait for the question and do not limit your testimony to that question, you might blurt out something that is inappropriate, such as the intent of the defendant, facts about the crime, or other specific testimony that is essentially a legal conclusion. In one case, I was asked questions about the intent and motives of the defendant, clearly issues for the jury, since they went to the issue of whether the crime was involuntary manslaughter, manslaughter, or second degree murder. I did not have to respond to those questions because the other side objected and the judge sustained the objection.

In all cases, the lawyers are responsible for objecting and the judge is responsible for determining rules of evidence, not you. Many forensic publications and seminars unnecessarily scare psychologists into feeling they have to be legal experts to testify in court. You do not have to know rules of evidence or all the ins and outs of the law to be a good witness. Naturally, the more you know the better, but it is more important to know your field and to respond precisely and carefully to the questions asked.

Actually, problems can arise from knowing too much (or thinking you know a lot) about the legal issues involved. I remember seeing a psychologist testify that it was not appropriate for him to respond to a question because it was a legal issue. The judge tore him up. The lesson there is that you never turn to a judge and say what you think about matters of law. The judge and lawyers will embarrass you if you attempt to assert yourself in a legal sense in a courtroom. If you think there may be an issue of privilege and the lawyers don't object, state your concern and let the judge decide.

When you do go to court, always take the chart with you. Never alter any of its documents. It will be extremely rare for the judge and jury to want to see the chart, since they are relying on your testimony and summary written report. However, if a lawyer wants to see your records, including your notes and raw data, this is not for you to object to. You were asked to perform a psychological evaluation for the court, so everything you did, from the moment you saw the client until the final written report was submitted, is a matter for the court to see. My clients are told from the beginning that everything I do with them will be subject to court disclosure. If one side has a problem with the request to produce records, it is up to their attorney to object.

I have seen psychologists foolishly turn to a judge and refuse to turn over a record. There is no one in higher authority than the person behind the bench. If the judge tells you to turn over a record, you hand it over. Even if you are testifying as a therapist, rather than in an evaluation role, it is the lawyer's job to object to the production of records, not yours. If a judge orders you to turn over records, even in a therapy case, you must do so. In those circumstances, you are not violating any legal or ethical principles. Again, you may hear some different things on this matter from seminars and books about court testimony. These are the same sources which assert that to be a forensic psychologist you have to be proficient in the law. I could not disagree more strongly. Psychologists are experts in psychology and that is what we should stick to; legal issues should be left to the lawyers and the judge.

When cross-examination starts, it will not be particularly hostile. Much ammunition is taken away from the cross-examining lawyer because everyone knows how you came to do the evaluation. Nevertheless, there may be times that the cross-examination will be vigorous and challenging. In such circumstances, it is important to remain calm and nondefensive. Just stick to your report and state your results. Never talk back, attack, or do anything but answer the questions.

You may be asked all kinds of hypotheticals. For example, you will be asked whether it would change your opinion if you knew certain information that you didn't know. In answering these questions, stick to common sense. If the information is profound, you might state that it could possibly change your opinion, but that, based on the information available to you, you stand by your report. For example, the cross-examining attorney might say, "Doctor, would it change your opinion to know that the mother whom you recommend have custody had a positive drug screen for cocaine two days ago?" You would look foolish to say no, since this factor would obviously cause you some concern. You cannot stick by your results with proposed information like that. You should respond, "Yes, if Mrs. Smith had a positive drug screen two days ago, which I am hearing about now for the first time, this would cause me concern." You could further add that you would have to study the facts presented, talk to the client, and determine what modifications you would want to make in your recommendations. Do not be tricked into changing your testimony wholesale, but acknowledge that this is new information that could change your opinion and that it would take a study of the presented facts and perhaps a revisit with the client to reevaluate your original recommendation.

At other times, so-called factual information presented to surprise you may not be relevant at all. It may even be information that you were already aware of. The point is to be sensible when answering these questions. Everyone will roll their eyes and dismiss your testimony if you stick to a previous conclusion when factual information is presented that anyone would know was important.

Other times you may be attacked on the basis that you could have done something more in the evaluation. You may be asked any number of questions along these lines, since there is no limit to what you have not done in a particular evaluation. In a child custody case, for example, you could have seen the father one more time. You could have performed additional tests on the child or on the opposing parent. You could have seen one of the grandparents or an aunt that had information relevant to the case. A related line of inquiry is whether you obtained records from other treatment sources. You can do some of this, but you should prioritize your time and energy, realizing the importance of completing the evaluation in as timely a manner as possible. You cannot interview the entire extended family, administer neuropsychological tests to each person, or obtain records from ten or fifteen years ago. If you didn't interview a particular person, administer a certain test, or request or obtain certain records, simply say so. Be confident and be as thorough as you can be and your practice will thrive.

Other challenges on cross-examination will be quite easy to handle. If, for example, you stated that a defendant with a history of schizophrenia was able to appreciate the criminality of his behavior at the time of the offense, the defense attorney may ask all kinds of questions about the nature of the defendant's mental illness and may suggest ways in which the defendant was not capable of differentiating right from wrong or was unable to control his behavior. The lawyer may emphasize how many times the defendant has been in the state hospital, all of which is irrelevant to the specific question about responsibility for a particular offense. In cases like that, there is no question of mental illness. The issue is whether the mental illness affected the defendant's ability to be responsible. Remember what you wrote in the report and why, and you should have no problem answering this line of questioning. Other times you may be handed test data and asked to reach a conclusion based on what someone else did. Don't do it. Have integrity and tell the lawyer that you can only reach conclusions based on your examination of the individuals and not on someone else's test data.

One challenge to testimony which is particularly popular on the forensic psychology seminar circuit is the Ziskin (1970) approach on cross-examination. Ziskin's position is that psychological test data cannot be defended as reliable, valid, or predictive and that such data is easily challenged as inappropriate for courtroom testimony. This approach on cross-examination is grossly overestimated in its effectiveness and is not a significant problem on a day-to-day practice level. In over fifteen years of testifying in court, I have never been discredited by this line of questioning on cross-examination.

The Ziskin method attacks the profession wholesale. It asks the judge or jury to believe that the testifying mental health expert has no expert testimony to offer at all. This position will be rejected by the court. Your presence on the witness stand is already a strong assertion that psychology is a scientific profession accepted by the court, since the court retained you to answer clinical questions related to the issues in dispute. Either the profession is valued for its expert testimony, including its test results, or it is not. If you are doing evaluations and testifying, you are obviously seen as an expert with something of value to contribute to the proceedings. The possibility of a Ziskin attack, however, does caution us to be careful about what we do and to make sure our techniques have some relationship to our conclusions.

There is a practical aspect of the Ziskin approach that works to the psychologist's benefit. As soon as the cross-examining attorney begins to apply this technique, everyone's eyes glaze over and the judge and especially the jury begin to tune out. This nitpicking about individual tests and scales is very boring to everyone in the courtroom and I have seen judges on many occasions become impatient with such questions. This approach rarely accomplishes its goal in the courtroom.

A typical attack using the Ziskin approach might start by asking detailed questions about the instruments used in the evaluation. The attorney might ask you to explain each MMPI scale, what the scale means, and what proof there is that it measures what you say it does. You might be asked question after question about the MMPI research literature and how you think the MMPI measures what it measures in your particular evaluation. Let's say you have an MMPI profile that suggests an individual has a psychopathic deviant personality and you state that it is likely that this person will continue to drink and put his children at risk. Using the Ziskin approach, you might be asked to explain how the psychopathic deviant scale predicts alcohol use and how that would result in danger to the child. The lawyer might say that a high score on Scale 4 on the MMPI does not preclude adequate parenting and might assert that there is no research establishing this scale as a criteria for parenthood or for decisions about custody. You can answer the question about the relationship between the profile and actual parenting by interpreting what this elevation means and what it means in this particular individual, based on your expert opinion. In addition, you can state that you have experience with similar profiles in a large number of cases.

If the attorney continues to attack the testing and ask research-related questions, the best defense is to acknowledge that you are not an expert on every research study on the MMPI or other tests being attacked, but that they are accepted techniques of practice and you are experienced in their use. If the instruments are customarily used by the profession, you have the right to draw conclusions from them and the court will uphold you in doing so.

When asked Ziskin types of questions, you should also state that your recommendations are based on your clinical judgment, considering all the information gathered in the evaluation, including the test results, background information, and interview data. You state that, in your professional opinion, *all* of the results, not just the MMPI or any other particular test, point to a certain set of conclusions about the parties involved. This is one of the most effective responses to this line of questioning, since it renders any particular criticism of one test or one scale on a test meaningless. In the example above, the man who obtained the Scale 4 MMPI profile might also have a high MacAndrew Scale, a history of drug abuse, a criminal record, and a history of spousal abuse. The answer to the attorney's line of questioning is that all of these indicators are relevant. You state that, in your experience and based on the test protocol and the interview data, this individual is psychopathic in personality and will place the child at risk or at least be a less desirable custodian than his ex-wife, who might have better psychological test data and a more stable background.

The cross-examining attorney may continue to ask questions along this line, perhaps saying that a parenting skill assessment test should have been given, since such a test actually measures the ability to parent. The answer is that such parenting tests, at least the ones I have seen, are very transparent and easily faked in a positive direction. Stick to your global conclusions, your recommendations in total, and the cross-examination attacking the validity of the instruments you used will be easily defeated.

The same attack has been used in cases involving IQ testing. I once testified in a Termination of Parental Rights hearing on a woman with a 55 IQ, very little family support, and a psychopathic, drug-using boyfriend. Her child had been removed by the juvenile court because of neglect. The background information indicated that she was not taking care of her child and there was little to suggest that she had the ability to change. The cross-examining attorney tried to imply that a 55 IQ did not measure anything regarding parenting. He attempted to say I didn't know anything about what kind of parent the mother was, based on the IQ test. I testified that, with an IQ of 55, she functioned no better than a fraction of 1 percent above the general population in her age group. I indicated some of the adaptive abilities with this IQ and with this particular individual. I emphasized that my conclusions were not based solely on her IQ score. During the interview she demonstrated a gross lack of understanding of basic child-care techniques and, even more important, she had a history of neglect, which predicted her parenting better than anything else. The point in that case was not to be cornered by the attack on the IQ score, but to broaden the discussion to include all the data that was used to make the decision.

Another line of inquiry is to ask research-related questions on certain aspects of your conclusions. You may be asked about research on the validity of joint custody or single parenthood or a host of other social issues and phenomena. Such abstract testimony about social trends is not appropriate for individual case dispositions. What difference does it make if ten studies can be cited that joint custody does or does not work? What matters is whether you have examined the particular parents involved and know whether they can work together. From time to time, lawyers approach me to testify on similar social issues in cases I have not evaluated. This is just another form of being a "hired gun," attacking someone else's conclusions. If you want to build a reputation as a clinical forensic psychologist who can accurately assess people and make helpful recommendations to the court, you should turn down this type of testimony that is supposedly research-based and makes broad social judgments.

Finally, I want to comment on the details of court appearances. As you receive subpoenas or telephone calls that you are needed in court, do not cancel your other appointments. Most of these will not materialize in actual testimony. When you get the subpoena, make a notation in your book and, if you can, talk to the attorney to see if he or she will need you. Sometimes the attorney will not know whether you will be needed until the day or the hour of the scheduled court hearing. Ask that the lawyer or his assistant call your office an hour or so before you need to appear. You can then leave the office, testify, and get back to work. If you tell the attorney you need to be put on the stand immediately, you will almost always be accommodated. Since you were appointed by the court or agreed to by both parties, you are a star witness and your testimony will take precedence over other witnesses. This has happened in my practice for years. This is not the case with psychologists retained as "hired guns" for one side or the other. They usually have to wait their turn to testify.

Having to rearrange schedules to go to court is one of the things that discourages many individuals from practicing forensic psychology. They imagine that they will be in court all the time and that they will lose entire days cooling their heels outside the courtroom. That does not happen in the type of forensic practice I am suggesting. First of all, most cases will never require your testimony, and, by being called an hour ahead of time and testifying immediately, your time in court will be minimized. In a forensic practice such as I am advocating, therapy clients will be few and far between and will not be waiting for you while you are in court. If you have assistants in your office, they can easily cover for you. They can give paper-and-pencil psychological tests, for example, while you are testifying.

Another thing most professionals worry about is being paid for court testimony. When the evaluation is court-ordered, either the court will be responsible for paying you or the parties will be ordered to share in the cost. You can expect a very high collection rate for court testimony. I do not suggest charging exorbitant fees for your testimony or any other aspect of your forensic work. When you go to court, your fee ought to be the number of hours involved, based on your actual travel time, testimony, and number of hours away from the office. Sometimes attorneys will send a very nominal witness fee with their subpoena. Send this fee back to the attorney and bill at your normal professional rate. This is just a little trick that some attorneys use to try to classify you as a witness, rather than an expert.

One final word of advice when testifying. You should dress conservatively, since that is the norm in courtrooms. If a male psychologist takes the stand wearing a ponytail or a female evaluator comes to court wearing jeans, that person will probably not be accorded much respect by the court. Since all the professionals in court will be dressed as businesspeople, even an open collar might suggest a lack of professionalism to the judge or jury.

Most psychologists who have a problem on the witness stand do so not because of incompetence, but because of self-doubt, intimidation, and devaluation of their own profession and role. You must always remember that you have a place in the courtroom and the court wants you there. Every time you take the stand, whether it is in a criminal court or a less formal family court, you will have the opportunity to state how you came to do the evaluation that you are testifying about. This will reinforce your reputation as someone who is objective, someone whose opinion can be respected. If you are professional, respectful, and calmly confidant in your testimony, you will steadily build your reputation as a forensics expert, both with the parties to the case at hand and with untold numbers of other persons who might be in the courtroom that day.

3

THE EVALUATION OF JUVENILE DELINQUENTS

All counties in this country have juvenile judges who must decide placement of juveniles who come before them. In smaller, rural counties, the juvenile judge may also be the chancery, probate, and circuit judge. Juvenile delinquents can be evaluated either before or after sentencing on misdemeanor or felony charges. In some cases, judges will ask that juveniles be evaluated before sentencing, so they will have more information to help them in determining disposition. In other cases, juvenile detention facilities (which could be diagnostic units, holding areas, or longer-term facilities) may ask for evaluations after the juvenile has been sentenced, since they have a constant problem with overcrowding and must move offenders into other facilities around the state or into alternative diversion programs.

Another type of juvenile who comes before judges for placement is the status offender. In this non-criminal matter, the juvenile or family is under the jurisdiction of the court, because the parent or child welfare agency has filed a Family in Need of Supervision (FINS) petition. This procedure may have other names in various jurisdictions, but the concept is the same: that a juvenile is in need of supervision, whether for truancy, running away from home, school behavior, or substance abuse. Status offenders might be held in detention for brief periods of time, but usually are not committed to long-term detention facilities unless there are also criminal charges.

There will be times when judges know exactly what they want to do with certain juveniles. This will be true in many cases in which an adolescent is charged with murder or robbery and the juvenile has an extensive rap sheet of prior convictions for serious crimes. In those cases, the judge will often want detention for as long as the law allows (until age 18 or, in some states, until the person has reached his early twenties). More and more juveniles, age 15 or over, who are accused of very serious offenses are not ending up in juvenile court at all, but are being tried as adults.

The cases in which evaluations are ordered are usually the most difficult cases, since many of the other juvenile cases are disposed of on the basis of the prior criminal record and input from the juvenile court staff. There is ample opportunity for a qualified forensic psychologist in the community to contract with the courts and the detention facilities to provide these evaluations, since there are not enough probation officers, county psychologists, and county social workers to provide the necessary evaluations. This is especially true now with the explosion in juvenile delinquency and gang activity. The psychologist will be paid by the court, not by the parents, although the parents may be required to reimburse the court for the cost of the evaluation. (Only infrequently will a family be found financially capable and ordered to pay the psychologist directly for the evaluation.)

In all of these evaluations, the question is basically the same: What is the best placement or disposition for this young person? The judges may have access to some background information on the juveniles before them, but they want more detailed information on which to base their decisions. Many different types of dispositional alternatives are available, depending on exactly what type of juvenile they are dealing with. As will be obvious from the reports in this chapter, two juveniles may be accused of similar crimes and yet have totally different psychological profiles and prognoses.

When an evaluation is ordered, the judge or county official making the referral wants very clear recommendations from the forensic psychologist as to disposition. There are many dispositional alternatives for the forensic psychologist to consider. If the evaluation results in a fundamentally antisocial character structure, a detention facility will usually be recommended. In different states this may be called a serious offender program, wilderness program, training school, boys' school, or various other names and euphemisms. If the juvenile offender has a psychiatric problem as well as a conduct disorder, a short-term or long-term psychiatric treatment center can be recommended. If the juvenile is a sex offender, recommendations can be made for an inpatient sexual offender program. Other dispositions could include inpatient alcohol and drug rehabilitation units, non-psychiatric community-based programs (such as shelters, ranches, or group homes), therapeutic foster care, or mental retardation facilities if the juvenile is retarded. Juveniles can be sent to community-based diversion programs, such as alternative schools, GED training, adult education, Job Corps, and boot camps. Probation and return to a parent, another relative, or foster care might be recommended, as well as outpatient therapy and/or psychiatric treatment and medication.

Making definite and clear recommendations to these programs by name is invaluable to the court and diagnostic units for which evaluations will be done. Many of the agencies and programs to which the psychologist is recommending placement will not admit the juvenile without such a psychological evaluation. A psychiatric program does not want to admit a criminally dangerous person who has no intention of changing his behavior. On the other hand, a detention center does not want to commit an adolescent who has a severe psychiatric or psychological problem. Despite all the talk about rehabilitation, detention centers, boys' schools, and training schools are set up mainly for punishment and are not equipped to handle psychiatric patients. Mental retardation facilities, which exist in most states, have specific requirements for IQ scores and adaptive levels of functioning. None of these determinations can be made without a complete psychological evaluation.

Juvenile evaluation reports should be written without reference to any personal or professional theory of delinquency. If the court or contracting agency begins to see that the evaluating psychologist has a particular view, the value of the reports will be diminished. For example, if these adolescents are viewed as poor and unfortunate or if psychopathology is used as a ready excuse for every offense, the reports will be disregarded. If every recommendation is for psychiatric treatment, regardless of the offense, it will not be long before everyone involved will begin to devalue the reports and the referrals will stop.

On the other hand, if the psychologist has some kind of vendetta against youthful offenders and recommends that they all be punished, then the courts and probation officers will also see that as a particular agenda. Judges, probation officers, community-based workers, and screening personnel are smart people. They see one youthful offender after another and it will not take them long to recognize quality reports. What they will respond positively to are individualized evaluations that recommend a variety of specific dispositions. Lofty reports that do not make specific recommendations are useless. It takes only a couple of reports like that for the courts to turn to someone else for the evaluations.

Perhaps the most serious impediment to writing useful evaluations of juveniles is naivete. There is a pervasive view among mental health professionals that young people are not antisocial. When the court sees that the psychologist can recognize an antisocial individual, there will be respect for the evaluations. The young people being evaluated often have criminal errors in thinking and it is vital to recognize a character disorder when we see one. Some of the pressure is taken off the detention facility or committing judge when the psychologist can identify someone who is antisocial and needs to be detained for a relatively long period of time. This is not to assume responsibility for anyone else's role, but there is a tremendous amount of leeway for juvenile sentencing, and these evaluations provide the juvenile court with a means of classifying the young people before them. It is also important to remember that the psychological evaluation is not the only information the court receives. The court also gets school records, probation reports, previous hospital discharge papers, family input, and reports from child welfare if the youth has been in foster care.

In many cases, the adolescents being evaluated will be brought to the psychologist's office by detention officers. These kids will be shackled and in orange uniforms. At other times, the court referral may require the psychologist to do the evaluation in the detention center, while the juvenile is detained pending his court hearing. Sometimes the adolescent or child is free in the custody of his parents and they are instructed by the judge to bring the child to the psychologist's office for the evaluation prior to the next court date. Sometimes parents are unavailable and the juvenile is brought to the office by a Department of Human Services worker. Evaluations for detention or diagnostic centers after adjudication has been made are always done at the facility.

Whenever possible, the psychologist needs to interview the parent or parents as part of the evaluation. This is important. The psychologist needs to know what the parents feel about the child and whether they want the child to continue living at home. This is also an opportunity to explore family problems that may be contributing to the juvenile's acting-out behavior.

When the adolescents or children have been released to their parents' custody, it will usually be possible to interview the parent who brings the child to the office. If the evaluation is to be done at a detention facility or when detention officers will be bringing the juvenile to the psychologist's office, it is important to let the court know that you want to talk to the parents. They can be ordered to show up for appointments at the same time their child is being evaluated. However, often this does not happen and parents are not interviewed. When parents are not seen, the psychologist should at least attempt to reach them by telephone.

Juvenile evaluations usually have to be performed quickly. Invariably, the psychologist will be asked to evaluate a juvenile who is in detention a day or two before the court date. Obviously, this requires the psychologist to have quick turn-around time on both the evaluation and report. Sometimes parents are not available and background information is not even supplied to the psychologist in the necessary time period. It is still feasible in these cases to produce useful evaluations. These are simply examples of compromises that are made in day-to-day forensic practice, meeting the demands of the court and dealing with limitations.

As you will see from the psychological evaluations presented in this chapter, all of my evaluations are reasonably short (three or four pages). Although psychological test data is interpreted in the reports, the language is as free of jargon and psychological terminology as possible. This makes the reports easily understood by the educated reader, namely the judge, probation officer, or detention center personnel.

Once the psychological evaluations are written and sent, they should be forgotten. The sentencing judge may or may not follow our recommendations and it is impossible, or certainly very impractical, to follow up on each case to find out what actually happened. In fact, that isn't even very relevant. If you had feedback on what actually happened in court, would you alter what you said for the next report?

The only kind of feedback the psychologist needs is whether or not the evaluations have been helpful. In soliciting feedback from the court, probation officers, or detention centers, the psychologist might learn that he or she needs to be more specific or needs to include diagnoses when writing the reports. Those recommendations would obviously be heeded in writing future reports.

These evaluations will be passed around, following the juvenile from placement to placement or from agency to agency. This is fine and does not require any releases. Releases were not obtained from the parents initially, since the evaluations were court-ordered. Sometimes an agency, detention facility, or treatment center may request a copy of a psychological evaluation two or three years after it was done. (Rarely is there a request for a juvenile's evaluation after the person turns eighteen.) In those cases, the report is released without permission from either the parent or the adolescent. These evaluations are court documents and they can flow just as easily as police reports.

THE TEST BATTERY

There is no one correct test battery for assessing juvenile offenders. This is true for any area of assessment, since clinicians will vary in their choice of instruments. Depending on the needs of the child, some tests will be deleted and some added. From the testing, the psychologist must be able to make Axis I–V diagnoses. Diagnoses are required, especially if the juvenile is being referred to a hospital or other facility. If a diagnosis is not included in the report, the psychologist will often be asked for one after the fact.

Intellectual and academic testing are critical for making accurate diagnoses and determinations about placement. However, it is not uncommon to come across evaluations of youthful offenders without such testing. These are not adequate evaluations, because intelligence and academic ability are central to the functioning of children and adolescents. These measures will not only contribute to an understanding of the juvenile's school behavior and failure, but will help the psychologist understand the extent to which the juvenile may be led by other brighter and more powerful peers and whether he has the capacity to benefit from therapy. For these reasons, this testing will provide some indication of prognosis. Because intelligence testing is critical when making determinations about placement, it is irresponsible to do a report that does not include these measures. Reports containing no intellectual measures are practically useless to the court and other users.

The Wechsler Intelligence Scale for Children–Third Edition (WISC-III) or the Wechsler Adult Intelligence Scale–Revised (WAIS-R) is administered for a measure of individual intelligence. If the adolescent is 16 years old, the WAIS-R should be administered rather than the WISC-III. The WISC-III is yielding low IQ scores, especially for minorities, and several colleagues have confirmed the same finding. The WAIS-R, given at age 16 to the same individual, seems to result in a higher IQ. Maximum performance is what is sought in testing. Another reason to administer the WAIS-R rather than the WISC-III, when the age requirements are met, is to avoid the effect of practice. Many of these kids have been in and out of facilities, so they have seen the WISC-R or WISC-III several times. Moving to the WAIS-R at age 16 can limit practice effects.

To test achievement, tests such as the Wide Range Achievement Test–Third Edition (WRAT-3), the Wechsler Individual Achievement Test (WIAT), or the Woodcock–Johnson Tests of Achievement–Revised (WJ-R) is administered. Many other academic or achievement tests are available. The important thing is to do at least a screening for academic ability. This permits comparison between intelligence and academic performance. Sometimes intelligence is low but achievement is higher. Other times, intelligence is high and achievement is low, suggesting a learning disability. Because evaluation for juvenile disposition is not primarily an educational evaluation, one measure of intelligence and one measure of achievement should be sufficient to obtain some idea about intellectual functioning and academic ability.

Personality measures typically include the Minnesota Multiphasic Personality Inventory (MMPI) or Minnesota Multiphasic Personality Inventory–Adolescent (MMPI-A), Incomplete Sentences Blank, Hand Test, House–Tree–Person Drawings, and Beck Depression Inventory. Elevations on Scales 4 (PD: Psychopathic Deviate) and 9 (MA: Hypomania) of the MMPI are especially notable in assessing juvenile offenders.

Two instruments that are routinely administered are the Jesness Inventory and the Carlson Psychological Survey (CPS). The Jesness is one of the few instruments specifically designed for assessment and classification of young delinquents. One of its weaknesses is the lack of validity scales, but the eleven critical scales and the "I-level" classifications are very useful. The eleven critical scores are Social Maladjustment (SM), Value Orientation (VO), Immaturity (IMM), Autism (AU), Alienation (AS), Manifest Aggression (MA), Withdrawal–Depression (WD), Social Anxiety (SA), Repression (REP), Denial (DEN), and Asocial (ASOCIAL). The I-level classifications are Undersocialized, Active (previously Unsocialized, Aggressive); Undersocialized, Passive; Conformist; Group-oriented; Pragmatist; Autonomy-oriented; Introspective; Inhibited; and Adaptive. The Social Maladjustment and Asocial indices are the two most powerful indications of delinquency and antisocial tendencies on this test. This test, which can be computer-scored, is appropriate for ages 8 to 18, but can also be administered to adults.

The Carlson Psychological Survey (CPS) was also designed for the criminal justice system and is very valuable for youthful offenders. People with a fourth-grade reading level should have no difficulty with the test. It has five scales: Chemical Abuse, Thought Disturbance, Antisocial Tendencies, Self-Depreciation, and Validity. CPS profiles that cause concern for delinquency and antisocial tendencies include spikes on the Antisocial Tendencies scale and the Chemical Abuse scale. Using scoring rules outlined in the manual, Carlson describes eighteen personality types among offenders and gives predictions related to their institutionalization, escape, parole, and four-year post-release adjustment. In addition, the CPS provides an excellent opportunity for item analysis. Its fifty items give specific information about the juvenile's attitudes and behavior. For example, item 50 says, "I have carried a weapon on me," and the choices are (1) never, (2) once or twice, (3) some of the time, (4) most of the time, or (5) all the time. This is valuable information in making an evaluation of juvenile offenders. (One criticism that has been made of the CPS is that it was developed for adults and might not be appropriate for adolescents. I do not think this is the case, since the normative group of 412 subjects had a mean age of 19. From the standard deviation of 3.33, this normative group certainly included 15- and 16-year-old offenders.)

The test battery outlined above is a comprehensive battery, and yet can be administered in a relatively short period of time. The adolescent will need two to four hours to complete the paper-and-pencil tests. Intelligence testing, academic testing, and the interview may require an additional two hours. Testing technicians should administer as much of the test battery as possible. Otherwise, there is no way to keep up the volume necessary in a forensic practice.

Cases are presented below to show exactly how these evaluations are done and the kind of recommendations that are made. All names and identifying information have been changed.

Case 1

Even though this adolescent was on probation and had committed another offense, he was not found to be antisocial or delinquency oriented.

Psychological Evaluation Report

Name: Bernard Williams
(Required identifying information, date of testing, etc.)

Tests Administered

> Wechsler Adult Intelligence Scale–Revised (WAIS-R)
> Minnesota Multiphasic Personality Inventory–Adolescent (MMPI-A)
> Wide Range Achievement Test–Third Edition (WRAT-3)
> Jesness Inventory
> Incomplete Sentences Blank (Sentences)
> Carlson Psychological Survey (CPS)
> House–Tree–Person Drawings
> Beck Depression Inventory (BDI)
> Hand Test

Clinical Interview
Bernard is a 16-year, 1-month-old black male brought to the office by detention. He said he was locked up for unauthorized use of a vehicle after he took his mother's car. This was both a violation of his curfew and a violation of probation. There

was initially a FINS petition, which had been prompted when he was taken to Children's Hospital for treatment of alcohol intoxication. After checking out of Children's Hospital, he went to CPC Pinnacle Point Hospital for four days. He says he has not had anything to drink since that time. He lives with his parents, both of whom are working, and his sister. He attends school and is in the eleventh grade at this time. He does not get in trouble in school, although he had one in-school suspension this year. He denies any gang membership or substance abuse, maintaining that the alcohol intoxication and poisoning was just a one-time thing. He said his parents want him to do better and would like him to be back home.

Test Results
Bernard was very cooperative during the testing. He did his best and was highly motivated. His WAIS-R scores were as follows:

Verbal Tests		Performance Tests	
Information	8	Picture Completion	8
Digit Span	3	Picture Arrangement	6
Vocabulary	6	Block Design	7
Arithmetic	7	Object Assembly	7
Comprehension	7	Digit Symbol	7
Similarities	8		

Verbal IQ	85
Performance IQ	82
Full Scale IQ	82

His IQ of 82 is in the Low Average range of intellectual functioning. The scores were very consistent across subtests. The 82 IQ is judged to be reliable and valid. Although his intellectual level is below average, I do not see any indications of a learning disability. In fact, he did quite well on the WRAT-3 and exceeded expectations based on the 82 IQ.

The WRAT-3 scores were as follows:

	Standard Score	Percentile	Grade Equivalent
Reading	105	63	HS
Spelling	100	50	HS
Arithmetic	86	18	6

He is weakest in arithmetic, but his reading and writing ability are in the solid average range. He is capable of finishing high school and, with some effort, he could receive some higher education.

The Jesness scores were as follows: SM = 30, VO = 42, IMM = 57, AU = 47, AL = 44, MA = 41, WD = 44, SA = 41, REP = 54, DEN = 60, ASOCIAL = 37. These scores are suggestive of someone who identifies with the larger culture and maintains support for his parents' values. All antisocial scales were very low. He is positive about himself, optimistic about the future, and positive toward his family. He did not show any hangups about authority and there was no evidence of hostility.

The MMPI-A scores were F = 40, L = 67, K = 63, HS = 35, D = 42, HY = 47, PD = 37, MF = 39, PA = 38, PT = 33, SC = 34, MA = 38, SI = 32. These scores are normal and there was nothing significant. He did his best to portray feelings of conformity and responsibility.

The CPS scores were good and he denied criminal behavior or tendencies. He portrays prosocial values and rejects delinquency. He had a BDI denying depression and he maintains that he has feelings of well-being and good adjustment. The Hand Test also looked good and he had no aggressive responses. On the Sentences he made several comments about wanting to be home and he was positive about his family.

Summary and Recommendations
Bernard's diagnoses are as follows:

Axis I	Parent/Child Problems (V61.20)
	Adjustment Disorder with Disturbance of Conduct (309.30)
Axis II	None
Axis III	None
Axis IV	Mild (2)
Axis V	Current GAF 75

There was nothing in the data or in the interview to suggest that Bernard is antisocial or delinquency-oriented. He made a very good first impression and, if there is antisocial behavior that I do not know about, it did not show up in the evaluation. If his offenses are no more than what he reported to me, then the test data suggests he is a positive young man with prosocial values and a solid family. If his parents want Bernard back in the home, then I think he can be returned, but with probation and court supervision. I think the problems with Bernard are related to his family and they may need family therapy to help work through his difficulties. Bernard should return to school as soon as possible. He does not appear to have a substance abuse problem, even though he had an overdose with alcohol on one occasion. This can be explored further if Bernard and his family are seen in therapy. Overall, the prognosis appears to be good and Bernard is ready for another try at home.

Discussion
Bernard was basically a status offender. He came from an intact family and there was no reason to consider him for punishment or for a boys' training school. He had had episodic alcohol use, which had been treated at a local psychiatric hospital. In spite of Low Average intelligence, he had fairly good academic ability. He had excellent Jesness scores and his profile was identified as Adaptive. The Adaptive I-level classification is one that internalizes values of the culture, which is very positive. This is the least rebellious and oppositional of the Jesness categories, along

with the Inhibited classification, which is a more neurotic type. Delinquent kids typically have very high Social Maladjustment and Asocial scores on the Jesness. Those were among Bernard's lowest scores, indicating that he is not someone who has a criminal mind or is interested in committing crimes.

The MMPI-A scores were also very good, because nothing was significant. The L and K scales suggested a little defensiveness, but perhaps reflected healthy ego development. Bernard also had a very positive CPS profile, with low scores in everything. That test indicated no significant chemical abuse or thought distur- bance and he had positive self-esteem on the Self-Depreciation scale. The Anti- social scale was also insignificant.

His Incomplete Sentences Blank included very positive sentence stems, which is not the case among the most delinquent and antisocial individuals. He said, I "love my family," dancing "is fun at parties," most girls "like me because I make them laugh." A typical antisocial response on the stem "most girls" might be "are bitches," which is not an unusual response among youth undergoing evaluation.

Bernard did well on the Hand test, not giving a single aggressive response. His Hand test responses were responses like waving, catching a ball, pointing at someone, grabbing something, holding something, shaking somebody's hand, and dropping something. He gave no antisocial or acting-out responses.

As the summary section indicated, Bernard was not antisocial. He only had parent–child problems and an adjustment disorder with disturbance of conduct. The Axis IV diagnosis was "mild" and his Global Assessment of Functioning (GAF) score was high. His diagnoses reflected a positive psychological evaluation. He was recommended for probation and court supervision, along with family therapy.

Profiles such as this point to the value of evaluations, since the judge might not have had any other way of determining the character of the juvenile before him.

Case 2

This adolescent was clearly antisocial and was referred to the Serious Offender Program.

Psychological Evaluation Report

Name: Edward Harton
(Required identifying information, date of testing, etc.)

Tests Administered

> Wechsler Adult Intelligence Scale–Revised (WAIS-R)
> Wide Range Achievement Test–Third Edition (WRAT-3)
> Beck Depression Inventory (BDI)
> Minnesota Multiphasic Personality Inventory–Adolescent (MMPI-A)
> Jesness Inventory

Carlson Psychological Survey (CPS)
Incomplete Sentences Blank
Hand Test
Clinical Interview

Clinical Interview
Edward is a 16-year, 6-month-old black male brought to the office by a detention officer. He was placed in detention for violation of probation. He was on 24-hour supervision for two different counts of criminal trespassing and an assault-and-battery charge that resulted from a fight in school. (He said somebody kicked him and he later assaulted the boy.) Connected with one of the trespassing charges was a fleeing charge. He denied that he was trying to run. He also has a circuit court charge pending for aggravated robbery. He said a friend of his picked him up in a vehicle that had been taken from the victim. He denies participating in the robbery, saying that the police pulled them over and three of them were arrested.

Edward is in the tenth grade. He lives with his mother, two brothers, and two sisters. I called his mother at home and she said her son has been skipping school, and when he does go to school he gets in trouble. She recounted the charges, especially the robbery charge in circuit court. She said Edward was standing by while this robbery was taking place. This places him at the scene during the robbery, which was different from his story. His mother said Edward likes trouble and she has little control over him. She said his biological father never took part in his life. He has always been with his mother, who has raised five children alone. She said he stays out all night, although he sometimes comes in at 1:00 or 2:00 A.M. (This was prior to the 24-hour curfew). Sometimes he is with his grandmother, but other times she does not know where he is. He has not had any psychological treatment.

Test Results
Edward was cooperative for the evaluation. His WAIS-R scaled scores were as follows:

Verbal Tests		*Performance Tests*	
Information	6	Picture Completion	8
Digit Span	11	Picture Arrangement	8
Vocabulary	5	Block Design	11
Arithmetic	9	Object Assembly	7
Comprehension	5	Digit Symbol	10
Similarities	9		

Verbal IQ	93
Performance IQ	94
Full Scale IQ	92

His IQ of 92 is in the Average range of ability at the 30th percentile.
The WRAT-3 scores were as follows:

	Standard Score	Percentile	Grade Equivalent
Reading	103	58	HS
Spelling	107	68	HS
Arithmetic	93	32	7

These scores are also in the average range, so Edward could do well if he did not have the behavioral and delinquency problems he has. He has fairly good ability and, so far, he is wasting the potential he has to do well in school and insure a future.

The MMPI-A scores were quite alarming because of the very high 4 and 9 scores. The scores were as follows: F = 70, L = 50, K = 44, HS = 46, D = 51, HY = 50, PD = 85, MF = 47, PA = 48, PT = 51, SC = 57, MA = 81, SI = 37. The 4–9 elevation is seen among psychopathic deviant individuals with very high activity levels and low impulse control. He does not delay gratification, has antisocial tendencies, very little moral development, and a high need for excitement and stimulation, usually of the antisocial variety. He has little endurance for anything that is boring or not exciting. He has difficulty getting along with others and certainly has trouble with authority.

The CPS scores were also extremely high for antisocial tendencies. He acknowledged drinking alcohol and using drugs. He checked the choice that he would use a weapon to rob someone, saying "have done it and would do it again." He said the staff at the detention center are "stupid" and said he has more problems than other people. He said he has been in gang fights and probably will be in trouble with the law again. He said he carries a weapon and describes his life as going badly.

On the Incomplete Sentences, he said that at bedtime he dreams "of shooting Demone," who I suppose is someone he knows. He said people are "animals" and he feels "furious and angry." He said he does not fear anything, cannot stop doing "stuff," and sometimes thinks of doing something "drastic." He said what pains him is "that I have no control over my anger" and he hates the juvenile system. He said he secretly "robbed, shot, and hurt people." He said he tries to change, but can't.

The Jesness scores were as follows: SM = 90, VO = 81, IMM = 72, AU = 76, AL = 83, MA = 84, WD = 60, SA = 52, REP = 38, DEN = 29, ASOCIAL = 73. This is an Undersocialized, Active (Aggressive) profile. It is one of the worst delinquency types on the Jesness. Edward has a negative attitude toward school, teachers, and authority. He is distrustful of people in general and his self-concept is negative and pessimistic with low morale. He has strong feelings of anger and frustration and he tends to blame others for his problems. He can be seen as hostile, even though face-to-face during the interview he was cooperative.

Edward had a score of 25 on the BDI, so he acknowledges that he does not feel happy, he is dissatisfied with his life, he feels he is being punished, and he is critical of himself. His responses on the Hand Test indicate that he displays poor insight, has difficulty expressing his emotions, and has a great deal of bottled-up tension and anger.

Summary and Recommendations
Edward has the following diagnoses:

Axis I   Conduct Disorder, Solitary Aggressive Type (312.00)
          Parent Child Problems (V61.20)
Axis II   Antisocial Personality Traits
Axis III None
Axis IV   Severe (4)
Axis V   Current GAF 30

Edward had very clearcut antisocial personality traits on the evaluation. He had very high scores on all scales indicating delinquency and criminal tendencies. He does not believe that he will change in the near future and he gives every indication that he will continue getting into difficulty. He even wrote on one of the responses that he has committed many more crimes than have come to the attention of the courts.

My recommendation is commitment to a Serious Offender Program which will require commitment to the Youth Services Center.

Discussion
Edward was 16 years old, just like Bernard, but that is the only thing they had in common. These two cases are placed side by side to show the contrast between a prosocial young person and an antisocial individual. Edward had many signs of aggressiveness beyond his assault and battery charge. He also had a circuit court charge pending for aggravated robbery, so he was probably on his way to adult court after his juvenile adjudication. Despite being on 24-hour supervision (which required him to be at home any time when he was not at school), he was staying out all night and pretty much doing as he pleased. Although he had average intelligence and academic ability, he was doing very little in school.

One could not ask for a more definitive MMPI-A than that which Edward produced. Spikes for Scales 4 and 9 clearly indicated the antisocial personality and his diagnosis of conduct disorder. On the CPS, he had a T-score of more than 100 for antisocial tendencies. He endorsed alcohol and drug use, and, item by item, he showed antisocial tendencies. This included endorsing items saying that he carried weapons and enjoyed fighting. His Sentence responses indicated his rage and the Jesness I-level classification was Undersocialized, Active, which was once referred to as Unsocialized, Aggressive. This is the worst type on the Jesness, indicating social maladjustment and very high alienation from authority.

While Bernard was recommended for placement back in his family, Edward was diagnosed with a conduct disorder and antisocial personality traits. It was recommended that he be committed to the Youth Services Center in the Serious Offender Program. In other states, this is the training school, boys' detention center, or youth detention center. The data that Edward presented left few dispositional alternatives. All aspects of the psychological evaluation indicated that his prognosis was very poor.

As with most juveniles who are evaluated, Edward was using alcohol and other drugs. Many of these juveniles will advance substance abuse as a primary symptom, since they would love to go to a drug rehabilitation program for thirty days and then return home. Don't be fooled into thinking that all of these juveniles need substance abuse treatment. You must be able to separate those with legitimate substance abuse problems from those whose drug and alcohol abuse is one component of a conduct disorder.

Case 3

This juvenile offender was found to be in the mild range of mental retardation.

Psychological Evaluation Report

Name: David Nogales
(Required identifying information, date of testing, etc.)

Tests Administered

> Wechsler Intelligence Scale for Children–Third Edition (WISC III)
> Minnesota Multiphasic Personality Inventory–Adolescent (MMPI-A)
> Wide Range Achievement Test–Third Edition (WRAT-3)
> Jesness Inventory
> Incomplete Sentences Blank
> Carlson Psychological Survey (CPS)
> House–Tree–Person Drawings (HTP)
> Hand Test
> Beck Depression Inventory (BDI)

Clinical Interview
David is a 13-year, 11-month-old Hispanic male brought to the office by detention. He had a gun charge. He said he had been riding in a truck which had a gun in it, although he denied the gun was his. The person driving the vehicle was about 20 years old. There was marijuana in the truck, so David was also charged with possession. He said he had curfew violations as well.

David lives with his mother, sister, and brother. He said his father, whom he did not know, died in 1990. His mother has received Social Security benefits since his father's death. David is in the seventh grade and denied having any suspensions this year. He said he was suspended once last year. He said that he smokes marijuana sometimes, but he denied any gang activity.

Test Results
The WISC-III scores were as follows:

Verbal Tests		*Performance Tests*	
Information	2	Picture Completion	8
Similarities	3	Coding	3
Arithmetic	4	Picture Arrangement	3
Vocabulary	4	Block Design	2
Comprehension	4	Object Assembly	4

Verbal IQ	63
Performance IQ	64
Full Scale IQ	60

His IQ of 60 is in the mild range of mental retardation. He was low on everything except Picture Completion. I thought he did his best and his low functioning is a valid and reliable measure of his retardation.

The WRAT-3 scores were as follows:

	Standard Score	Percentile	Grade Equivalent
Reading	60	0.8	2
Spelling	62	1.0	1
Arithmetic	47	0.04	1

These scores are also low and support the validity of the low IQ. His academic ability was consistent with his level of intelligence. He was able to spell a few words, such as "will," "run," "boy," and "cat." He could read a few words, like "letter," "city," and "jar." Arithmetic ability was even less and he missed problems as easy as 6 + 2.

He had help reading the personality tests, but still his comprehension was very poor. The MMPI-A scores were as follows: F = 93, L = 80, K = 59, HS = 68, D = 65, HY = 74, PD = 67, MF = 44, PA = 76, PT = 60, SC = 64, MA = 56, SI = 54. These scores appear to be invalid because the validity scores were so high. It is clear that David did not understand the questions on the MMPI-A. The CPS was also a problem, because he had the most extreme scores on everything. He may have been very negative and angry, marking the most ridiculous items. Basically he marked the most extreme answer for every single item. He did the same thing on the BDI, answering most items in an extreme way, saying that he is depressed and has emotional problems.

On the Sentences, David said he likes "to have fun all day" and that he is happiest "being in the street." He said he likes to have his freedom and he feels "like a good boy." He said his nerves are bad and his mind "is not right." He said he is best with his friends, that he hates himself, and that he wishes he could go home. David was very negative about himself throughout the test, when he did understand and comprehend the items.

The Jesness scores were as follows: SM = 66, VO = 59, IMM = 66, AU = 58, AL = 55, MA = 50, WD = 44, SA = 59, REP = 57, DEN = 61, ASOCIAL = 68. He does not engage in blatantly antisocial behavior and he tends to be quiet and to follow the group. He shows little tendency to make appropriate choices, but follows whatever the circumstances happen to be and whoever he might be associating with.

The HTP drawings were very immature and clearly reflected his mental retardation. The Hand Test was also typical for someone with low intelligence. He had a Description and a Failure response, which are usually given by mentally retarded individuals. He had two Tension responses, indicating he feels some bottled-up anger and anxiety. There were not any Aggressive responses, and overall he did not appear to be aggressive. I do not think he is assaultive at this point, nor is he interested in planning criminal behavior.

Summary and Recommendations
David has the following diagnoses:

Axis I	Conduct Disorder, Group Type (312.20)
Axis II	Mild Mental Retardation (317.00)
Axis III	None
Axis IV	Moderate (3)
Axis V	Current GAF 55

The most salient finding in this evaluation is David's mental retardation. I do not see him as particularly aggressive at this time. Acting-out is not likely to occur on his own. The key for David is supervision. If he is properly supervised, off the streets, and in school, there should not be a problem. Because of his mental retardation, he is going to be easily group-influenced. His adaptive ability is commensurate with his mental retardation. He requires special education. If David cannot be returned home or if additional offenses occur, then I recommend placement at Mill Creek. He may not need placement at Mill Creek if he can receive proper supervision while on probation.

There is a concern, and that is the undercurrent of anger, resentment, and feelings of futility in David's test results. This could lead to additional criminal behavior if he is not properly supervised. I think he needs some positive experiences, since he could be so easily influenced by more delinquent peers.

Discussion
David was a 13-year-old boy who had a gun charge against him. The evaluation results indicated he had a 60 IQ and very poor academic functioning. He had help on the paper-and-pencil tests, but, for the most part, his comprehension of any of those items was questionable. His responses on the Sentences were also childlike. He had an Introspective Jesness typology, which reflects a more withdrawn and introverted individual.

David was diagnosed with a conduct disorder, but the primary finding in this case was mental retardation. The court was advised that he could make it at home with special education services and serious supervision of his activities. The court was also advised that, if he re-offended or required residential placement, he should be placed in a residential mental retardation facility located in the state. Most states, if not all, have such facilities. The facility that was recommended for him was a mental retardation facility that is licensed as an Intermediate Care Facility (ICF) and must meet the same standards as nursing homes.

David was not appropriate for a psychiatric facility. He would not benefit from treatment and there was no particular issue of depression or anxiety. It was also inappropriate to consider him for the boys' school or the training school, since he would be at risk there of being adversely influenced and affected. David clearly was mentally handicapped and, if anything, he needed habilitation, rather than punishment or psychiatric treatment.

Case 4

Treatment in a psychiatric facility was recommended for this young person with antisocial tendencies and borderline intelligence. It was recommended that he not return to his family for two years.

Psychological Evaluation Report

Name: Robert McNeese
(Required identifying information, date of testing, etc.)

Tests Administered

> Wechsler Intelligence Scale for Children–Third Edition (WISC III)
> Carlson Psychological Survey (CPS)
> Jesness Inventory
> Wide Range Achievement Test–Revised (WRAT-R)
> Hand Test
> Bender Gestalt Drawings

Clinical Interview
Robert is an 11-year, 9-month-old white male brought to the office by detention. I attempted to contact his parents by telephone, but could not reach them. Juvenile Detention did send some background information.

During testing Robert tried to act very bored with the tests. He is an 11-year-old boy who attempts to act much older. He said he wanted to return home. There was another juvenile in the office being tested and Robert stuck his head in the doorway and swore some obscenity at the other juvenile. He apparently has engaged in this kind of disruptive, hostile behavior toward other students while in detention. He has no respect for adults whatsoever.

Robert said he is in the fourth grade. He told me his parents are separated and he lives with his father and his father's girlfriend. He said his brother lives with his grandmother. I asked him about his mother and he said, "She don't want to see me, she's an asshole." He said his mother is an alcoholic. He said he smokes marijuana and drinks alcohol. I asked him if he plans to continue the substance abuse if released home, and he said he would. He said he has no intention of stopping.

Robert comes from a chaotic family and there is a history of physical and verbal abuse in the family. Robert and other family members are abusive to the mother, hitting and assaulting her. There is little discipline in the home and Robert has friends who are anywhere from 15 to 21 years of age. The children are often left on their own, completely unsupervised. Robert skips school and has been suspended before. He told me he breaks into places and he had no remorse or regret about it.

Robert has attended counseling at Professional Counseling Associates. Robert was in Pinewood on one occasion. The background information indicated he has assaulted staff at Pinewood and threatened to kill people. The family has a FINS petition filed on him.

Test Results
The WISC-III scaled scores were as follows:

Verbal Tests		Performance Tests	
Information	1	Picture Completion	7
Similarities	3	Coding	7
Arithmetic	6	Picture Arrangement	6
Vocabulary	5	Block Design	1
Comprehension	7	Object Assembly	6
Verbal IQ	75		
Performance IQ	72		
Full Scale IQ	71		

His IQ of 71 is in the Borderline range of intellectual functioning. He is low in all areas.

The WRAT-R scores were as follows:

	Standard Score	Percentile	Grade Equivalent
Reading	46	.03	1
Spelling	46	.03	<1
Arithmetic	46	.03	<1

Robert is basically not able to read and write. He was able to spell a few words, such as "and," "will," "in," "cat," and "go." He was able to read "red," "to," "big," "work," "book," and a few other simple words, but he missed words like "letter," "jar," and "deep."

The personality tests were read to him so he could give his answers.

The Jesness scores were as follows: SM = 90 , VO = 66, IMM = 69, AU = 81, AL = 65, MA = 81, WD = 59, SA = 50, REP = 51, DEN = 40, ASOCIAL = 75. These scores are about as high as any juvenile delinquent will score. The SM and Asocial Index are both very high, indicating strong antisocial tendencies and criminal thinking and behavior. His basic type is Undersocialized, Active. His Jesness profile was highly deviant for Social Maladjustment, Value Orientation, Immaturity, and Asocial thinking. He identifies with psychopathic, asocial, and amoral people. Lying, stealing, drinking, and drugging are the behaviors that he seeks to model. There is little satisfaction in life, much family dysfunction, and no regard for authority. There has been almost no socialization of this young man and he does not incorporate the values and standards of society. He engages in a wide range of asocial and antisocial behavior. Lying, cheating, and stealing are a way of life and a way of thinking for him. His family relationships are extremely stormy and there is almost no interest in achievement or school. To make matters worse, he is in the borderline range of mental retardation, so his ability is very limited. Since he has little academic ability, he experiences even more failure and isolation in school. He acts without considering the consequences of his behavior. He has almost no frustration tolerance and is completely impulsive from moment to moment. He has no judgment and he enjoys risk-taking. This is only an 11-year-old child and people dealing with him will not see a more antisocial individual for his age.

On the CPS Robert had high scores on Antisocial Tendencies and Thought Disturbance. He said he uses drugs and alcohol, gets a kick out of seeing people hurt, would "make someone sorry" if they tried to cheat him, and would beat the person up if someone hit him. He is proud that he tells people off at every opportunity. He acknowledges that all of his friends have been picked up by the police.

Robert made very little effort on the Bender Gestalt drawings. He does not try very hard on school tasks, because he has low self-esteem and experiences failure. He would rather reject the task than do poorly.

His Hand Test responses showed very little imagination and he is unable to process much information or display any kind of empathy or introspection.

Summary and Recommendations
Robert's diagnoses are as follows:

Axis I   Conduct Disorder, Undifferentiated Type (Severe) (312.90)
              Parent/Child Problems (V61.20)
Axis II   Borderline Intellectual Functioning (V40.00)
              Developmental Disorder NOS (315.90)
              Antisocial Personality Traits

Axis III   None
Axis IV   Extreme (5)
Axis V   Current GAF 25

In my opinion, Robert should be in the custody of the Department of Children and Family Services. Given my understanding of the family background and the assessment of Robert, there is no way he can function or be properly supervised in his family. This is someone who could seriously hurt another person if allowed to live in an unsupervised setting. He will not control himself now and at the first opportunity he will be in the streets. The little boy in him wants to live with his father, but Robert cannot point to anything that would be different if he returned home. In fact, he does not believe anything should be different about his life or behavior.

I think Robert should initially be in a residential psychiatric treatment facility, such as Rivendell or Elizabeth Mitchell Children's Center. From there, he should be transferred to either a group home or a therapeutic foster home. I think it is critical to remove this child from his family and begin some socialization and prosocial education, while it still can make a difference. This young man is over the edge on the scale of criminality and juvenile delinquency.

I realize child welfare policy generally is to attempt family reconciliation and family support. Perhaps this would be possible after about two years in state custody. If Robert does well in treatment, group home, or foster care placement, then perhaps placement with the family would be possible. This should not happen until the family makes significant changes and Robert can demonstrate some control over his own behavior.

Discussion
Both the background information and test data on Robert were alarming. Nothing was working for this 11-year-old child—not his family, his intellect, or his social development. This evaluation demonstrates again the importance of the intellectual assessment. In this case, an 11-year-old illiterate boy with an IQ of 71 is at a significant disadvantage. The test behavior, apart from the test scores, revealed someone who did not know how to behave, even when it was in his own interest to be more appropriate. He had no respect for authority. The disrespect for the examiner, office personnel, and other people encountered in the office was representative of this young person's typical behavior.

In spite of antisocial tendencies that showed up in the test data, this young person at age 11 was not recommended for the boys' school or the Youth Services Center. Instead, it was recommended that he be in the state's custody, first in a psychiatric facility for treatment and then in a foster home or group home. It would have been unrealistic to recommend that Robert be returned to his family. There was no discipline in the home, other than whippings administered by the father. (His father was later referred for psychological evaluation, but refused to complete the evaluation.) Robert was already drinking alcohol and using marijuana and test data indicated near mental retardation and highly antisocial behaviors and attitudes.

There is a big difference between an 11-year-old antisocial youth and one who is 15 or 16 and engaging in crimes. Most of the young people evaluated have been in psychiatric facilities and there is good reason for this. These young offenders are given opportunities to work out their problems. In fact, they often have four or five admissions to various psychiatric facilities, before they are committed to a detention center. (There are exceptions, but these usually involve more serious crimes, such as manslaughter, murder, robbery, and rape. In those cases, if they are tried as juveniles, they are directly committed to the boys' training school. Often, depending on state law, they are tried as adults.)

It is imperative that the court receive a realistic recommendation for a case like this. Most juvenile courts and social service agencies have a fundamental goal and philosophy of returning the child to the home and attempting reconciliation and family preservation. The court may not follow recommendations for alternate placement, but our obligation as psychologists is to identify those young people who need to be removed from their families.

While the court may or may not follow a recommendation at a particular point in time, this does not mean that the evaluation is a failure. Children like Robert are often put on probation and sent home, but if they get into more difficulty, the evaluation is still in the court record and the recommendations are often revisited by the court. On many occasions, when juveniles re-offend, they return to court and the initial recommendations are implemented. In those cases, the court or probation officer may contact the evaluating psychologist for an updated report or a letter reiterating the original recommendations months or even a year or two after the initial evaluation.

Case 5

This 13-year-old adolescent with a conduct disorder and history of committing sexual abuse was recommended for commitment to the Youth Services Center.

Psychological Evaluation Report

Name: Ken Lowrey
(Required identifying information, date of testing, etc.)

Tests Administered

> Wechsler Intelligence Scale for Children–Third Edition (WISC III)
> Wide Range Achievement Test–Third Edition (WRAT-3)
> Minnesota Multiphasic Personality Inventory–Adolescent (MMPI-A)
> Jesness Inventory
> Incomplete Sentences Blank
> Carlson Psychological Survey (CPS)
> House–Tree–Person Drawings (HTP)
> Hand Test

Beck Depression Inventory (BDI)
Clinical Interview

Clinical Interview

Ken is a 13-year, 2-month-old white male brought to the office by detention. When asked to describe his problems, he said he broke into a church with his friends. He also broke into a school. He was running away at the time. When I asked him why, he said he likes to "because it is fun." He said he loves to drink and smoke weed, get drunk, and get high. He said he likes to use speed, crack, and other drugs. He said his mother does not know about his substance abuse. He associates with gang members and aspires to be in one. He stays out with his friends, runs away for weeks at a time, and does not go to school very much. He was unapologetic about his behavior and, in fact, boasted about his escapades.

Ken said his mother is an alcoholic and still drinks, but not as much as before. He said that when his stepfather and mother were drinking more, they were always drunk and his stepfather was abusive to his mother. He said he was also abused by his stepfather. He said he was hit with a two-by-four and punched for no reason when his stepfather was drunk. He said he used to stay with his sister when his mother and stepfather were drunk. His stepfather and mother are now separated and he said his stepfather just got out of prison.

Ken likes to do what he wants to do. He said, "I take care of myself." He was in Florida last year staying with his father and his paternal grandmother, but they could not control him. He got in trouble there and had to return here. He said he returned because his stepmother thought "I was a pain in the ass."

Ken's mother admitted she is an alcoholic. She said she has been working and not getting drunk for the last two years. She said, "I am an alcoholic, but I'm getting better," so she seemed to suggest that her recovery is an ongoing process and she may be drinking a little bit at this time. She has five children and four of them are with her. She has lost her children before to DCFS custody. She has also been in a battered women's shelter. She admitted that Ken has been exposed to a very unstable background. She said that his stay in Florida was a disaster because he would not behave there. She said she works some at night now, but she has a roommate, so an adult is always present in their home.

Ken's mother confirmed that Ken has a constant problem running away from home and getting into trouble. She said he enjoys being in the streets and will stay gone for two weeks at a time. He does not get along well with her roommate and he steals from family members whenever he can. She was not aware of the substance abuse that he bragged about. He has been in Turning Point twice and Bridgeway once. Treatment in these psychiatric facilities has had no effect on Ken's behavior. He has been prescribed medication before, such as Ritalin, but he refuses to take it.

Ken's mother told me that Ken sexually abused her daughter and her daughter's playmate. These children were six when the abuse occurred six months ago. She said she found out about the sexual abuse several months ago and she thinks it was immediately reported. However, it was not reported. She said Ken attempted to have intercourse with his sister and apparently had some success penetrating the other girl, who is the daughter of her roommate. She said Ken made no attempt to deny that he did this and had no remorse about it. I asked Ken about this and he admitted trying to have intercourse with the two girls. He said it happened on one occasion, but he put it at two years ago. He laughed about it and had no remorse.

Test Results
The WISC-III scaled scores were as follows:

Verbal Tests		Performance Tests	
Information	6	Picture Completion	8
Similarities	8	Coding	11
Arithmetic	6	Picture Arrangement	9
Vocabulary	5	Block Design	10
Comprehension	2	Object Assembly	12

Verbal IQ	74
Performance IQ	100
Full Scale IQ	85

Ken's IQ of 85 is in the Low Average range and he was especially poor in verbal ability.

His academic scores on the WRAT-3 were as follows:

	Standard Score	Percentile	Grade Equivalent
Reading	87	19	5
Spelling	76	5	3
Arithmetic	86	18	5

These scores are commensurate with his intelligence. Ken is able to do school work at the elementary school level and would likely be behind due to his behavior problems and academic neglect over the years.

His CPS scores were markedly antisocial. His social adjustment is poor and he demonstrates little ability to control his behavior. He has difficulty relating to others and is very intolerant and hostile. There may be feelings of inadequacy and depression from time to time.

The MMPI-A scores were likely invalid because the F score was 80. The other scores were as follows: L = 46, K = 37, HS = 63, D = 69, HY = 45, PD = 78, MF = 34, PA = 82, PT = 83, SC = 75, MA = 56, SI = 65. He either answered the items randomly or he endorsed a large number of pathological items.

He said on the Sentences that he was happiest when he was in Florida. He wants to know why his mother will not let him go to Florida, so he has absolutely no insight about his behavior and how problematic he is to others. He thinks Florida was a vacation, which is why he wants to return there. He said boys "are boys—will never change" and a mother "is the best mom a kid could have." He said he can't stop getting in trouble and he is very "tired of this place." He said he hates his stepfather and swears he would kill him if he had the chance. A very telling response is when he said he suffers "nothing at all."

The Beck Depression Inventory had a score of 21. He said he has nothing to look forward to, he feels he is going to be punished, and he would like to kill himself. Many of these responses have everything to do with his detention.

The Jesness scores were as follows: SM = 84, VO = 76, IMM = 56, AU = 68, AL = 73, MA = 84, WD = 60, SA = 51, REP = 30, DEN = 20, ASOCIAL = 66. These scores indicate an Undersocialized, Passive individual who perceives the world in concrete and self-centered terms. He views reality as something quite distorted and usually to his own benefit. He has limited understanding of the world around him and he believes things just happen. He has little or no remorse about anything, except when he is confined.

Summary and Recommendations
Ken has the following diagnoses:

Axis I	Conduct Disorder, Undifferentiated Type (312.90)
	Parent Child Problems (V61.20)
	Adjustment Disorder with Mixed Emotional Features (309.28)
Axis II	Antisocial Personality Traits
Axis III	None
Axis IV	Severe (4)
Axis V	Current GAF 30

This is a 13-year-old who is very unstable and will do almost anything if he gets the opportunity and he believes it will be fun and exciting. He has a history of committing sexual abuse, for which he was never charged. He admits this and makes nothing of it. There is no way that he will obey his mother or comply with any conditions of probation, if returned home. He has been in three psychiatric units, one for a repeat admission. These have done little to change his behavior. My recommendation is commitment to the Youth Services Center and Serious Offender Program.

Discussion
In many ways, Ken was typical of adolescents in front of the court. Low IQs seem to be the rule, more than the exception. Verbal IQs are almost always lower than Performance IQs, as in this case. Academic functioning is usually far behind. Certainly there was some anxiety and the Beck Depression Inventory indicated feelings of depression. These children vacillate between feelings of depression and despair and defiance. His I-level classification on the Jesness was Undersocialized, Passive and he seemed to be someone who had little understanding of the world around him.

Ken, like many of these children, had a history of rejection and abuse. As in most of the juvenile court cases, the family background was poor and extremely chaotic. There was a family history of substance abuse. Unfortunately, little can be done about these factors at the time juveniles are evaluated. The psychologist's job is to state the facts as they exist at the time of the evaluation and to make recommendations.

Ken also had a history of sexually abusing his sister and her friend. However, he was not recommended for sexual offender treatment, since his sexual offenses were symptomatic of an antisocial personality. I do not recommend a juvenile for sexual offender treatment if the sexual offense is particularly vicious or if it is one among many other offenses, that is, part of a conduct disorder. Sex offender treatment will probably be the recommendation if the juvenile's overall personality appears to be inadequate, the victim was younger, there was a history of victimization of the offender, and there were no other criminal behaviors.

In this case, Ken had been hospitalized at least three times in psychiatric facilities, but treatment had little impact, as is often the case when the primary diagnosis is a conduct disorder. This was a 13-year-old who had no remorse, no regard for consequences, and a very high need for excitement, fun, and danger. He associated with gang members, taking off for weeks at a time from home and bragging about his behavior. He was also a drug user. There was no indication that he could return home and comply with his mother or the conditions of release.

Since psychiatric units did little to change his behavior, the recommendation was for commitment to the Youth Services Center and the Serious Offender Program. This particular commitment involved nine months' detainment in a wilderness program. In most states there are equivalent juvenile detention centers of varying lengths of stay. The type of facility offered in different jurisdictions would not affect the recommendation for someone like Ken. The recommendation is still confinement in a youthful offender program—with security. The more treatment and rehabilitation that is available at such programs, the better the prognosis, but this varies a great deal from one facility to another and from one state to another.

4

CRIMINAL COMPETENCY AND RESPONSIBILITY EVALUATIONS

Criminal competency and responsibility evaluations have traditionally been done at centralized locations, either at state hospitals or special state forensic units. To save money, many jurisdictions are now decentralizing forensic evaluations and contracting with mental health centers or private practitioners to perform evaluations in the community. Instead of hospitalizing all defendants for thirty days for evaluation, forensic evaluations can be performed in the community and cases can be disposed of more quickly. With the decentralized system, psychologists will not only have opportunities to perform community-based evaluations, but may also contract with inpatient forensic units to perform evaluations. (Federal competency and responsibility evaluations are still performed at federal hospitals, so this chapter will focus on opportunities for state outpatient forensic evaluations.)

Outpatient forensic evaluations are ordered by the court and fees are normally paid for by the court or by the state Division of Mental Health. These evaluations are done either in county jails, or in the practitioner's office if the defendant is free on bond. In only a few cases will defendants be referred to the hospital for a more complete evaluation. After the evaluation report is submitted, the defense attorney has the option of appealing to the judge for an inpatient evaluation, but the judge may not grant that request, since the purpose of outpatient evaluations is to reduce the forensic inpatient population. However, if the defense continues to insist on an inpatient evaluation, the judge may go along with the request, lest the case be overturned on appeal. Still, most cases are resolved at the outpatient level, without the need for inpatient evaluation.

Despite my practice of taking referrals only from neutral fact-finders, defense attorneys will often call and request an evaluation of a defendant. When attorneys call with such requests, they generally do not have in mind traditional competency and responsibility evaluations. They usually realize that their defendant was competent and responsible, but they want a report suggesting that there were mitigating circumstances or a mental condition which reduced their client's culpability. This is the traditional use of psychology and psychiatry in the courtroom: psychologists for the defense and prosecution doing battle in court. However, in the type of forensic practice I am advocating, the only referrals accepted are those done for a court or forensic unit to answer narrow questions of competency and responsibility. When defense attorneys call, they are encouraged to request a court-ordered mental evaluation. If a forensic practice is to be built following the guidelines outlined in this book, namely, accepting referrals from courts, decision makers, and other third parties, then all requests for evaluations coming from defense attorneys must be rejected.

Forensic evaluation reports should answer very directly the question of whether the defendant is currently competent to stand trial and whether the defendant was responsible for the offense. The court, judge, or jury will ultimately decide those questions, but the forensic report is expected to deliver a clear opinion regarding those issues. Anything short of a direct statement answering these questions is not acceptable, unless the recommendation is that the defendant be hospitalized for further evaluation.

The most common finding in these evaluations is that the defendant is competent and responsible and should proceed to trial. Many of these evaluations are done on defendants with no serious mental health or psychiatric history and are, in essence, frivolous mental defense motions. In most of these cases, the defense lawyer will accept the outpatient forensic evaluation and then proceed to trial or plea bargaining. The lawyer may have hoped that something would turn up in the mental evaluation, although he or she knew perfectly well that the client was competent and responsible. It is with these cases that the outpatient evaluation system has been successful in drastically reducing the number of defendants evaluated at state inpatient forensic units and saving the state mental health division or forensic unit a significant amount of money.

The next most common finding is that the patient is competent to stand trial, but suffered from mental illness at the time of the offense, making him not responsible for the offense. In these cases, the defendant will go back to court and, if both sides agree, the "not guilty by reason of mental illness" plea will be entered and the defendant will be sent to the state forensic unit. Such persons will stay there until they meet the civil requirements for release, which in most jurisdictions is that they not be a danger to themselves, others, or property.

The third most common finding is that the defendant is not competent to stand trial and was not responsible for the offense. In essence, the defendant is so impaired as to not be able to assist in his own defense, but enough information was gathered in the evaluation to make a finding that the defendant was also not responsible. This type of defendant is also sent to the state hospital, either on the incompetency alone or on both the incompetency and irresponsibility. The court may not make a finding of irresponsibility, but may send the defendant to the state hospital to restore competency and then consider the question of responsibility after competency has been restored.

The final and least frequent case is one in which the person is incompetent to stand trial, but the level of responsibility cannot be judged while he or she is untreated. These defendants are so impaired that you cannot get enough information about their version of the offense to make a judgment about responsibility. In these cases, final determination is deferred to the state forensic unit. If a defendant is sent to the state hospital for evaluation, this should not be considered an incomplete evaluation, since you have done exactly what the decentralization of forensic evaluations was meant to accomplish. State forensic units are usually pleased to get the occasional referral, compared to 100 percent of the evaluations that were performed there before the decentralization.

Once the forensic report is submitted, it is possible to be called as a witness to defend the report. However, if you were appointed by the court to perform the evaluation, a court appearance will rarely be necessary. More often than not, the report will be accepted and stipulated by both sides. This is in contrast to forensic work done for defense attorneys. In those cases, you can be sure that you will be called to court and vigorously cross-examined by the prosecution.

Occasionally there are cases, such as high-profile murder cases, in which the prosecuting attorney does not wish to accept findings of criminal insanity. In those cases the forensic psychologist will have to defend the results during preliminary hearings or trial. (Because these evaluations have been performed for the state, the prosecuting attorney is not likely to obtain another evaluation.) The prosecuting attorney will cross-examine the psychologist regarding the results and argue in front of a jury for a finding of responsibility. However, this is somewhat difficult to argue, once a state forensic psychologist has determined that the defendant was not responsible.

In some of the cases mentioned above, the defendant will be sent to the state hospital or forensic unit until he is judged to be competent to stand trial. While on the forensic unit, the staff psychologists and psychiatrists may form their own opinions about whether the defendant was responsible for the offense. In that case, there might be two differing opinions and you will be called to defend your findings. With state mental health divisions contracting criminal forensic evaluations to community psychologists, there is always a risk of such a difference of opinion, but this occurs in a small percentage of cases. The psychologist doing the initial evaluation should not be concerned about what the state hospital will say about a defendant who is found to be either not competent or not responsible. Although the inpatient staff will have the advantage of observing the defendant over a longer period of time, the outpatient psychologist will have the advantage of evaluating the person closer in time to when the offense occurred. The psychologist must simply form his or her own opinion from the evaluation and testify about those conclusions if called to court.

Although this chapter freely discusses deciding competence and responsibility, you should avoid testifying in front of the jury or judge that a defendant is not competent or not responsible. Those are ultimate findings that will be made by the jury or judge. If you use the words responsible or competent in the courtroom, the other side will object and the judge will tell the jury to disregard your statement—I know this from experience. If you can't use the terms responsible and competent in court, what can you say? When testifying about responsibility, you state whether the defendant "was able to conform his conduct to the requirements of the law at the time of the offense" and whether he "was able to appreciate the criminality of his or her conduct." In testifying about competency, you simply state whether the defendant "is able to assist in his own defense or understand the charges against him." You can use the terms competency and responsibility in your written reports.

COMPETENCY TO STAND TRIAL

Competency is a relatively simple question to answer. The definition of competency is based on *Dusky v. the United States*. It states that the accused must have sufficient present ability to consult with his lawyer with a reasonable degree of rational understanding and have a rational and factual understanding of the proceedings against him. The defendant must be able to cooperate with his attorney in his own defense and have an understanding of the nature, object, and consequences of the proceedings.

The Competency to Stand Trial Assessment Instrument, developed by A. L. McGarry in 1972 (see Table 4–1), is used to assess issues related to competency. It covers appraisal of available legal defenses, degree of unmanageable behavior, quality of relating to attorney, ability to plan a legal strategy, appraisal of the role of various participants in the proceedings, appreciation of the charges and possible penalties, and other related issues.

Defendants will often begin answering the question of competency even before they are asked. It is not unusual for defendants to immediately start talking about plea bargaining, reduced charges, sentences, jury trials, and issues of wrongful arrest. When defendants begin discussing these issues, their level of competency is obviously intact.

Retardation, if very significant, can interfere with competency. However, the threshold of competency is quite low, so it is only when IQs are legitimately in the low 50s and lower that competency may be compromised or absent. Most individuals with IQs in the 60s will be competent to stand trial. They have basic educable ability to learn something about the courtroom and to follow the directions of their attorneys.

Table 4–1. Competency to Stand Trial Assessment Instrument

	(Note Degree of Incapacity)
1. Appraisal of available legal defenses	_____
2. Unmanageable behavior	_____
3. Quality of relating to attorney	_____
4. Planning of legal strategy, including guilty plea to lesser charges where pertinent	_____
5. Appraisal of role of:	
a. Defense counsel	_____
b. Prosecuting attorney	_____
c. Judge	_____
d. Jury	_____
e. Defendant	_____
f. Witnesses	_____
6. Understanding of court procedure	_____
7. Appreciation of charges	_____
8. Appreciation of range and nature of possible penalties	_____
9. Appraisal of likely outcome	_____
10. Capacity to disclose to attorney available pertinent facts surrounding the offense including the defendant's movements, timing, mental state, actions at the time of the offense	_____
11. Capacity to realistically challenge prosecution witnesses	_____
12. Capacity to testify relevantly	_____
13. Self-defeating v. self-serving motivation (legal sense)	_____
Examinee_____	Examiner_____
Date_____	

[Developed by A. L. McGarry, M.D., 1972, under NIMH Grant Project No. 7R01-MH-18112-01: DHEW Publication No. (ADM) 74-103]

If a defendant is delusional, the defendant may not be competent to stand trial. The defendant must reasonably be able to recount the alleged charges and provide his or her lawyer with factual and historical information. The defendant has to understand that the judge or jury will make a decision and that his attorney is there to help him. A defendant who is delusional or paranoid about his own attorney, for example, would not be found competent. These are very basic questions, however, and only the most grossly disturbed individuals will not pass the threshold for criminal competency. If defendants are so psychotic that their behavior cannot be controlled in the courtroom, they will be found incompetent and will be hospitalized until they can be restored to competency.

At times defendants are seen who are extremely hostile and present a courtroom management problem, although they are not suffering from a mental illness. These defendants might be refusing to cooperate with their attorney or with the psychological evaluation as a political decision, for example, thinking they are "prisoners of war." This type of volitional lack of cooperation does not lead to a finding of lack of competency. It is only when refusal to cooperate is based on a mental illness or mental defect that there is incompetency.

CRIMINAL RESPONSIBILITY

Responsibility, which is entirely different from competency, is the essence of the insanity defense. It asserts that the defendant was too insane to be responsible for the offense, that is, that he is not guilty by reason of insanity. The McNaughton Rule in 1843 established a defense of insanity if the defendant was laboring under a defective reasoning from a disease of the mind, so as not to know the nature and quality of the act or not to know that it was wrong. Most states now rely on the test drafted by the American Law Institute (ALI) which states that a person is not responsible for criminal conduct if the conduct is the result of mental disease or defect and the person lacks substantial capacity to appreciate the criminality of his conduct or to conform his conduct to the requirements of the law. Many states also include the inability to have the culpable mental state to commit the alleged act. A defendant must have the cognitive capacity to appreciate the wrongfulness of the act (a standard which almost no one fails), the capacity to conform his conduct and not be subject to irresistible impulses, and the ability to have a guilty mind. Only the most grossly mentally ill person does not understand right from wrong. It also takes a seriously ill person to not conform his behavior to the requirements of the law.

Having a mental illness, however, is not enough by itself to lead to a determination that a person was not responsible for his actions. To make that determination, the mental illness must relate in a meaningful way to the criminal act. The criminal behavior must occur *because of* mental illness to establish lack of responsibility. In such cases, there is usually a delusion that is consistent with the behavior. For example, someone with paranoid schizophrenia who burns his mother's house because he thought it was possessed with evil spirits is not responsible. However, someone who is diagnosed with paranoid schizophrenia, but who steals to support a cocaine habit, is responsible. There is no provision across the country for a lack of responsibility based on substance abuse. Antisocial personality disorders and other personality disorders are not included as mental diseases which relieve defendants of responsibility.

Defense attorneys routinely make the motion for a mental examination if there is any mental health background or if defendants offer some explanation that they were not responsible, do not remember the offense, were drunk or using drugs, had an uncontrollable rage, or any number of other mitigating circumstances. Ninety percent of the time this line of defense is not successful, since defendants will be found to be responsible for their actions. These defenses may still be argued before the jury by psychologists hired by the defense.

THE EVALUATION

When a referral for a forensic evaluation is received, whether it is done in the community or at an inpatient forensic unit, a packet must be received before the evaluation can begin. At the very least, the information must include the arrest report, which outlines the charges against the defendant and describes the offense. It is impossible to question the defendant unless you understand the official version of the alleged offense. These packets are sometimes very thin and may just be a single page indicating the facts for probable cause. This is enough to proceed, since all that is needed is enough information to question the defendant about the alleged crime.

A defendant should be told at the beginning of the evaluation that you are conducting an evaluation for competency and/or responsibility. The defendant is told that the report will be supplied to the defense and prosecuting attorneys, but that the prosecution cannot use the forensic evaluation to prove guilt based on facts related during the forensic evaluation. Copies of the report will also be furnished to the judge, circuit clerk, and to the mental health division which initially contracted for the evaluation. The defendant has a right not to participate in the evaluation, but cooperation is usually secured because it is the defense, for the most part, that has made the motion for a forensic evaluation.

Records for previous mental health treatment will probably not be included in the packet provided by the prosecuting attorney. If you discover during the evaluation that the defendant has been treated at the state hospital or another psychiatric facility, you should have the defendant sign a release and obtain those reports before writing the forensic report.

Each state or jurisdiction may have a particular format for forensic reports. State forensic units generally have an established format to follow. What follows is a typical format for a forensic evaluation:

Forensic Report

Defendant's Name:
Defendant's Hospital Number or Case Number:
Date of Referral for Forensic Evaluation:
Date Forensic Report Submitted:
Date Forensic Report Typed:
Referred by: State Law or enabling legislation regarding mental evaluations
(example: CCO ACA-5–2–305) (name of county)

Sources of Information
You should indicate all sources of information. For example: "This evaluation is based on: a clinical interview with Mr. Jones on October 13, 1996; review of a Forrest City police report dated July 5, 1996; review of psychiatric records from Mr. Jones' previous hospitalization at Little Rock Psychiatric Hospital

in 1995; a telephone conversation on October 13, 1996 with the defendant's mother; psychological testing which included the WAIS-R (Wechsler Adult Intelligence Scale–Revised) and the MMPI (Minnesota Multiphasic Personality Inventory)."

Official Version of Alleged Offense
Relate the official charges against the defendant. Then provide a brief synopsis of the police report.

Defendant's Version of Alleged Offense
Include the defendant's account of his/her behavior, thoughts, and feelings related to alleged offense, including information about the context of the alleged offense. Use quotes when possible.

Relevant History
Historical facts pertaining to prior arrests, convictions and sentences, prior inpatient or outpatient mental health treatment, prior alcohol or drug use/abuse. Use judgment about what is included.

Clinical Evaluation
Include here mental status and other aspects of the individual's behavior and personality dynamics. Results of psychological testing should be included as well. A diagnostic formulation should be included.

Mental Condition
Give DSM-IV diagnosis.

Legal Questions
First address competency to stand trial. If indicated, describe factors which were important in reaching your decision. Then make a statement such as "Mr. Jones is (is not) currently able to understand rationally and factually the legal proceedings against him and is (is not) currently able to assist effectively in his own defense. Thus he is (is not) competent to stand trial."

Next address the issue of criminal responsibility. Discuss and evaluate the evidence regarding the various elements of the criminal responsibility issue: presence/absence of mental illness; ability to appreciate wrongfulness of behavior; ability to conform conduct.

Incorporate the following statements: "Mr. Jones was (was not) able to appreciate the criminality of his conduct at the time of the alleged crime and was (was not) able to conform his conduct to the requirements of law at the time of the alleged crime. Thus, it is my opinion that he was (was not) responsible for his behavior at the time of the alleged crime."

Some orders require that you address the issue of whether the defendant had the capacity to form the culpable mental state necessary to be found guilty of the specific offense he is charged with. This question should be dealt with in this section as well.

As can be surmised from the above format, this is one area of forensic evaluation in which testing is helpful, but not the most critical component of the evaluation. A person's MMPI protocol might be extremely abnormal, but if his mental illness was not related in a causative way to the criminal act, he will be found responsible, even if he is seriously mentally ill. In these evaluations, it is critical to determine from police reports and from the defendant's statements what was happening at the time of the event. You must determine what the mental state of the defendant was at the time of the offense and if mental illness caused the defendant to act in a criminal manner. The rest is standard clinical evaluation, utilizing good clinical judgment, with a great deal of reliance on background information and the person's history of mental illness.

The testing should always include intellectual measures. In fact, IQ may be the most important psychometric test in these evaluations, because there is a threshold at which point mental defect becomes relevant. If a defendant's IQ is less than 60, there will be a problem with competency and responsibility. Other projective and objective tests can be included in the evaluation, in addition to the Competency to Stand Trial Assessment Instrument or another check-off instrument guiding the psychologist through the categories and components of competency. The forensic evaluation report should include a diagnosis, as well as a clear answer to the legal questions of competency and responsibility. There is no limit to the kind of recommendations that can be made. If the defendant is found not to be responsible, suggestions can be made for disposition other than commitment to the state hospital. These might include mandatory attendance at a local mental health center or placement in a rehabilitation center. Courts are usually appreciative of such recommendations.

Following are cases showing the range of competency and responsibility evaluations that will be done in a typical forensic practice. The initial six cases show defendants who were psychotic or retarded and whose competency and/or responsibility were compromised because of it. The last four cases are representative of other types of cases in which defense attorneys requested competency evaluations, even though there was little reason to suspect the defendants lacked either competency or responsibility for the crime.

Case 6

This is an example of a defendant who was found to meet the minimum standards for competency to stand trial, but who was not responsible by reason of mental disease.

Forensic Evaluation Report

Name: Paula Ledwig
(Required case numbers, referral information, etc.)

Sources of Information
This evaluation is based on a clinical interview conducted at the Arkansas State Hospital, lower unit 2, on 8/19/94. I reviewed information from the Polk County Prosecuting Attorney's office, information from the Western Arkansas Counseling and Guidance Center, and state hospital records. Ms. Ledwig was administered the Wechsler Adult Intelligence Scale–Revised (WAIS-R) and the Competency to Stand Trial Assessment Instrument. She did not complete the Minnesota Multiphasic Personality Inventory (MMPI) and other personality tests which were left at the hospital for her. The staff reported that she was obsessing about each item, so the testing was finally discontinued.

Official Version of Alleged Offense
Ms. Ledwig is charged with terroristic threatening, a class D felony. On April 30, 1994, the police received a call from Denise Baker of Channel 5 about Paula Ledwig, who had been calling her at work. Baker is a television news reporter in the Fort Smith area. The police questioned Paula Ledwig and she promised not to call again. Ms. Ledwig called the television station again on May 7, 1994. The person who took the call said, "She told me she was deranged and if Denise was going to be on TV next week, she would have to kill her. I told her I hoped she wouldn't do that and she repeated herself—how if Denise was on TV next week she would just have to kill her." When the police questioned Ms. Ledwig, she admitted saying that.

Defendant's Version of Alleged Offense
When I asked Ms. Ledwig about the charges, she said her mother died when she was only 10 years old and she has been looking for another mother since then. There was another woman by the name of Tamara Massey, whom she pursued for several years. Ms. Massey moved to Texas and Ms. Ledwig had legal sanctions placed against her not to contact Ms. Massey again. Ms. Ledwig said Denise Baker appears to have the same traits as Tamara Massey and she thinks Denise Baker could be a mother to her.

   Ms. Ledwig said she first contacted Denise Baker using the excuse that she was upset about one of the stories Ms. Baker did about mental patients. She really wanted to talk to her and thought that would be something to talk about. She was visited by a police officer after that initial contact with Ms. Baker. When she called the station again on May 7, Ms. Ledwig said she talked to the receptionist and said that *if* she were threatening Ms. Baker, she would tell her that she would kill her if she got on the air the next week. Ms. Ledwig insisted to me that she was just using an example of what a threat would be. She said she told Ms. Baker earlier that if she were going to hurt her, she would notify her. Ms. Ledwig stated that she will again contact Ms. Baker if she has the opportunity. She thinks Ms. Baker acts the same as her mother and, if she could tell her this, she would understand "she is supposed to be my mother." She also said, "I'm not going to kill her. I can't imagine why Ms. Baker would be frightened." She said she has never met Ms. Baker in person.

Relevant History

Ms. Ledwig was seen in the state hospital, where she has been hospitalized on several occasions (Ms. Ledwig said it was five times). She has been seen at various mental health centers around the state. She has also been hospitalized twice at Rusk State Hospital in Texas. She said she was sent to the state hospital in Texas for threatening Tamara Massey and she is on probation for that offense.

At the mental health center in Waldron she was seeing Dr. Jerome Hall for medication and a counselor by the name of Catherine Carlson. She also saw a Dr. McManus at the Western Arkansas Counseling and Guidance Center and a psychologist in Mena she called Dr. Dennison, who she said was her most recent therapist. She said she would go back to the mental health center, if she is released from the state hospital. She has been on numerous medications, including Haldol, but she said she usually takes herself off her medicine when she feels better. She said she has tried to commit suicide before and she has trouble with her memory. Ms. Ledwig said she thinks she will be killed at the penitentiary because the prosecuting attorney will make plans to kill her.

Ms. Ledwig grew up in Texas. She has lived in the Mena area near her grandmother for six or seven years. She dropped out of school in the ninth grade. Tamara Massey was her physical education teacher. She said she was in the Hot Springs Rehabilitation Unit in 1990 for a year because she had an adverse reaction to medication and was paralyzed. The hospital records indicate she was paralyzed for a time.

Clinical Evaluation

Ms. Ledwig is a nervous 24-year-old white female with very poor hygiene. In talking about Ms. Massey and Ms. Baker, she said, "I don't pick these people out, they come, it's their personality and attitude. . . . I have to talk to them." The relationship she had with Ms. Massey vacillated between love and hate. She wrote threatening letters and was finally arrested when she allegedly pulled a knife on her in Texas. She said she threatened Ms. Massey and sent her four bullets in the mail because "if she wouldn't accept me, I'd get even with her." She said, "I'm not ashamed because she deserved it." Even in the face of her current arrest, her delusional beliefs are so strong that she said she would continue contacting Ms. Baker if she could.

Ms. Ledwig has a Verbal IQ of 80, Performance IQ of 81, and Full Scale IQ of 79, which is in the Borderline range of intellectual functioning.

In spite of her psychosis, Ms. Ledwig did fairly well on the Competency to Stand Trial Assessment Instrument. She knew the prosecuting attorney "wants to have me put away." She said the judge makes the decision and if there is a jury "they make the decision." She said the defense attorney "helps you." The witness "tells what happened." She understood the role of her attorney and basic court procedures.

She has the mental capacity to appreciate her presence in relation to time, place, and things. She has sufficient intelligence to grasp the basic facts of the court system. She understands there is a judge on the bench and attorneys who are adversarial. She understands she is expected to tell her lawyer the circumstances of the case. She understands that her guilt or innocence can be determined by a judge or jury and she has sufficient memory to relate those things in her own experience. She is competent to understand rationally and factually the legal proceedings against her. She understands what the state maintains she did. Even though she defends herself with a delusional belief system, she still has the ability to meet the minimum threshold to assist her attorney.

Mental Condition

> Axis I   Delusional Paranoid Disorder, Persecutory (297.10)
> Axis II   Personality Disorder, NOS (301.90)

Legal Questions
As stated, Ms. Ledwig is able to understand rationally and factually the legal proceedings against her and is able to assist her attorney in her defense. Although she is psychotic, she is still able to meet the minimum standards of competency. With regard to criminal responsibility, Ms. Ledwig was not able to appreciate the criminality of her conduct and conform her conduct to the requirements of the law at the time of the alleged offense. She did not have the capacity to form the culpable mental state to commit the alleged crime. She did not believe that what she was doing was a crime and she could not suppress her own criminal behavior. She was not responsible for her behavior at the time of the alleged crime. She is still a threat to continue similar acts in the future against the same person or a future victim.

She is currently in the state hospital and, if discharged on the appropriate medication and compelled to attend the mental health center, she will be competent to stand trial. Long term treatment will require that Ms. Ledwig be compelled to continue her medication and continue attendance at the mental health center with strong sanctions against contacting Ms. Baker or other persons.

Discussion
This defendant was evaluated at the state hospital instead of in the community. This was an example of the forensic unit contracting with a psychologist in private practice to perform the evaluation in the unit. This defendant was so disturbed that she did not complete the MMPI. This report points to the fact that sometimes tests cannot be administered other than an intelligence test. However, an

adequate evaluation can still be done, since these types of forensic reports often rely more on the clinical interview than other types of assessment.

This report is also an example of how one can be competent and not responsible. This defendant understood the charges against her and had the ability to argue her case, but this did not change her delusional state, especially at the time of the offense. As a result of her delusional paranoid disorder, she was unable to suppress her own behavior. She simply did not believe that what she did was a crime. She also had a history of stalking another individual, whom she similarly saw as a mother figure. Her diagnosis of delusional paranoid disorder, persecutory type, was directly related to the commission of the offense. She continued to be a threat at the time of the evaluation, since she had gained no insight into her behavior. She was found not guilty by reason of mental illness and sent to the state hospital where she stayed for over a year, rather than receiving treatment at a local mental health center.

In addition to the forensic report, a cover letter attesting to the accuracy of the report is always included. The notarized letter asserts the truthfulness of the report, which is a legal document. Following is a copy of the letter which was sent in this case:

(Date)
Honorable Judge Brown
Circuit Court of Polk County
Polk County Courthouse
Mena, Arkansas 71953

     Re: Paula Ledwig
     Arkansas Code ANN section _____
     Date of Evaluation: _____
     Polk County Docket # _____

Dear Judge Brown:
     This is to certify that this is a true and correct report of the findings in the above case, as derived from a psychological evaluation of Paula Ledwig, review of information from the Polk County Prosecuting Attorney's office, and material from Western Arkansas Counseling and Guidance Center and the Arkansas State Hospital.
     Ms. Ledwig has the following diagnoses:
     Axis I   Delusional Paranoid Disorder, Persecutory (297.10)
     Axis II   Personality Disorder NOS (301.90)
     The defendant appears to be aware of the nature of the charges and proceedings taken against her. She is capable of cooperating effectively with an attorney in the preparation of her defense.
     At the time of the commission of the alleged offense, the defendant did not have the capacity to appreciate the criminality of her conduct or to conform her conduct to the requirements of the law. She was not able to form the culpable mental state to commit the alleged act. While she is able to assist her attorney in the

preparation of her defense, she was not aware that the offense was wrongful and she did not have the ability to stop herself when committing the alleged offense.

Although competent at the most minimal level to stand trial, she continues to be delusional and is a threat to commit the same alleged act of terroristic threatening against the same victim or someone else in the future.

She is currently at the state hospital and should be discharged to the care of the mental health center with the appropriate antipsychotic medication. I think there is a good chance she can do better, if she complies with the mental health center and takes her medicine as prescribed, but she has a history of discontinuing her medication.

Sincerely,

Paul L. Deyoub, Ph.D.
Clinical Psychologist

cc: Attorney for Defendant
      Prosecuting Attorney
      Circuit Clerk
      DHS Mental Health Division

Subscribed and sworn before me on this _____ day of _____, 19___ .

_____
Notary Public. My commission expires _____ .

Case 7

This defendant was clearly competent to stand trial, but was not criminally responsible.

Forensic Evaluation Report

Defendant's Name: Norman Reed
(Required case numbers, referral information, etc.)

Sources of Information
This evaluation is based on a clinical interview conducted at this office. Norman Reed, who is currently in detention in Saline County, was brought to the office by the sheriff's department. He was administered the Wechsler Adult Intelligence Scale–Revised (WAIS-R), Wide Range Achievement Test–Third Revision (WRAT-3), Minnesota Multiphasic Personality Inventory (MMPI), Incomplete Sentences Blank, and the Competency to Stand Trial Assessment Instrument. Information was reviewed from the Saline County Prosecuting Attorney's office, the Arkansas State Hospital, and Birch Tree Communities, Inc.

Official Version of Alleged Offense
The defendant is charged with two counts of first degree battery. On 7/11/94 officers were dispatched to an address in Alexander (Saline County) to a shooting. When police arrived, they found that a white male, Ben Jamison, 40, had been shot. The bullet entered his neck and exited his back. Mr. Jamison said Mr. Reed shot him, but he had no idea why. Officers went to the residence next door and found a black male, Willie Jones, 31, who had been shot in the right arm. Mr. Jones said Norman Reed shot him and he did not know the reason. Mr. Reed was found standing on the roadside, down the street from where the shootings occurred. He was arrested, but not interviewed, because he requested an attorney. He had a gun in his possession. There were two spent rounds in the weapon.

These shootings took place at the home of Susan Edison, who is employed by Birch Tree Community. She brought the three men, all from Birch Tree Community, home with her as part of their therapy. Ms. Edison stated that they were sitting on the couch, with her sitting between Mr. Jamison and Mr. Jones. Mr. Reed was sitting on the end of the couch. She said Mr. Reed got up, took a Smith and Wesson .357 magnum from the entertainment center, and shot the other two men. The weapon belonged to Don Edison, Susan Edison's husband, who was not home at the time. Ms. Edison then ran from the home and went next door for help. Mr. Jones followed her.

Defendant's Version of Alleged Offense
Mr. Reed first said he thought he should be out now because he had been locked up since July 11th. He said he shot the other two men because of "jealousy." He said he saw the weapon on the entertainment center and got it first, because he was afraid the other guys would get the gun before he did. He said the other two men were patients at Birch Tree, as he was. He said Mr. Jones was getting up a lot and he thought Mr. Jones believed he was better than him because Mr. Jones "had a girl." He said Mr. Jamison was "relaxed" and he did not think that much about him, since he was focused on Mr. Jones. He denied ever having an altercation with either man.

Mr. Reed said he thought Susan Edison wanted to have sex with him and he was worried that Mr. Jones would have a relationship with her. He said he shot Mr. Jamison first and then Mr. Jones. He said he had been feeling angry because he did not have his money and he was tired of being reprimanded at Birch Tree Community. He said he was angry at the staff for making him do chores at Birch. He said he scared a woman before in a store and was accused of touching women in the community.

He said he felt "destroyed" after the shooting. He said he was scared and sat on the roadside. I asked why he did not shoot Ms. Edison and he said he was protective of her. He also said, "I had the opportunity. They could have got the gun as well as I." He said he was scared at the time and he never had a thought of shooting anyone before this. He thinks he can now go live with his father.

Relevant History
Norman Reed is a 35-year-old black male. He said his father is alive but his mother died in 1991. He said he has four brothers and one sister. He did not graduate from high school. He said at age 19 he was "broken into" by his cousin and brother. He finally said he was sexually abused anally by these individuals, which is what he meant by being broken into. He has a history of hearing voices and having delusions. His family reports that he has been threatening for many years. He stabbed someone six years ago and received probation. He also has a history of substance abuse, which exacerbates his psychosis, especially when he discontinues his medication.

Mr. Reed has had more than twenty-six admissions to the Arkansas State Hospital. He has been taking Clozaril and has a long history of using various antipsychotic medications with periods of noncompliance. He has been receiving medication and day treatment services at Birch Tree Communities, as well as supervision of his residential placement. He receives SSI.

Clinical Evaluation
Mr. Reed has a Verbal IQ of 74, a Performance IQ of 72, and a Full Scale IQ of 72, which is in the Borderline range of intellectual functioning.

On the WRAT-3, his standard scores were as follows: Reading–86, Spelling–73, Arithmetic–78. With his borderline intelligence he is able to understand basic information about his environment and the legal system.

The MMPI scores were very extreme and were as follows: L = 43, F = 99, K = 40, HS = 61, D = 77, HY = 64, PD = 76, MF = 59, PA = 99, PT = 71, SC = 101, MA = 57, SI = 65. These scores are very extreme and indicate strange symptoms and delusional thinking. He acknowledges bizarre experiences and is suspicious and paranoid.

On the Sentences he said the best "year of my life was in control." He said he feels "destroyed" and other people "excites me." He said he needs money "to get me out of trouble" and he is very "sorry for what I did."

On the Competency to Stand Trial Assessment Instrument he seemed to understand the legal system. He understood that his attorney is to help him and the judge "sentence people." From the description of the arresting officer, he did not talk because he wanted an attorney. He seemed to understand his offense because he said, "I'll go to the state hospital." He also said the authorities are likely to "just drop it, every day people get shot, they don't have room." He said that when he goes to court, he will just tell his side. He said he will plead "not guilty . . . guilty of insanity . . . because the gun was there."

I asked him if he could do such a thing again and he said, "I could, mad about my life." He said he could have had accomplishments in his life and he is angry because he has "no control." Mr. Reed is oriented at this time and in contact with reality, but he has delusional thinking.

Mental Condition

Axis I   Paranoid Schizophrenia, Chronic (295.32)
Axis II   Antisocial Personality Disorder (301.70)

Legal Questions
Mr. Reed is able to understand rationally and factually the legal proceedings against him and is able to assist effectively in his own defense. He is competent to stand trial. With regard to criminal responsibility, he was not able to appreciate the criminality of his conduct or to conform his conduct to the requirements of the law at the time of the alleged offense. He did not have the capacity to have the culpable mental state to commit the alleged act. He was not responsible for his behavior at the time of the alleged offense.

Norman Reed was delusional about the two victims and believed he was going to be shot by one of them. There were also peripheral delusions about Ms. Edison. Norman Reed continues to be dangerous and even acknowledges that he could do the same thing again. My recommendation is commitment to the Arkansas State Hospital, until he is determined not to be a threat to others and/or a secure facility is located for long term placement.

Discussion
Norman Reed lived in a facility for the chronically mentally ill, where he had an individual apartment. He was also attending a day treatment program for the chronically mentally ill run by the local mental health center. At the time of the offense, he and several other patients were visiting in the private home of one of the case workers. He was delusional about the female case worker and, while he sat with two other patients on the couch, he decided that one or both of them were going to shoot him with a gun that was in the living room. Why this case worker had a gun in open view and easily accessible when she had chronically mentally ill patients in her home is beyond comprehension. She was probably liable for negligence and, of course, open to discipline by her employer, the mental health center. Her negligence is beside the point, however, since the issue is whether or not Norman Reed was responsible for his actions.

This individual had twenty-six hospitalizations at the state hospital, where he was diagnosed with paranoid schizophrenia and an antisocial personality disorder. Despite his mental illness, there was little doubt that he was competent to stand trial. He did not have significant retardation, but had a Full Scale IQ of 72, making him capable of understanding the charges against him. He understood the legal system and was able to assist his attorney with his defense.

However, he was found not responsible for his actions because the shooting was a direct result of his delusional system. Being paranoid schizophrenic would not have been sufficient to make him irresponsible if his delusional system had not been related in a causative manner to the offense. His MMPI was abnormal, but that was not a critical factor in making this determination. He was antisocial, angry about his treatment in the program, and resentful, but he probably shot the other two patients because he believed he was about to be shot. He also thought the other two patients were jealous of his special relationship with the caseworker.

This defendant was committed to the state hospital and found not guilty by reason of mental disease. The only way he could win his release was to prove to the mental health judge that he was no longer a danger to himself, others, or property. Once a defendant is found not guilty by reason of mental illness and committed to a state forensic unit, the burden is on that defendant to prove that he is no longer a danger to others. This standard for release is the same throughout the United States for all patients who are committed.

Case 8

This is an example of a defendant who was found not competent to stand trial and not responsible for her actions by reason of her psychosis.

Forensic Evaluation Report

Defendant's Name: Sharon Smithson
(Required case numbers, referral information, etc.)

Sources of Information
This evaluation is based on a clinical interview with Sharon Smithson on July 13, 1994 at the Garland County Jail. She was administered the Wechsler Adult Intelligence Scale–Revised (WAIS-R), Bender Gestalt Drawings, Carlson Psychological Survey (CPS), Minnesota Multiphasic Personality Inventory (MMPI), Incomplete Sentences Blank, and Competency to Stand Trial Assessment Instrument.

She was interviewed for approximately an hour and tested for another hour and a half. Information obtained from the Garland County Prosecuting Attorney was also reviewed.

Official Version of Alleged Offense
Ms. Smithson allegedly took a 1983 Pontiac automobile and is charged with theft of property over $200 and under $1000, a Class C felony. The owner of Leeland Shell service station in Hot Springs reported that a 1983 Pontiac was left by the owners for repair. The attendant said he noticed on 3/30/94 that the vehicle had disappeared and immediately called the police and reported it stolen. Shortly thereafter, an officer was dispatched to the scene of a vehicle accident and upon arrival observed that the stolen vehicle had crashed into the side of a building and that Sharon Smithson was behind the wheel of the vehicle. When Ms. Smithson got out of the car, she had a strong odor of alcohol on her breath. She was transported

to St. Joseph Hospital and later charged with driving while intoxicated. The vehicle was totally damaged.

Defendant's Version of Alleged Offense
Ms. Smithson was not able to say much about the alleged offense. When I asked her if she wanted to tell me what happened, she said she was driving a friend's car and was drinking too much. She denied that the car was stolen and said very little about the accident. It was very difficult to interview Ms. Smithson, since she was easily derailed and not able to hold a thought for more than a few seconds.

Relevant History
Ms. Smithson said her mother died when she was 14 and her father is also deceased. She said she has a ninth grade education and she was not able to indicate any work history. She thinks she had her first child when she was 14 years of age and she claims she is getting AFDC at this time. She said she has four children, ages 12, 13, 14, and 17. While she said she has custody of her children, it is not clear that she does, since she was unable to describe her living arrangement or childrearing practices. She also said she has been living with a lady named Ms. Browning. Before that she had an apartment and, before that, she said she stayed with friends. She said she likes to drink and does it whenever she is able to. She denied any admissions to the Arkansas State Hospital or any other hospital. It could be, based on her diagnosis, that most of this history is not true or distorted.

Clinical Evaluation
Ms. Smithson is a short, obese, 30-year-old black female evaluated at the Garland County jail. She wore a white towel wrapped around her head. Her hygiene was very poor and I was told other inmates were complaining about her personal habits. She never understood what my purpose was, even though I explained very carefully why I was there. She asked maybe twenty-five times if I would release her, since she was convinced that she could just walk out of the jail with me. She was extremely persistent about getting out of jail. She did not understand that she has charges to face, that she has been unable to make bond, and that she faces court hearings and a possible trial.

She was tearful when she explained, "I lost my brain." She thinks she hurt her head and her brain literally poured out of her head. She was quite upset when she described this. Later in the interview she talked about a snake biting her head and then claimed that caused her brain to drain out. There was not much consistency from one moment to the next in her story.

She pulled up her pant leg to show me where she said a computer is placed in her leg. She said water gets inside her leg and makes her leg bubble. She said she needs to go to Little Rock to get her leg drained. She believes the computer in her leg records movements and watches what she and other people do. The wound on her leg that she thinks the computer was implanted in was from kicking a window. She was apparently arrested at some other time for kicking out that window.

Her WAIS-R Verbal IQ was 71, Performance IQ was 64, and Full Scale IQ was 66. Her IQ of 66 is in the Mild Range of Mental Retardation. This score of 66 appears to be a reliable and valid measure of her intelligence.

The Bender Gestalt Drawings were very poor and consistent with a low IQ. She did not complete the CPS and MMPI and it was almost impossible to keep her on task. She requires one-on-one supervision. During the testing and interview, she often made stereotypic hand movements or startle movements. She put her hands up in the air, as if jolted or surprised. A couple of times she had auditory hallucinations and answered as if someone were talking to her. Others in the jail have also observed her talking to no one, but apparently hearing someone talking to her. This occurs whether she is alone or with someone.

She wrote on the CPS booklet incomprehensible phrases, such as "we ride love boberts" and "svella blue bleak." The patient was obviously both delusional and suffering from auditory hallucinations. On the Sentences most of her statements were incoherent. She said she feels "no one watching" and at bedtime "I want be told tight a close." The items on the Sentences were a combination of mental retardation, illiteracy, and psychosis.

It was clear on the Competency to Stand Trial Assessment Instrument that she did not understand the various roles of the participants in the legal system or her particular legal situation. She did not understand the seriousness of her offense and she thought if convicted she would get "a week or two in jail." She had no idea how she could plea or what her legal defense could be. Her behavior in court is likely to be poor and it would be difficult for her to sustain her attention on the proceedings. She has no ability to plan legal strategy or to assist her attorney in her defense.

The results of the evaluation indicate Ms. Smithson was also grossly confused at the time of the alleged offense.

Mental Condition

Axis I   Schizophrenia, Paranoid, Chronic with Acute Exacerbation (295.34)
Alcohol Abuse (305.00)
Axis II   Mild Mental Retardation (317.00)

Legal Questions
Ms. Smithson is currently unable to understand rationally and factually the legal proceedings against her and is unable to assist in her own defense. Therefore she is not competent to stand trial. With regard to criminal responsibility, Ms. Smithson was not able to appreciate the criminality of her conduct or conform her conduct to the requirements of the law at the time of the alleged offense. She did not have the culpable mental state to commit the crime. Although she was abusing alcohol and mentally retarded, these two diagnoses are not the main reasons for incompetency and lack of responsibility. The mental disease or defect responsible for her

incompetency and irresponsibility is paranoid schizophrenia. The patient is not on any medication to control her psychosis and should be sent to the state hospital.

Discussion
This defendant's diagnosis of schizophrenia was directly related to her offense. She was unable to provide any meaningful history and she demonstrated total lack of competency related to her current circumstances. She seemed to have no understanding or memory of the offense at all. There was no faking or malingering when she talked about losing her brain and then showed her leg where she thought a computer was implanted. She had very little ability to complete any of the tests. It was concluded that she was grossly psychotic at the time of the evaluation and at the time of the offense.

At the time of the offense, this defendant had apparently been drinking, but alcohol abuse alone is never sufficient for a finding of irresponsibility. She was also retarded, with a 66 IQ, but this was also not sufficient by itself to escape competency and responsibility. If there had been mental retardation and alcohol abuse without psychosis, she would have been determined to be competent and responsible for the offense.

This person was determined to be not guilty by reason of insanity and sent to the state hospital. She was evaluated a year and a half later for stealing cars again and she was again determined to be not competent to stand trial and not responsible for her behavior. She is a chronic paranoid schizophrenic who seems to commit random property offenses whenever she is out of the hospital and not taking her medication.

Case 9

In this stalking case, notes written by the defendant were extremely informative about his paranoid state of mind. He was found incompetent, even though he understood much of the legal proceedings against him. The finding of incompetence was moot because he was found not responsible.

Forensic Evaluation Report

Defendant's Name: George Waller
(Required case numbers, referral information, etc.)

Sources Of Information
This evaluation is based on a clinical interview conducted at the Pike County Jail on 1/17/95 with Mr. Waller. He was administered the Wechsler Adult Intelligence Scale–Revised (WAIS-R), Minnesota Multiphasic Personality Inventory (MMPI), Carlson Psychological Survey (CPS), Incomplete Sentences Blank, Millon Clinical Multiaxial Inventory (MCMI), and the Competency to Stand Trial Assessment

Instrument. Information from the Pike County Prosecuting Attorney's office and treatment notes from Community Counseling Services were reviewed.

Official Version of Alleged Offense

The defendant is charged with stalking. The alleged victims are Dawn and Sam Liston. Sheriff Moore stated that in July 1994 a person called Dawn and Sam Liston at home one night at 3:00 A.M. The next Monday they got a call at the same time. Mrs. Liston's father's gravestone was defaced at Mount Tabor Cemetery in Montgomery County. Sheriff Moore said that in mid-October 1994 a person called the Liston residence and left a message telling Mrs. Liston that if she would kill herself he would marry Deanna. On October 24, 1994, a magazine was found on their front porch and on November 1, 1994, their business was shot into twice. Dawn Liston also says she was followed by a vehicle that day. Sheriff Moore stated that later on November 1, 1994, while he was present at Dawn Liston's business, a call was received. The caller stated that he had heard about her trouble at the office the night before. Mrs. Liston asked who it was and the caller stated, "your friend Zak." At that time, no one except Sheriff Moore and Mrs. Liston knew about the gunshots into the building.

Sam Liston said George Waller came into his office in August 1992 to inquire about a job at the Farmers Insurance Group. George Waller later came to the Liston home and threatened to kill Mr. Liston. Mr. Liston talked to George Waller's father about that incident prior to the November 1, 1994, shooting. Mr. Liston stated that George Waller is infatuated with his wife Dawn. Mrs. Liston received a call and the person said, "Dawn, I figured out a way to fuck Deanna." This call was traced to a local convenience store. Mr. Waller had been seen making calls from that store previous to this phone call. On December 17, 1994, Mrs. Liston was at Dillard's at the Hot Springs Mall when a man walked up to her and said, "Dawn, I haven't seen you in a long time." The man was identified as George Waller. On December 18, 1994, at 10:30 P.M., George Waller called and identified himself. He made no threats, but asked about Shirley, a relative of the family. A pornographic book was left on the doorstep of the Liston's business. On December 23, 1994, the Pike County Sheriff's Department received a call that George Waller was pacing in front of the Liston's business. Upon their arrival, George Waller was found in front of the store and was arrested for stalking. During the arresting incident, Sheriff Moore took a .22-caliber semiautomatic rifle, which was in the small vehicle.

Defendant's Version Of Alleged Offense

When asked about the stalking charges, Mr. Waller said that Mr. and Mrs. Liston are friends of his parents. He said he does not get along with the Listons and "we don't see eye to eye." He said he talked to Mr. Liston about employment at the Farmers Insurance Company owned by the Liston family in 1992. He said he talked to him for twenty minutes and, when he ended the conversation, he claims Mr. Liston called him "a goddamn faggot." Mr. Waller said he tried to fight Mr. Liston because he had called him a name. He said he bumped into Mrs. Liston once at the mall and spoke to her. He denied that he threatened or stalked her. He said he did not make the calls that the Listons have been receiving. Later he said, "I may have made phone calls. I don't know." He denied having anything to do with shooting the building.

Relevant History
George Waller is a 30-year-old white male who has been treated at Community Counseling Services since September 1991. He said he was seeing the doctors because his parents thought he was depressed after he lost a job. Counseling notes from 8/18/92 indicated that his parents were concerned about his threatening Mr. and Mrs. Liston with violence. Mr. Waller insisted at that time that Mr. Liston hit him in the back of the head. He also reported he had a call from President Bush. He was diagnosed with a delusional disorder, persecutory type, and possible schizophrenia and schizotypal personality disorder. He was treated with Haldol. Presently Mr. Waller is taking Effexor 75 mg. twice a day and trifluoperazine 5 mg., half at bedtime. Mr. Waller has a degree in agri business but has been unemployed. He has lived at home continuously since returning from college four years ago. He said he worked at USDA for twenty-nine months but was fired for starting a rumor. He said he started a rumor about a man sexually abusing or raping his daughter. He later denied that he started this rumor. He had a disorderly conduct charge at a Rolling Stones concert in November 1994.

Clinical Evaluation
George Waller was seen at the Pike County Jail. He was extremely flat in affect, made poor eye contact, and was in no distress whatsoever about his detention. He displayed absolutely no insight that he might have a mental illness. He was verbal and cooperative throughout the evaluation. He was in contact with reality and he would not reveal any delusional material. His thought processes and content were very guarded and paranoid.

I had access to notes he had written during his detention and before. The notes, which he was writing to himself, were extremely bizarre and said things such as, "The government doesn't control weather. The government doesn't kill its own people. No one is out to get hurt or kill you. You're not in the CIA." When I asked him about these, he did not respond. He did not deny the notes were his, but he seemed embarrassed and secretive about it. He looked away and would not respond. Other notes said, "Mom and Dad approve of Sam Liston cutting your rectum and Dawn Liston putting toothpicks in your penis and cutting your penis and rectum with a razor blade." I asked Mr. Waller about this and he finally admitted that he felt they did this to his body parts. He has very strong feelings of inadequacy. He is particularly distressed about his inability over the last four or five years to hold a job. He wrote, "Working (it seems like one big mistake), gestures are mean SOB's." He also wrote, "When you get married and your wife is with another man, when you get home, don't worry, ask what to do." Another note said, "Dawn Liston cut my penis and rectum and burnt me. Sam Liston beat me and hot shoted me." There were many other similar notes.

On the WAIS-R, Mr. Waller had a Verbal IQ of 97, a Performance IQ of 75, and a Full Scale IQ of 86. This is in the Low Average range of ability.

He had MMPI scores as follows: L = 43, F = 65, K = 40, HS = 36, D = 67, HY = 44, PD = 66, MF = 63, PA = 91, PT = 69, SC = 75, MA = 40, SI = 66. He retreats into an autistic fantasy world to avoid the stress of reality. He is socially isolated, withdrawn, and awkward. He is preoccupied with strange paranoid thoughts. His paranoid delusional system appears to be well crystallized. He has persecutory delusions, but apparently no hallucinations. He may otherwise appear to be intact, but he incorporates jealousy, grandiosity, and feelings of persecution into his delusional disorder. He is able to perform everyday tasks, but with diffi-culty. He cannot hold a job and has a mild degree of depression. He is very worried and self-conscious. He tends to be a hostile individual, capable of explosive and dangerous behavior.

On the CPS he endorsed items saying that his future will be bad, he thinks he does not do the best thing, he has disturbing dreams, and he gets scared and sick about problems he has. He also believes that most laws are bad and says he has carried weapons. On the Sentences he said, other people often "influence my behavior and actions" and he suffers "slight depression." He is resentful and said he is bothered by "self-righteous people." He also said that most women "want independence" and that he is worried about "mental and physical abuse."

The MCMI was very high for social withdrawal, schizotypal adjustment, anxiety, and depression.

On the Competency to Stand Trial Assessment Instrument, he said he is going to plead innocent and wants a jury trial. He indicated who his attorney was and he seemed to understand the charge of stalking and the possible penalties. On the other hand, his competency is compromised because he does not believe he is mentally ill. He stated that he is not schizophrenic or paranoid and he does not understand how he could be accused of bothering the Liston family, since they were bothering him.

Mental Condition

Axis I   Schizophrenia, Paranoid Type (295.30)
Axis II   Schizotypal Personality Disorder (301.22)

Legal Questions
Mr. Waller does have some ability to understand rationally and factually the legal proceedings against him, but because he is actively psychotic, disorganized, and delusional about this particular offense he is not able to assist his attorney effec-tively in his own defense. Thus, he is not competent to stand trial. In my opinion, the issue of competency is somewhat moot, because I believe he is not criminally responsible. Mr. Waller was not able to appreciate the criminality of his conduct or conform his conduct to the requirements of the law. At the time of the alleged

offense, he did not have the ability to have the culpable mental state to commit the alleged act. He believed Mr. and Mrs. Liston were harming him and this delusional belief was directly related to his conduct. Therefore, his mental illness affected and determined his criminal behavior.

If he is found not guilty by reason of mental illness, my recommendation is commitment to the state hospital until he is determined not to be dangerous. If the court chooses not to make a finding at this point, he should be committed to the state hospital for further evaluation until he is competent to stand trial.

Discussion

This individual had a chronic history of schizophrenia, very poor adjustment, and dependency on his parents. The MMPI was a valid profile and the elevations for Scales 6 and 8 clearly indicated his schizophrenia. There is also no better psychological test than the handwritten notes this defendant presented. The notes were clearly bizarre, paranoid, and suggested an active psychotic state.

Although this defendant and Paula Ledwig, the defendant in Case 6, were both accused of similar crimes and both had some understanding of the legal system, she met the minimal standards of competency while he did not. Ms. Ledwig was diagnosed with Delusional Paranoid Disorder, a diagnosis suggesting that her mental impairment or psychosis was confined to the delusional belief itself. This defendant was diagnosed with Schizophrenia, Paranoid Type, a much more pervasive mental and emotional disorganization, which affected his competency.

As stated in the report, issues of competency are often moot if the determination is that the defendant was not responsible. In this case, the defendant's schizophrenia was directly related to and responsible for his stalking offense. He was committed to the state hospital after he was found not guilty by reason of mental illness. For eventual release from the forensic hospital, he would have to show that he was not a danger to himself, others, or property, the standard for release in most jurisdictions.

Case 10

This defendant, a juvenile, was found not competent and not responsible by reason of mental retardation.

Forensic Evaluation Report

Defendant's Name: Leah Ford
(Required case numbers, referral information, etc.)

Sources of Information

This evaluation is based on a clinical interview with Leah Ford and an interview with her sister, Georgia Matson. The defendant was administered the Wechsler

Intelligence Scale for Children–Revised (WISC-R), Wide Range Achievement Test–Revised (WRAT-R), Peabody Picture Vocabulary Test (PPVT), Carlson Psychological Survey (CPS), Bender Gestalt drawings, House–Tree–Person drawings, Incomplete Sentences Blank, and the Adaptive Behavior Scale (AAMD).

Official Version of Alleged Defense
The defendant Leah Ford was charged with first degree battery for allegedly participating in the physical abuse of 6-year-old Daniel, who received multiple injuries, including amputation of a leg. Daniel is a neighbor child apparently left by the mother. He lived with the Fords for three or four years. Leah's mother, sister, and brother are in prison for participating in the abuse of Daniel. There was another boy involved in the abuse who is also being adjudicated through Juvenile Court. Leah is accused of spanking and striking Daniel throughout the time he lived with her family.

Defendant's Version of Alleged Offense
The defendant said she did not hurt the child, although she admitted slapping him on the hand "one time when he did something wrong." She blamed other members of the family, especially her brother Troy, with most of the abuse. She said her brother abused her as well as the child.

Relevant History
Leah is a 15-year-old black female who now lives most of the time with her grandparents but spends considerable time with her sister, Ms. Matson. There are seven children in the family, not from the same father but from the same biological mother. Leah attends Forest Heights in the eighth grade in special education. Her sister said Leah has not been abused herself, but said she may have spanked the victim.

Clinical Evaluation
The defendant had very strong body odor and was poorly groomed. She had a significant overbite and is a thin, emaciated female who looks more like 9 or 10 years of age. She seems to have long-term failure to thrive. She had pressured speech and significant stuttering. She talked very rapidly and was very inappropriate in the way she related. She moves very close to the person with whom she is talking and one has to back away from her, since she has little understanding of social cues. She was a poor historian about her personal and family circumstances.
    The WISC-R scaled scores were as follows:

Verbal Tests		*Performance Tests*	
Information	1	Picture Completion	1
Similarities	1	Picture Arrangement	2
Arithmetic	4	Block Design	3
Vocabulary	1	Object Assembly	1
Comprehension	2	Coding	4

Verbal IQ   49
Performance IQ   48
Full Scale IQ   44

Her IQ of 44 is in the moderate range of mental retardation at less than the first percentile rank. Her PPVT score was less than 40, also in the mentally defective range.

Her WRAT-R scores were:

	Standard Score	Percentile	Grade Equivalent
Reading	66	1.0	3B
Spelling	73	4.0	3E
Arithmetic	49	0.06	<3

All of her academic scores are in the defective range, but are better than her 44 IQ. Apparently she has picked up some basic academic information from special education. Still, her reading is poor and she is not able to do calculation.

On the CPS she endorsed many pathological items and her highest score was on thought disorder. She denies antisocial behavior, but she says she has had a poor life, she worries a great deal, she has little success in her life, and she feels sad and depressed. She denies drug and alcohol abuse.

Her Bender drawings were equivalent to those of a child about 7 years of age. She had several mistakes and had visual–motor problems.

On the House–Tree–Person drawings, this 15-year-old drew extremely immature figures. Her drawings resembled those of a 5- or 6-year-old child. She was not able to take the MMPI because she had poor reading comprehension and inability to understand the items.

Her Incomplete Sentences Blank was consistent with her mental retardation and lack of social development. She said that she regrets hitting the boy (so she does admit hitting this child) but she minimizes her involvement in the abuse. She said she does not like boys, and I doubt there has been any sexual activity unless she has been abused. She is generally fearful of strangers.

On the Adaptive Behavior Scale she has adequate eating and toilet skills. Vision and hearing appear to be normal and motor development is adequate. She has adequate body balance, walking and running, and control of extremities. She has full use of language, although she does stutter. She is able to perform acts of personal hygiene, but obviously she does not do it unless supervised. At present no one is supervising her personal care, so she does not take care of herself. She does not have a sense of direction and would not be able to handle her own transportation. She has minimal telephone use. She does not have any ability to handle money or shop independently. Under supervision she is able to engage in domestic activities, such as cleaning and simple cooking. She has inappropriate interpersonal skills. There is no apparent self-abuse or sexually aberrant behavior. Her sister did not think Leah was violent or destructive. She also denied antisocial behavior. Overall, Leah's social functioning appears to be in the mild range of mental retardation, while her intellectual deficits are in the moderate range.

The defendant had little to no understanding of the various roles of the participants in the legal system. She did not understand the charges against her or the possible penalties. She did not know what her defense would be or the various roles of her attorney, the prosecuting attorney, or the judge. She does not meet the minimal requirement for competency to stand trial.

The defendant has an IQ of 44 and has been an abused and neglected child herself. Family members around her were allegedly abusing the child, Daniel, and with her low IQ, if she did participate, she was mimicking the behavior of the adults around her. She lacked any appreciation of the cumulative effects of the abuse or the significance of her own behavior or that of her family members.

Mental Condition

> Axis I: No diagnosis (V71.09)
> Axis II: Moderate Mental Retardation (318.00)

Legal Questions
Leah Ford is not able to understand rationally and factually the legal proceedings against her and is currently unable to assist effectively in her own defense. Thus, she is not competent to stand trial. With regard to criminal responsibility, she was not able to appreciate the criminality of her conduct or conform her conduct to the requirements of the law at the time of the alleged crime. She did not have the culpable mental state to commit the alleged offenses. Thus, Leah Ford was not responsible for her behavior at the time of the alleged crime.

The defendant should be a protective service case herself with the Department of Children and Family Services. It is not in her best interest to remain in her home and she is in need of services, possibly residential care at an ICF facility.

Discussion
This was a well-publicized case, in which a 6-year-old boy was abused and lost a leg at the hands of an entire family. This juvenile defendant had the right to file for a mental evaluation of competency and responsibility. Such evaluations are not the same as standard evaluations for juvenile delinquents.

In this case a mental defect, rather than mental disease, resulted in an inability to be competent or responsible. This defendant had a 44 IQ and there was no question that she was very defective in her ability to think and solve problems. Her mental retardation was pervasive. She had no ability to discuss the juvenile court system. She failed to appreciate the impact, consequences, or wrongfulness of her behavior. Not only was she not able to understand rationally and factually the legal proceedings against her, which resulted in incompetence, but she was also unable to appreciate the wrongfulness of her behavior at the time of the offense. She was recommended and placed with the Department of Human Services, a child protective services agency. Another alternative given the court was placement in a mental retardation facility.

Case 11

This case shows a person who was too psychotic to be fully evaluated. He was found incompetent to stand trial, but the issue of his responsibility for the crime was deferred until evaluation by state hospital staff.

Forensic Evaluation Report

Defendant's Name: Lonnie Galton
(Required identifying information, date of testing, etc.)

Sources of Information
This evaluation is based on an attempted clinical interview with Lonnie Galton at the Washington County Jail on 9/1/95 and review of information from the Washington County Prosecuting Attorney's office.

Official Version of Alleged Offense
Mr. Galton is charged with commercial burglary, a class C felony. On 8/15/95, patrol officers responded to Vera's Trading Post in downtown Springdale, Arkansas, in reference to a burglary in progress. Upon arrival at Vera's Trading Post, Officer Trenton found a front window of the business broken out and blood drops by the glass fragments. Officer Trenton yelled into the business, identifying himself as the police, and suspect Galton yelled back from inside the business that he was coming out. The suspect walked to the broken window, was ordered to climb back out, and was taken into custody.

Defendant's Version of Alleged Offense
Mr. Galton was so psychotic that he could not offer his version of the offense.

Relevant History
No history could be obtained from Mr. Galton because he was uncooperative and in a psychotic state.

Clinical Evaluation
Mr. Galton is a 26-year-old black male. When he was brought into the examination room at the jail, he walked in the room swearing, using bizarre profanity, making derogatory and obscene sexual statements, and talking continuously. He could not be asked any questions because he was hypomanic and had a stream of obscene speech that would not stop. He never knew who I was, did not allow me to explain what the evaluation was all about, and immediately became hostile. He grabbed my cellular phone and threw it against the wall. Deputies were summoned and the interview was ended.

     Mr. Galton is taking Haldol, Tegretol, and Cogentin. Jail records indicate he has been isolated because of his psychotic behavior, which other inmates could not tolerate. It was noted by jail personnel that some days he is calmer than other days, but usually he is just as I saw him: out of control, banging on the door, and making no sense in his speech and thought processes.

No tests could be administered to Mr. Galton and no interview or background information could be obtained. He could not discuss the offense or provide his version of the offense.

Mental Condition

>Axis I   Provisional Psychotic Disorder NOS (298.9)
>Axis II   Deferred until further examination

Legal Questions
Mr. Galton is in a psychotic state and is not able to understand rationally and factually the legal proceedings against him. He is unable to assist effectively in his own defense. His behavior at this time would not be appropriate for a court appearance, since he is aggressive and difficult to manage. He is not competent to stand trial and referral to the Arkansas State Hospital Forensic Unit is necessary at this time.

Although he is not competent, there was no way to assess his responsibility for the offense, since he could not be evaluated. Evaluation of responsibility is deferred to the State Hospital staff, who will have ample opportunity to make this determination.

Discussion
Because his behavior was so bizarre and disruptive to the other inmates, Mr. Galton had been kept in a holding cell since his arrest for burglary. Not only was he psychotic, ranting and raving, but he was also dangerous. Guards were called as quickly as possible to end the interview.

On the basis of my report, this defendant was sent to the state hospital for further evaluation and treatment. After treatment with antipsychotic medication, he would be evaluated by state hospital psychologists to determine his level of responsibility for the crime. One might think that a person this psychotic would automatically be found innocent by reason of mental illness for the offense itself. That is not necessarily the case. Mr. Galton may well have been able to appreciate his behavior and to conform his behavior to the law at the time of the offense. He may not have been as psychotic, or psychotic at all, at that time. He was charged with commercial burglary and that charge alone suggests he may have known what he was doing. If the offense had been more bizarre or a personal injury offense, there might have been more reason to suspect irresponsibility. The point, however, is that he had to be treated for his acute psychosis before the allegations could be explored and evaluated. As an outpatient forensic psychologist, I could never determine levels of responsibility in someone as totally incompetent as this defendant.

Nationally, there are findings of incompetency or irresponsibility in less than 10 percent of the criminal forensic cases evaluated. The defendant who is found to be criminally insane is placed in the state hospital or forensic unit until such time as he or she is judged not to be dangerous.

The cases presented above may seem to be obvious because of the presence of delusions or a history of psychotic behavior. There are other cases more complicated involving more atypical claims of mental illness. Defense attorneys may argue a whole range of mental disease and defect strategies based on temporary insanity. These include post-traumatic stress disorder, battered wife syndrome (in which a wife who kills her husband alleges self-defense), and other uncommon defenses. These "exotic" defenses, as I choose to call them, should be left to defense attorneys and psychologists for hire. If a defendant claims blackouts and memory loss, uncontrollable fear, jealous rage, or similar emotional states, those are arguments that the jury can hear, but they do not involve mental illness.

Other times attorneys will argue that defendants are incompetent or irresponsible simply because of a history of mental health treatment. Because of the present system of private psychiatric hospitals, many people receive inpatient treatment who are not psychotic. Many adolescents and adults with conduct disorders and antisocial personality disorders receive psychiatric diagnoses in order to ensure that insurance will pay for treatment. Many people receive antipsychotic medications for behavior control, not for psychoses. Therefore, histories of inpatient treatment should be closely evaluated. A prior psychiatric diagnosis or treatment with antipsychotic medication does not necessarily raise serious questions about a defendant's competency to stand trial or responsibility for the crime. Substance abuse, anxiety disorders, depression, and bipolar illness do not excuse a person from responsibility for his or her actions. Conduct disorders and antisocial personality disorders certainly do not fall under the definition of "mental disease or defect" in determining competency and responsibility. Even a legitimate diagnosis of psychosis does not mean that a defendant will automatically be found incompetent and irresponsible.

Another strategy used by defense attorneys is to argue that competency and responsibility are compromised because of neurological impairment. I have evaluated defendants with histories of seizure disorders and head injuries, including one with left side paralysis because of trauma to the right side of his brain. If you come across these issues while evaluating a defendant, you need to administer a Luria–Nebraska Neuropsychological Battery or a Halstead–Reitan Battery in addition to the intellectual and personality tests.

There might be isolated cases in which a neuropsychological impairment would have a critical impact on competency or responsibility. Competency would be compromised if the defendant is so demented, disoriented, and neurologically impaired that he is unable to understand his current circumstances. Responsibility would be compromised only if there was the grossest level of dementia at the time of the offense. These standards will not be met in the overwhelming number of cases. In most cases of remote head trauma there is good compensation and recovery. Although some neuropsychological impairment may still show up on the testing, these defendants will often have a history of antisocial behavior that is more

germane to the issue. Even if the neurological problems contribute to the antisocial behavior and poor impulse control, this does not constitute a mental disease
or defect for a particular crime. Having some neurological impairment is no more
significant, for example, than having a 65 or 70 IQ, which also does not qualify as
a "mental defect" under the law. You should find these defendants both competent and responsible, unless they meet the criteria mentioned above.

All of these exotic claims of incompetency and irresponsibility should not
be a problem for a psychologist performing criminal forensic evaluations for the
state. The rule to follow in performing evaluations for the state is to be conservative, to rely on classical and traditional definitions of irresponsibility, and to be
grounded in well-established principles of mental illness. To be found not responsible, the defendant must not appreciate the criminality of his conduct and must
be unable to conform his conduct to the requirements of the law by reason of mental
disease or defect. That normally entails psychosis and delusional behavior or IQs
below 60.

The following cases show how various defendants were found to be both
competent and responsible using these traditional standards.

Case 12

This case points out how the psychologist should not confuse self-defeating, irrational, impulsive, and totally irresponsible behavior with mental illness. This clinical profile also indicated an exaggeration of symptoms.

Forensic Evaluation Report

Defendant's Name: James Clason
(Required case numbers, referral information, etc.)

Sources of Information
This evaluation is based on a psychological evaluation and clinical interview conducted at the Clark County Jail on 2/14/95, review of information from the Clark
County Prosecuting Attorney's office, and administration of the Wechsler Adult
Intelligence Scale–Revised (WAIS-R), Minnesota Multiphasic Personality Inventory (MMPI), Millon Clinical Multiaxial Inventory (MCMI), Carlson Psychological Survey (CPS), Incomplete Sentences Blank, Beck Depression Inventory (BDI),
and the Competency to Stand Trial Assessment Instrument.

Official Version of Alleged Offense
James Clason is charged with aggravated assault, terroristic threatening, and possession of a handgun on school property. On or about the fifth day of December,
1994, Arkadelphia police were dispatched to the Headstart location at Sixteenth
and Caddo Streets. Three officers responded. James Clason had entered the school,

gone room to room, and then spoken to Alicia Montez. She said Mr. Clason asked if his child was in the class at Headstart and she said no. Mr. Clason said that was good, because if his child had been there and he had not been permitted to see him, he would have started shooting. She said he made comments about a gun and eventually showed her a semiautomatic handgun. She said she did not know if the gun was loaded, so she talked very nicely to Mr. Clason until he left the facility. She then notified the police. The officers responded and picked him up a block from the school. Officer Tysdale asked Mr. Clason to place his hands on a citizen's vehicle, with Sergeant Wilson standing behind the defendant. Before he could be searched, he stated that he had a gun in his back, meaning his waistband, and a .40-caliber Beretta handgun was removed from him. The weapon was fully loaded and one round was in the chamber. At the time James Clason entered the school, small children were attending class and children were all about the area.

Defendant's Version of Alleged Offense
Mr. Clason was asked about the alleged offense. He said he does not usually carry a weapon, but at that time he was going into a more dangerous neighborhood to get drugs. He said he had the gun for possible protection. He said he ran into a girlfriend on his way to get drugs and she had business in the area of the Headstart facility. That is when he decided to walk into the Headstart program, because he thought his son might be in attendance. He said he walked in and a lady asked him if she could help him. He said Ms. Montez looked for his son's files and said he was not in the school. Mr. Clason said he told Ms. Montez that "I guess it's good. No one will get hurt about messing with my kids." He said Ms. Montez asked him if he had a gun and he showed it to her. He said he has not been seeing his children, which is why he decided to walk into the Headstart program to see his child. He said he realized he was carrying a concealed weapon and he is a convicted felon. He knew it was against the law to have a firearm on school property. He denied that he was going to hurt anyone or that he threatened Ms. Montez.

Relevant History
James Clason is a 33-year-old white male who appeared to be physically healthy. He grew up in Arizona. When he was 16 he moved to Arkansas with his mother and two sisters. He dropped out of school in the seventh grade and later obtained a GED. He said his father, who is still alive, is an alcoholic and a "child molester." His mother is working at Henderson State University. Around the age of 17, he married and had one child who died of crib death. After that divorce, he said he had another child with a different woman and that child also died in infancy. When he was 21 years of age, he moved back to Arizona. He said he has worked as a roofer, carpenter, mechanic, cook, and laborer. He said he has a history of substance abuse, including alcohol, marijuana, cocaine, LSD, methamphetamine, and mushrooms. He said he was depressed in 1989 and 1990 and thought about or attempted suicide. He said he was seen at the University Medical Center in Arizona.

At the age of 17, James Clason stole a car and was sentenced to the Job Corps in Oklahoma. He had a theft of property in 1981 and received probation. He stole another vehicle after probation and received two years at the Department of Corrections in Arkansas. He was 18 or 19 years old at the time of that first incarceration. When he was free at about age 21, he said he took another car and received ten years probation. He moved to Arizona and took a vehicle there. He served nineteen months in Arizona and then served two additional years in Arkansas. He said he was out of prison in 1988.

James Clason was married in 1992, after living with his wife for two years before the marriage. She had an affair with his brother, as well as a two-year affair with one of his friends. After having two children, they separated and his wife moved back to Arizona. When he attempted to join her in the summer of 1994, she wanted a divorce. He stayed in Arizona from July until the fall of 1994, but was not able to see his children. He said his wife relocated to Arkansas in late 1994 and he has seen his children only twice since then. He said he was unable to go to court to get them. He was staying with a girlfriend in Arkansas when the present offense occurred.

Clinical Evaluation

Mr. Clason was verbal and cooperative throughout the evaluation. He was in good contact with reality and his general fund of information was adequate. His thought processes and content were basically normal and there was no indication that he was experiencing hallucinations, delusions, or any psychotic symptoms. He had no unusual or bizarre behavior and he did not seem to be anxious or depressed. His level of motivation was good.

On the WAIS-R, his Verbal IQ was 107, Performance IQ was 113, and Full Scale IQ was 109. His IQ of 109 is in the Average range at the 73rd percentile, so it is close to the High Average range. He has very good ability and does not have any intellectual deficits.

The MMPI scores were L = 54, F = 116, K = 38, HS = 75, D = 87, HY = 62, PD = 76, MF = 57, PA = 102, PT = 86, SC = 101, MA = 66, SI = 77. These scores were so extreme as to be invalid. He is attempting to emphasize a need for treatment and help. He did the same thing on the MCMI, with very extreme scores on the Schizoid, Avoidant, Dependent, Passive Aggressive, Anxiety, and Dysthymia scales. The profile indicated exaggeration of symptoms.

The CPS was elevated for all of the scales and he indicated extensive substance abuse.

His BDI was 35 and again he emphasized feelings of depression and despair. Most of this is related to his present circumstances.

On the Sentences he said he regrets "having ever been born," people "usually just piss me off," he feels "lonely, angry, and depressed," his greatest fear "is that I'll never see my children again," and his nerves "are shot." He said the future looks bleak and he feels like giving up.

On the Competency to Stand Trial Assessment Instrument he was clearly aware of the legal system, the charges against him, possible options for his defense, and possible penalties. He has no difficulty understanding the legal system.

Mental Condition

Axis I	Polysubstance Abuse (304.8)
Axis II	Antisocial Personality Disorder (301.7)

Legal Questions

Mr. Clason does not have a mental disorder that would affect either competency or responsibility. His problems are longstanding and, for the most part, represent an antisocial personality disorder with a history of substance abuse. At times he probably has been depressed, but nothing in his mental health history would suggest loss of control or impairment of judgment. He is able to understand rationally and factually the legal proceedings against him and is able to assist effectively in his own defense. He is competent to stand trial. With regard to criminal responsibility, he was able to appreciate the criminality of his conduct and conform his conduct to the requirements of the law at the time of the alleged offense. He had the capacity to have the culpable mental state to commit the alleged act. He was responsible for his behavior and he is fit to proceed at this time.

Discussion

This defendant's behavior was totally self-defeating, irrational, and impulsive, but not indicative of mental illness. Behaving in ways that the average person regards as completely irrational does not constitute mental illness or irresponsibility. Committing crimes that make no sense is what defendants do and we cannot use the standards of rational, prosocial beliefs and behaviors to judge criminal behavior. We can continue to be baffled by criminal behavior, but at the same time we know that this has nothing to do with mental illness. These individuals are competent and responsible.

James Clason, who was fundamentally an antisocial personality, had a long history of self-defeating behavior and substance abuse. In all jurisdictions in the United States, substance abuse is not considered to be a mental illness or sufficient for lack of responsibility. (The only rare exception is when intoxication resulted from involuntary ingestion of a substance. For example, if someone working with chemicals became intoxicated and committed a criminal act, that person would have a legitimate defense.)

Although this defendant was a substance abuser, there was no evidence that he was mentally ill. He had no history of mental illness and no previous inpatient psychiatric treatments. He had average intelligence. His MMPI scores were extreme, as was the Beck Depression Inventory. It is not unusual for some defendants to exaggerate symptoms on objective tests to somehow plea that they have mental illness or need help. This is why test data on forensic criminal evaluations cannot stand alone and must be evaluated in context. On the Sentences, Clason said he regretted being born, he feared he would never see his children, and he felt his nerves were shot. These statements certainly indicate his personal distress, but it must be remembered that he was in serious trouble with the law. While he may have needed counseling, his distress had nothing to do with incompetence or irresponsibility for criminal behavior.

Case 13

This defendant, a substance abuser with borderline intelligence, was found to be both competent and responsible.

Forensic Evaluation Report

Defendant's Name: A.C. Watson
(Required case numbers, referral information, etc.)

Sources of Information
This evaluation is based on a clinical interview with Mr. Watson conducted at the Pike County Jail while he was free on bond, review of information from the Pike County Prosecuting Attorney's office, and administration of the Wechsler Adult Intelligence Scale–Revised (WAIS-R), Wide Range Achievement Test (WRAT-3), and the Competency to Stand Trial Assessment Instrument.

Official Version of Alleged Offense
The defendant is charged with two counts of delivery of a controlled substance, which was marijuana. On January 4, 1995, an agent made contact with A. C. Watson for the purpose of obtaining the controlled substance LSD from a residence in Pike County, Arkansas. No one was present at that residence. During the ride back to Mr. Watson's residence, he stated he knew of marijuana available for $35 per bag. The agent agreed and, at Mr. Watson's direction, the agent drove to the residence of David Watson. At approximately 8:25 P.M. the agent gave A. C. Watson $35 in U.S. currency for the purchase of one bag of marijuana. He entered the residence, returning a short time later with a clear plastic bag containing a green, leafy substance, which the agent recognized as marijuana. The agent drove Mr. Watson back to his residence and left the area.

On 1/15/95 the same agent was involved in an undercover drug investigation in Pike County. She came into contact with a white male, known to the agent as A. C. Watson. She asked him if he knew where the agent might obtain marijuana. Mr. Watson replied that he did and directed the agent to a trailer house located in an area known as Rock Creek, south of Glenwood. This trailer is known by the agent as the residence of David Watson. Upon arrival, the agent gave A. C.

Watson currency in the amount of $35 to purchase marijuana. He entered the residence and returned about five minutes later with a bag of what appeared to be marijuana. Mr. Watson asked that a joint be rolled for his part in going in and getting the bag for the agent. The agent complied. Mr. Watson rolled a joint, which he lit and handed the agent. The agent simulated smoking and handed the joint back to A. C. Watson and declined any further. The agent and A. C. Watson parted company.

Defendant's Version of Alleged Offense

Mr. Watson denied that he sold marijuana on January 4 or 15, 1995. He said on January 4th the agent picked him up and bought him beer. He said they smoked marijuana together and he kissed her. He had known the agent, whom he knew as Sandy, for about a year. He said he never sold her marijuana. He said that he and Sandy were at the same party on January 15 and that they both smoked marijuana there.

Relevant History

A. C. Watson is a 46-year-old white male. A friend brought him to the Pike County Jail for the evaluation. He said he has never been in prison and has never been found guilty of a felony. He said he smokes marijuana if it is around, but it is not a habit. He said he has an alcohol problem and has been to the Benton unit for detoxification. He said a previous drug charge against him was dropped. He said drugs were planted on him by the police.

Mr. Watson was born and raised in Pike County. He has a fourth grade education. He has always lived at home. He currently lives alone with his father; his mother died about five years ago. He has five brothers and five sisters. He has been married three times and is married now but separated. His present wife is living in California. He has five children, all from his first marriage, which lasted 13 years. He said all his children are married and he sees them frequently. He said he lost his house and property because of the last drug charge. Although that charge was dropped, he said he had to spend all his money on his defense. He said he is receiving SSI and has not worked in seven or eight years. He said he spends his time smoking marijuana and drinking. He has three DWI's.

Clinical Evaluation

A. C. Watson presented himself as a low-functioning individual, but in very good contact with reality and not experiencing any psychotic symptoms or mental illness. His thought process and content were basically normal, and there was no indication of delusions or hallucinations. His Verbal IQ is 68, Performance 76, and Full Scale IQ 71. This is in the Borderline range of intelligence. The subtest scores were consistent, suggesting he has always functioned at this level. On the WRAT-3, he had a Reading score of 49, a Spelling score of 45, and an Arithmetic score of 46, all of which are below the first percentile. He functions at no better than the second grade level.

Mr. Watson's responses to the Competency to Stand Trial Assessment instrument indicated he had a good understanding of the various roles of the participants in the legal system. He appreciates the seriousness of the charges against him and the possible penalties. He said that he would defend himself and he understood the role of his lawyer and the prosecuting attorney.

The results of the evaluation indicate he has borderline intelligence, but no psychosis or mental illness. He does have a history of substance abuse. While his intelligence is clearly below average, it is more than adequate to meet the minimum standards to be judged competent to stand trial.

Mental Condition

Axis I   Alcohol Dependence (303.90)
           Cannabis Dependence (304.30)
Axis II   Borderline Intellectual Functioning (V62.89)

Legal Questions
A. C. Watson is currently able to understand rationally and factually the legal proceedings against him and he is able to assist effectively in his own defense. He is competent to stand trial. With regard to criminal responsibility, he was able to appreciate the criminality of his conduct and conform his conduct to the requirements of the law at the time of the alleged offense. He had the capacity to form the culpable mental state to commit the alleged act and he was responsible for his behavior at the time of the alleged offense.

Discussion
Forensic evaluations are frequently requested on clients such as this who have no history of mental illness. The defense lawyer, often the public defender, files a motion for forensic evaluation almost as a routine procedure when he comes across a client who has a history of substance abuse or low intellectual functioning.

This defendant had a history of drug and alcohol abuse and had previously been treated at a rehabilitation unit for alcohol detoxification. He was receiving Social Security disability benefits, which is not unusual for drug addicts and alcoholics around the country. His IQ was 71, so he had more than adequate ability to meet the requirements for competency. During the evaluation, he denied that he engaged in the alleged offence. This type of denial is not unusual in individuals who are evaluated. Defendants such as this are not advancing any defense based on mental illness themselves. They are simply denying that they engaged in the offense at all.

Cases like this are very straightforward and conclusions are easily reached. This case had no merit, as far as meeting the criteria for lack of competency or criminal responsibility, but the defendant received a thorough evaluation in an effort to determine whether there was any mental illness or defect involved. This was a waste of the state's resources and the court's time, but clearly it was the defendant's right to have a forensic evaluation at the state's expense. It is not the forensic psychologist's place to say which cases should receive forensic evaluations and which cases should not. Results in cases such as this are hardly ever challenged, because the defense attorney probably realized all along that his client did not meet the criteria for lack of competency or responsibility.

Case 14

This adolescent, who was being tried for murder as an adult, had a history of inpatient psychiatric treatments. Although the issue to be decided was competency and responsibility, he was given a test battery similar to that given juvenile delinquents.

Forensic Evaluation Report

Name: Gene Boardman
(Required identifying information, date of testing, etc.)

Sources of Information
This evaluation is based on a clinical interview conducted at my office on January 12, 1995, administration of the House–Tree–Person drawings, Incomplete Sentences Blank, Jesness Inventory, Wechsler Intelligence Scale for Children–Third Edition (WISC-III), Minnesota Multiphasic Personality Inventory–Adolescent (MMPI-A), Carlson Psychological Survey (CPS), Beck Depression Inventory, Wide Range Achievement Test–Third Edition (WRAT-3), the Hand Test, Competency to Stand Trial Assessment Instrument, and review of information from the Yell County Prosecuting Attorney's office and review of records from the adolescent unit at Bridgeway Hospital.

Official Version of Alleged Offense
Gene Boardman is charged with murder in the first degree, a Class Y felony. On January 2, 1995, the Yell County Sheriff was dispatched to a shooting in Delaware, Arkansas. When Officer Lane arrived, he was advised that the victim was upstairs. The victim, Wayne Darling, a 17–year-old black male, had been shot four times in the chest and side area. Gene Boardman was taken into custody and taken to the Criminal Investigation Division. After being advised of his rights with his parents, he gave a video- and audiotaped interview. He stated that Darling had become disrespectful, so he threw his clothes out the window and told him to leave. He said at that point Darling came toward him, as if he were going to fight him, but grabbed for a gun. He stated that he was faster than Darling and got the gun. They struggled and the gun went off. He remembers shooting at him when he was across the room. He stated he did not know how many times he shot the victim. In the statement, he described the shooting as both accidental and self-defense.

Defendant's Version of Alleged Offense
Gene was asked about the alleged offense. He said, "I'm not supposed to discuss my case without an attorney present." His statement was accepted and his refusal to discuss the case was not due to mental illness.

Relevant History
Gene is a 15-year-old black male brought to the office by the Yell County officer. He said he lives with his father in Delaware, but used to live with his mother in Little Rock. He said he attended alternative school most of last year, his ninth grade year. He said he has never had juvenile charges against him.

Gene said his first inpatient hospitalization was at Bridgeway in June 1991. He said he was hospitalized because he was in constant trouble at school and was fighting with his stepfather. Following that, he had other hospitalizations at CPC Pinnacle Point Hospital, Charter Hospital, and Youth Home. He described all of these as the result of "family dysfunction." He said he just didn't like his stepfather. He said that every time he left the hospital and returned home to his mother's house, he encountered his stepfather and had the same problems again. He said he would leave the house after a fight and would always end up in another placement. He said he finally began living with his father, but he had trouble getting along with him, too. He denied alcohol or drug abuse and said he is not a member of a gang.

Clinical Evaluation
Gene presented himself as a healthy looking 15-year-old male. He was in good contact with reality, verbal, and cooperative, but he chose not to discuss the alleged shooting incident. There was no evidence of psychosis or serious mental illness. His thought processes and content were normal and he displayed no unusual or bizarre behavior. He was not particularly anxious or depressed, although he did talk about being uncomfortable in jail and wanting to go home. His level of motivation and cooperation were very good throughout the evaluation.

The records from Bridgeway Hospital indicated that Gene was diagnosed with conduct disorder and attention deficit–hyperactivity disorder. Depression was considered a possibility. The staff at Bridgeway described his behavior as uncooperative, manipulative, and argumentative. He was disruptive to the unit and would not accept responsibility for his behavior. Bridgeway recommended longer term residential treatment and he was placed at other facilities, including Youth Home. While at Bridgeway he was diagnosed with mild mental retardation, but the testing at this time indicates that he is not retarded.

Gene obtained a WISC-III Verbal IQ of 81, a Performance IQ of 82, and a Full Scale IQ of 80. This is in the borderline range of intellectual functioning at the 9th percentile. His academic scores were much better and, with the exception of arithmetic, he has average academic ability. His reading and writing scores exceed his 80 IQ. The WRAT-3 scores were as follows:

	Standard Score	Percentile	Grade Equivalent
Reading	102	55	HS
Spelling	99	47	8
Arithmetic	78	7	4

The MMPI-A scores were F = 52, L = 76, K = 55, HS = 41, D = 71, HY = 61, PD = 80, MF = 59, PA = 54, PT = 54, SC = 48, MA = 46, SI = 63. The elevations on the MMPI-A are consistent with a conduct disorder and oppositional defiant behavior. The highest elevations were on scales 4 and 2. This profile indicates impulsiveness, a problem delaying gratification, little respect for social standards, and a tendency to be in conflict with authority. His acting-out behavior includes problems at school and home. The 4–2 elevation indicates some depression when he is in difficulty. After a period of acting-out, he may express a great deal of remorse and guilt, but the depression usually lifts if there is not a particular environmental problem. He tends to be energetic, sociable, outgoing, and creates a favorable impression. This profile suggests that the hospitalizations at various adolescent facilities were directed toward behavior control and not significant depression or emotional turmoil.

On the CPS he indicated that he drinks alcohol sometimes and that he has used drugs once or twice. He denied antisocial criminal tendencies and denied ever carrying a weapon, but admitted causing trouble in school. His scores on the Jesness suggested group affiliation, denial of emotional problems, and lack of interest in school.

On the Sentences he said he regrets "what I've done," he feels "terrible," and he can't "believe why this happened." He said his nerves are bad and that other kids seem to do better than he does. He said he suffers a lot in life and failed at being a teenager. Certainly he has some despair and depression about his particular circumstances. He indicated on the Beck Depression Inventory that he feels depressed, but again this is related to his current circumstances. On the Hand Test he gave a wide range of responses which were consistent with an adolescent conduct disorder. His House–Tree–Person drawings were unremarkable.

On the Competency to Stand Trial Assessment Instrument, he clearly understood the roles of the legal participants and the court system. He understood the charges against him and he is able to refer to his attorney and assist his attorney in his own defense.

Mental Condition

Axis I:	Conduct Disorder, Undifferentiated Type (312.90)
	Adjustment Disorder with Depressed Mood (309.00)
Axis II:	None

Legal Questions

Gene is able to understand rationally and factually the legal proceedings against him and is able to assist effectively in his own defense. Thus, he is competent to stand trial. With regard to criminal responsibility, he was able to appreciate the criminality of his conduct and to conform his conduct to the requirements of the law at the time of the alleged crime. He had the capacity to have the culpable mental state to commit the alleged act. There is no evidence of psychosis, hallucinations, delusions, or mental defect contributing to the alleged offense. He was responsible for his behavior at the time of the alleged crime and he is ready to return to court for disposition.

Discussion

This adolescent had an 80 IQ, so he had no mental defect that would compromise his competency and responsibility. He refused to give his version of the offense, but that was a rational decision that went directly to his ability to defend and protect himself. I read the official description of the offense and the transcript of his previous statement, as well as some of his mental health records, and determined that he had the ability to conform his conduct to the requirements of the law and that he was able to appreciate his conduct. In short, he was both competent and responsible.

On the MMPI-A, he had a 4–2 profile, indicating that he was basically someone with a conduct disorder who was depressed because of the situation he found himself in. He received diagnoses of oppositional defiant disorder and/or conduct disorder in the past. However, the more he was hospitalized, the more he was diagnosed. It is typical today for private psychiatric hospitals to overdiagnose adolescents, since insurance will not approve hospital admission with a diagnosis of conduct disorder. Teenagers who act out are being diagnosed with depression, bipolar disorder, and other major psychiatric disorders. It is only when their behavior is particularly obvious and undeniable and they will not benefit from further hospitalization that they receive a diagnosis of conduct disorder.

The adolescent in this case received a diagnosis of bipolar disorder a year prior to this offense and was given Haldol, Stelazine, Mellaril, and other major antipsychotic drugs. However, there was no evidence from this evaluation that he was bipolar. He had a conduct disorder and, because of his middle-class background, had been put in a psychiatric hospital every time he acted out. This young man even stated himself that he ended up in the hospital each time he had a conflict with his mother and stepfather.

Because his parents had resources, this defendant had a very vigorous and aggressive defense team. After my evaluation, his lawyers made a motion for state hospitalization for assessment, which was granted. He stayed at the state hospital for eighteen days and the state hospital staff concurred with my findings that he was competent and responsible. After that finding, the defense hired a psychologist to evaluate the defendant independently and testify at the trial. That psychologist eventually testified that the defendant could not control what he was doing because of his conduct disorder.

In Arkansas and many other jurisdictions, the statute for the mental illness defense excludes antisocial personalities. Just based on law, the testimony of that "expert" should have been disregarded. However, it is unlikely that the judge would interfere, leaving it to the prosecution and cross-examination. Right or wrong, our judicial system invests ultimate authority in the jury. The jury could decide that this defendant was not responsible because he had a conduct disorder, notwithstanding the fact that the law excludes conduct disorders from consideration in the mental illness defense. Even if the judge instructed the jury not to consider the defendant mentally ill on that basis, the jury could still disregard those instructions and find him not guilty by reason of mental illness.

In this case, the psychiatrist who diagnosed this adolescent with bipolar disorder was also called to testify. She testified that, in her opinion, he had bipolar disorder and was not responsible for his behavior. She apparently came to that conclusion based on her treatment of him at least a year prior to the alleged crime. She talked about prescribing Haldol, Stelazine, Mellaril, and other major antipsychotic drugs to him. When I testified, I was asked whether these medications are given for major psychiatric illnesses. I testified that they can be, but that it is not uncommon for adolescents who have intractable behavioral problems and multiple psychiatric hospitalizations to receive drugs like that. In those cases the drugs are, in effect, used as chemical restraints.

As can be seen from this case, the defense will sometimes go to great lengths to put their own "hired guns" and experts on the stand. Our job, however, is to use the well-established standards described by law to determine whether a defendant is competent to stand trial and responsible for his actions.

Case 15

This evaluation, done on a defendant who was charged with aggravated robbery and rape, shows the extent of the information that the psychologist can put in a forensic evaluation, even if it is incriminating to the defendant. The official version of the offense, which was quite lengthy in the original report, has been abbreviated.

Forensic Evaluation Report

Defendant's Name: Larry Johnson
(Required case numbers, referral information, etc.)

Sources of Information
This evaluation is based on a clinical interview conducted at the Garland County Jail on September 30, 1994, review of information from the Garland County

Prosecuting Attorney's office, and administration of the Wechsler Adult Intelligence Scale–Revised (WAIS-R), Wide Range Achievement Test–Third Edition (WRAT-3), Beck Depression Inventory, Minnesota Multiphasic Personality Inventory (MMPI), Incomplete Sentences Blank, Carlson Psychological Survey (CPS), and the Competency to Stand Trial Assessment Instrument.

Official Version of Alleged Offense
Johnson is charged with aggravated robbery and rape, both Class Y felonies. On August 17, 1994, a reported rape and aggravated robbery occurred at 4008 Bower. Upon arrival at that location, Detective Williams observed the victim, Janet Yang, age 78, sitting outside of the residence. She had numerous abrasions on her face and a black right eye. She had blood on her face.

Ms. Yang stated that two white males, later identified as Larry Johnson and Louis Hayward, came to her house looking for yardwork. Over the next two hours, they beat her, raped her, held a razor to her neck, and threatened to kill her with a gun. She also gave them money.

Defendant's Version of Alleged Offense
When asked about the alleged charges, Johnson said that for five days before August 17 he was with Louis Hayward using drugs. Johnson told Hayward that he needed money for more drugs and knew where he could get money. He told Hayward they could ask Ms. Yang for work and she would unlock the door while they were asking. He said Ms. Yang had no work, so Hayward asked for a glass of water to get into the house. Johnson said Hayward threw her down and hit her in the head. Johnson said he grabbed her and told her to calm down and she threw a glass at him. He said he tried to help her, but Ms. Yang reached for a knife and tried to stab him. He said, "I was in slow motion and threw her around like a rag doll." He said he could hear her talking in tongues and he told her to shut up. He said Hayward hit her with a loud-speaker. Johnson said he found a gun in the bedroom. He said he loaded the gun and Hayward made a silencer from a bottle. He said he never used the gun. He said that Hayward told him later that he shot the woman. When Johnson was told that he raped the woman, he said, "That's impossible." He said, "I only hit her two times with my fist and kicked her because she pulled me down." He said he does not remember the victim writing two checks, but only one. Johnson said he was smoking crack, shooting crank, and taking acid before this happened. He said he had been under the influence of drugs for five days prior to the offense, as well as on the day of the incident.

In the statement to police, Johnson said he told Ms. Yang to take her clothes off, so she would not run out of the house. He said she took her clothes off and sat on the bed with a blanket pulled across her. He said he saw that Ms. Yang was trying to hide a razor blade, so he hit her and knocked her off the bed. He said he hit her on the back of the head with his fist and she fell to the floor. He said he picked up the razor blade and called her a "stupid bitch." He picked her up, put her on the bed, and unzipped his pants and started to play with himself. He said the next thing he knew, he picked up her blue jumpsuit and told her to put it on. He stated he could not feel if he had sexual intercourse with her or not, but that he was playing with himself about "an inch away from her privates."

Relevant History
Larry Johnson is a 18-year, 9-month-old white male who was interviewed and evaluated at the Garland County Jail. He said his mother and her husband are both alcoholics. His parents have been divorced since 1986. Johnson has been getting SSI since age 13 for Attention Deficit Disorder. He was in Rivendell one time at age 13 or 14. He claims he had blackouts and was sleepwalking. Around that time he was also in trouble for theft, fighting, and trying to stab someone. Johnson said he was also at Ouachita Children's Center once. He thinks he has been put on probation three times. He said he got probation for shoplifting and stealing a truck. He was committed to the Alexander Youth Services Center one time for theft by receiving. He said he got a GED while he was there. When he got out of the training school, he lived with his father. He said his father told him not to work because he was getting the Social Security check. He said after that he did burglaries, sold drugs, and stayed out most nights using drugs. He said that when he ran out of money, he thought about burglarizing the Yang house. He said he would probably go to prison for this offense and "If I do, I'll get worse."

Clinical Evaluation
Larry Johnson presented himself as a healthy looking 18-year-old with absolutely no evidence of mental illness or psychosis. He was verbal, cooperative, and in good contact with reality. His general fund of information was good and his contact with reality was normal. There was no evidence of hallucinations or delusions. He displayed no unusual or bizarre behavior. His speech was normal without any pressure.

His WAIS-R Verbal IQ was 96, Performance 92, and Full Scale IQ 93. This is in the Average range.

The WRAT-3 scores were as follows:

	Standard Score	Percentile	Grade Equivalent
Reading	100	50	HS
Spelling	97	42	HS
Arithmetic	94	34	8

He has a GED and average academic ability. There are no intellectual deficits.

The MMPI scores were as follows: L = 33, F = 99, K = 39, HS = 63, D = 58, HY = 64, PD = 84, MF = 61, PA = 67, PT = 62, SC = 78, MA = 62, SI = 54. These scores are not valid because he wanted to dramatize a need for treatment and he exaggerated all symptoms. He did the same thing on the CPS, answering the items in the most extreme manner.

On the Beck Depression Inventory, he said he feels life is hopeless, he feels he is a failure, he believes he is being punished, he hates himself, and he would like to kill himself. He endorsed many other extreme responses for depression and anxiety.

On the Sentences he said he suffers "blackouts in which I do things I don't remember." He said he needs help, he regrets "the crimes that I have committed," and that the happiest time "is when I am on drugs."

On the Competency to Stand Trial Assessment Instrument, he indicated a good understanding of the various roles of the legal participants. He appreciated the seriousness of the charges against him and possible penalties he could face. He asked me what Hayward said about him and I told him I could not say anything about that.

Mental Condition
Diagnoses are as follows:

> Axis I: Mixed Substance Abuse NOS (305.90)
> AXIS II: Antisocial Personality Disorder (301.70)

Legal Questions
Larry Johnson is able to understand rationally and factually the legal proceedings against him and is able to assist effectively in his own defense. He is competent to stand trial. With regard to criminal responsibility, he was able to appreciate the criminality of his conduct and conform his conduct to requirements of the law at the time of the alleged offense. He had the capacity to have the culpable mental state to commit the alleged act. He was responsible for his behavior at the time of the alleged offense.

Even if he had Attention Deficit Disorder when he was younger, this had no bearing on his mental state at the time of the offense and does not affect his competency at this time. He claims drug use and lack of memory. The intellectual and academic scores did not indicate any cognitive deficits. He is ready to return to court for disposition.

Discussion
This is another example of a criminal forensic evaluation which was the result of a motion made by a defense attorney without any apparent justification. The defense probably knew there was no issue of mental illness and that his client was competent and responsible. It is possible that the motion for an evaluation was made in an attempt to appear to be thorough, to ensure that there was no legal malpractice, or to fish for any possible mitigating circumstances.

This was clearly the case of an antisocial 18-year-old engaging in a horrendous crime, with no issue of mental illness contributing to the offense or resulting in mitigating circumstances. He had average intelligence and a long history of delinquency and drug abuse. He was clearly able to understand the charges against him and could assist his attorney in his defense. It is not unusual for defendants in cases such as this to describe themselves as experiencing blackouts or not remembering, which Johnson did.

There was quite a bit of information in the forensic evaluation that was incriminating to the defendant. As in all cases, the defense attorney had the choice of whether or not to introduce the report. If the defense chooses not to introduce a report like this, the prosecution cannot present it. This procedure gives the defense some protection against incriminating information, since the prosecution cannot use the report to establish guilt. In this particular case, the jury never saw the report or heard the results. If the defense had chosen to introduce the report, the prosecution would have had an open door to explore the results of the evaluation. The defense could have also objected to portions of the report being presented to the jury and could have argued that in front of the judge.

The point here is that we can perform the forensic evaluations without concern about incriminating the defendant, since the defendant is represented by an attorney. All the information gathered in the evaluation can be included in the report. It is the psychologist's job to do exactly what was done in this report—to explore issues of competency and responsibility regarding a particular crime. It is then the defense's job to decide what information in the report will be introduced.

Over the years, psychologists doing defense work have tried to expand the "mental illness or mental defect" defense to the point that it is almost meaningless. Any type of antisocial personality, drug or alcohol abuse, anger, or passion seems to be enough for a "hired gun" to say that the defendant was not responsible for his or her actions. Fortunately, juries in most jurisdictions are smart enough to understand mental illness and what "not guilty by reason of mental illness" really means. Juries are also smart enough to recognize the inherent bias in psychological testimony that is paid for and presented on behalf of one side.

All of the evaluations presented in this chapter were done by court order. In order to have this type of practice, you must turn down all requests to do work for defense attorneys and keep insisting that all requests for evaluation come through the court. This may mean losing work in the short run, but it will make for a better practice and better reputation in the long run. This type of practice is the exception today, but will hopefully become the norm in the future, as more and more psychologists who want to do professional, objective forensic work give up the role of "hired gun."

5

CUSTODY EVALUATIONS

There are many ways in which the issue of mental health and fitness can be opened in a custody trial. Even mental health professionals who primarily do psychotherapy and do not have a forensic practice will probably be involved in custody court cases at some time during their careers. The therapist may begin the relationship thinking it is a confidential therapeutic relationship only to find that it changes later when the client is involved in a custody dispute.

Let's say you have been seeing a client over a fairly long period of time for depression. That patient divorces and her husband sues for custody, raising her mental health as an issue. He contends that the very mental illness you have been treating her for disqualifies her as the main custodian of the child. If the lawyer from the other side contacts you wanting information, or if you receive a subpoena, the issue of confidentiality is fairly clear. As long as the patient you saw wants her sessions held in confidence, that is your obligation. In all cases, the patient is the one who owns the privilege of confidentiality. If she chooses to relinquish her right to confidentiality by signing a release, it is your obligation to disclose the information. However, in the absence of such a release, the therapist must always assume that the client would invoke confidentiality.

When you receive a request for information from the husband's attorney, you must say that you cannot answer any questions and you cannot confirm that you have or have not seen the patient. If you receive a subpoena, your obligation is to show up in court, unless you have your lawyer quash the subpoena ahead of time. Assuming that your patient invoked her privilege of confidence, has not signed a release, and wants you to fight disclosure, your response on the stand is that your patient has instructed you not to disclose any information based on the doctor/ patient relationship. Since you are already on the stand, the judge will have an opportunity to rule on confidentiality. The judge may support the patient's right of confidentiality, rule that the information is not admissible, and excuse you. However, if the judge instructs you to answer, for whatever reason, you are obligated to respond.

Don't be foolish enough to think that you should defy the judge's order in an effort to protect the patient's confidence. Clients should be told from the very beginning that, if there are marital problems or a custody dispute, you will respect their wishes for confidentiality until ordered by a judge to testify. Once the judge rules on the matter, it is finished—and you can defend any lawsuit or complaint to your state Board of Examiners. This is not to say that your client cannot file either an ethics complaint or a lawsuit, but you will be successful in defending the charge as long as a circuit or chancery judge ordered you to respond.

Why would the judge rule that you must disclose information from a confidential therapeutic relationship? The usual reason is that the patient herself has either alleged that her husband is mentally unfit or somehow opened up the issue. Another reason is that the judge may feel that the patient's mental health or illness plays a vital role in determining custody. The judge will order that this is discoverable information necessary to make a custody determination that will be in the best interest of the child.

There are other ways that psychologists get involved in custody disputes. Sometimes a child will be brought in by a parent who is contemplating divorce but has not filed. The parent may be fishing for mental health issues regarding the child to support his or her eventual claim to custody. Parents are extremely manipulative in these circumstances and often are not straightforward with therapists when bringing their children for counseling. If you suspect that the parent might be fishing for information against the other parent, you should be very conservative in your treatment and should not make any recommendations about custody.

If you treated a child while the parents were together and the couple then files for divorce, you will probably be right in the middle of a custody dispute. One parent may have brought the child in and signed the release for treatment, but the other parent presumably has just as much say about the child's medical records. If the parties were married when you saw the child and custody has not been decided, you have to disclose the records to either parent who wishes to have them. If you receive a release of information, you should provide either the notes or a summary of sessions to that parent or that parent's attorney. If you were primarily involved with one parent and the other parent signs the release for information, you should call the parent you were involved with and perhaps that parent's attorney and let them know that you must release information. At the same time, it would be wise to send the same information to that other spouse and his or her attorney. This is perfectly legal. Just be sure that the parent requesting disclosure still has custody.

If there has already been a separation and one of the spouses was awarded temporary custody, you cannot disclose information to the noncustodial parent without the consent of the custodial parent. If the noncustodial parent continues to press for the records, you may have to go to court, explain the situation to the judge, and let the judge decide. If you have any doubt about disclosure of information in any of these matters, the safest thing to do is to state that you think the information is protected and appear in court so the judge can rule on the matter. This will always protect you.

Other times a custodial parent will bring a child in, saying that the child is afraid of the noncustodial parent or does not want to visit the parent. This could happen after a temporary custody hearing or long after custody has been decided. If you do see a child in such circumstances and later end up in court, you should testify only as a therapist, not as an evaluator. You should report only the content of your sessions, what the parent with custody is saying, and what the child seems to be saying about the noncustodial parent. These limitations in your testimony should be explained to the parent when the child is initially brought in. The parent should be told that unless all parties can be seen and evaluated you will refrain from any conclusions about the noncustodial parent and certainly refrain from any conclusions about custody or visitation.

When a custodial parent brings a child in under such circumstances, I require that a release of information be signed so that information from the sessions can be given to the noncustodial parent. In one case, for example, a mother brought her 10-year-old son to me, presumably for counseling, because he was feeling anxious and was resisting visiting his father who lived 40 miles away. When I questioned her, she admitted she was referred by her lawyer. In such cases, it is tempting just to see the mother and work with the son about his anxiety, but it will never remain a simple counseling case. It will end up in court, with the mother attempting to get some change in the visitation. In this case, the mother and her lawyer were told that the father would be invited to participate in therapy and that the mother, who had custody, would have to sign releases of information, making information from all sessions available to the father and his attorney. What each parent said about the other parent would be revealed in the report.

Psychologists with primarily therapy practices may find this policy hard to justify at first. It may not seem fair that parents cannot get treatment for their children, or really even for themselves, without everything being available to the ex-spouses and attorneys. However, after you have been burned a few times, getting called into court and attempting to defend your assessment without involving the noncustodial parent, or not being able to reveal information about one side because you do not have a signed release of information, you will see the only way to get control of cases like this from the outset is with the kind of policy I have outlined above.

Before I had a firm policy in cases like this, I did get burned. One such case involved an anxious mother who was creating a problem in the child and obstructing visitation. Since I had no release to communicate with the father, there was little I could do with that information. When I was later contacted by the father, who wanted to know something about his son's treatment, I was unable to tell him anything or give him a copy of my report. What I wanted to do was to talk with him and assess his side of the story and eventually release a report that addressed the entire visitation and custody issue. However, I could not do any of that, since treatment began with the mother and she controlled issues of confidentiality.

In that case, the father's lawyer eventually subpoenaed me to court and the judge overruled any issues of confidentiality and required my testimony. I should never have been in that position. If I had insisted upon a release of information to talk to the noncustodial parent, which I do now, that situation would have been avoided. In some cases, the noncustodial parents will live out of state and you will not have the opportunity to meet with them. You can still proceed with treatment and/or evaluation of the custodial parent and the child as long as releases of information are obtained beforehand. Both parties will then have access to any report that is written.

In some cases in which you have access to just one parent, the custodial parent may have very legitimate concerns about visitation and the environment the child is being exposed to during visitation. I have seen cases in which there were reports of substance abuse in the home of the noncustodial parent, frequent changes of address, frequent changes in sexual partners, and reports of the child being left unattended. If the noncustodial parent is unavailable for evaluation and/or treatment in such cases, you can still proceed as long as you have a signed release of information to the ex-spouse and his or her attorney. However, as in all cases in which only one side has been seen, you must limit your conclusions. You should never conclude that the noncustodial parent, for example, is an alcoholic or an unfit parent, since you didn't evaluate that parent. You can only state what the child and the custodial parent reported and what your concerns are for the child. If you do end up sending in a report or testifying in such cases, you can always say that you would be happy to do a full evaluation of the parents and child, should the court order it or both sides agree to the evaluation. Unfortunately, a lot of therapists will not even see the noncustodial parent in such circumstances and will testify that visitation should be restricted or supervised. This is ridiculous and very unethical.

At times it will be the noncustodial parent who brings a child in for evaluation or treatment. This usually occurs during extended visitation periods over holidays or during the summer. The noncustodial parent may allege some type of abuse or mistreatment that has been reported by the child. In these circumstances, it is unethical to treat or evaluate the child without the consent of the custodial parent. Remember, it is the custodial parent that has the legal right to make decisions about treatment. One possibility in those cases is to contact the custodial parent and get his or her consent for treatment. If that consent cannot be obtained and the allegation is a serious one, such as sexual abuse, you should refer the parent and child to the Department of Human Services or a local children's hospital for emergency evaluation.

Despite my policy of always evaluating both parents in custody matters, there will be occasional situations in which it is appropriate to do a complete evaluation on only one party, even when all parties are available. I saw one case, for example, in which a father had custody all along and the mother had a series of hospitalizations for schizophrenia. In another case, the mother had custody and the father had just been released from prison. In both cases, the issue was the same: to evaluate the noncustodial parent and make suggestions about visitation. In both cases, I did a complete psychological battery on the noncustodial parent. The fitness of the custodial parent was not at issue, so that parent was not formally evaluated. However, it was still critical to see the custodial parent and child in collateral visits. In those visits, the custodial parent can express any concerns he or she has about visitation and whether the visits should be supervised. I can see what the child's attitude is toward the noncustodial parent and whether any fearfulness is being expressed about visitation. After all the information is gathered, the court receives a report on the noncustodial parent's mental health and suitability for visitation. Recommendations are made about how visitation should proceed, whether it should be supervised, gradual, or daytime only, two or six weeks in the summer, or whether extended visitation should be avoided.

In a formal custody battle, however, it is necessary to evaluate both sides if you are to make statements or recommendations about who should have custody and what the visitation should be. You should continue to state this policy when attorneys call you to do custody evaluations. You will be happy to do the evaluations, as long as both parties are evaluated. Without seeing both sides and having a signed consent so information can be given to all parties, you will simply be a "hired gun." If you do reach a conclusion which is unfavorable to the side that hired you, they will seek to keep that information from the other side. This situation should be avoided. As forensic psychologists, our interest should be to discover what is best for the child. To do this, we must have access to both parents, any other significant family members, and all prior mental health records on the parents and the child. Only in this way can we do a complete evaluation and make final recommendations about custody, which is a grave matter.

As in all areas of forensic work, you have to believe in this work to be successful. You have to believe that you can learn something of value from the evaluation and make useful recommendations to the court. Judges who do not value psychological testimony will not refer cases for evaluation, but will simply make the determinations themselves. On the other hand, when a judge appoints you to do an evaluation, that judge places value on psychological results and wants your recommendation. In such cases, you should always attempt to make clear recommendations. That is not only helpful to the judge in that particular case, but helps build your reputation as a professional with something of value to add in similar cases.

Case 16

This was a custody evaluation on two parents who were divorcing and both seeking custody of their child.

Psychological Evaluation Report

Names: Jeremy Freeman
        Allison Ernst
(Required identifying information, dates of testing, etc.)

Referral
Dr. Allison Ernst and Jeremy Freeman were referred for a psychological evaluation by Hon. Judge Dana Cooper. The couple is disputing custody of their son, Charles, who is 3 years of age. Both Dr. Ernst and Mr. Freeman were administered the Wechsler Adult Intelligence Scale–Revised (WAIS-R), the Minnesota Multiphasic Personality Inventory (MMPI), the Millon Clinical Multiaxial Inventory (MCMI), Beck Depression Inventory, and Incomplete Sentences Blank. Charles was interviewed. Since neither party was alleging that Charles had any problems or that he was resisting the visitation with the other parent, developmental and IQ testing were not administered. Mr. Freeman asked that I interview Janice Rudder, with whom he is currently involved, and I did so on 8/18/95. I also reviewed information that Dr. Ernst provided: her notes of incidents she was concerned about and school records on her children. Records were reviewed from Dr. John Scott, who treated Mr. Freeman, and Dr. Shawna Westin, who treated Dr. Ernst.

Interview Information
Jeremy Freeman is an attorney in private practice and Allison Ernst is a physician in residency. Allison Ernst has three children from a previous marriages, ages 12 through 19. One of these children is in a gifted and talented school, one is in college, and one is home with Dr. Ernst.

   Jeremy Freeman reported that he and Dr. Ernst met when she was in medical school. They dated and lived together for a year and a half to two years prior to their marriage in 1990. Not long after they were married, Dr. Ernst went to Kentucky to study for the medical boards for six months, leaving the children with Mr. Freeman. They had around four visits during that time. Mr. Freeman said he was going to Kentucky for the purpose of trying to have a baby, since this is what they both wanted. He said she apparently conceived during one of his visits there. Mr. Freeman said he and Dr. Ernst were separated in May 1993, after which they made an attempt to get back together. Since that did not work out, they are now proceeding with the divorce and custody hearing over their son, Charles. He said he wants custody so his ex-wife will not leave the state. He said he does not want to keep Charles from his mother, but he wants legal control.

   Mr. Freeman said he was more immature during the first part of their marriage than he is now. He said he went from school to taking care of three children, which was a difficult adjustment for him. He apparently got out of law school shortly before their marriage. While Allison was in Kentucky, he said the children missed their mother, but he did the best he could. He said he did inappropriate things during the marriage. He said he "mooned" his wife for the video camera, but he claimed it was a bet between him and Allison that she could not get it on video-tape without the other guests in the room knowing. There was another incident in which he mooned outside the car, going down the highway, along with Allison's youngest son, who did it with him. They were mooning Dr. Ernst's father. There were other incidents in which he pulled down the pants of his stepdaughters, but he said he was just pulling down an extra pair of shorts covering spandex type of shorts. He said nothing was exposed and he claimed everyone was participating in this. He acknowledged making a comment to Dr. Ernst's oldest daughter when she started wearing a bra. He also admitted shooting fireworks in the direction of Allison's youngest son when he was 9. Mr. Freeman's explanation for all of these incidents was that the entire family, including Allison, had a habit of horseplay. He tended to minimize and rationalize every incident that was brought up about his behavior.

Mr. Freeman said he is not drinking very much, although he might have an occasional drink. He said Dr. Ernst does as much drinking as he does. He acknowl-edged that his drinking might have been a problem at one time. He talked about one incident in which he had too much to drink and he cut her pubic hairs. He said, "I didn't know she would act that way." He said he just cut the "split ends" off and he did it to "joke with her." He said they were both drunk when it happened.

Mr. Freeman said Allison is more "liberal" in childrearing practices than he is. He said he was always close to her two younger children, but that he had prob-lems relating to the oldest daughter. Now he said the younger two have "turned against me." Mr. Freeman is worried that if he does not have custody of Charles he will not be able to see him or have a good relationship with him. He believes the father of her other three children was shut out of their lives and he worries the same will happen to him. He described Dr. Ernst as selfish and as someone who can never say she is sorry. He worries that she will move out of state with Charles, making it more difficult for him to have a relationship with his son. He also com-plained that she will be working all the time and will not have enough time for a good relationship with Charles. Mr. Freeman said he has the time and flexibility to be a full-time parent. Mr. Freeman said Allison's mother is deceased, one brother committed suicide, another brother is drug-dependent, and her father currently lives with a woman. He contrasted this with his parents who have been "married all my life." He said his brother and sister have been married only one time. Mr. Freeman had a first marriage from 1978 to 1985 with no children. He said his wife at that time did not want children.

Mr. Freeman said he and Dr. Ernst had counseling at the medical center. They had about three sessions and he had several individual sessions. I read the notes from Dr. Scott, who diagnosed Mr. Freeman with depression, but said bipolar disorder should be ruled out. Mr. Freeman took Prozac for a short period of time. He said he stopped treatment at the medical center because he was going to have to switch therapists, his wife was not going to participate, and the marriage was coming to an end.

Mr. Freeman said Dr. Ernst has custody until there is a final determination and he has Charles every other weekend and one weeknight a week. Mr. Freeman has a three-bedroom house. He is in the National Guard. He said Charles is very close to Janice Rudder's sons. He seems to have an intense relationship with Ms. Rudder at this time. Ms. Rudder was interviewed and she relayed most of the same history that Mr. Freeman talked about. She was also concerned that Mr. Freeman would not have enough access to Charles should the mother be awarded custody. She said Charles relates very well to her children, a point everyone seems to agree on. She said her children adore Mr. Freeman and he is very good with them.

Allison Ernst said she was in her first year of medical school when she met Mr. Freeman. She said he came on very strong, saying that she and her children were all he ever wanted. She feels he is doing exactly the same thing with Janice Rudder and her children. She said there were problems even before they married and she called off their engagement. She related all the incidents that Mr. Freeman told me about, including the firecrackers, pulling pants down, mooning, and the rest. She added other things, such as crude sexual comments to her and her two daughters, constant comments about old girlfriends and other women, sexually inappropriate jokes, derogatory comments about her body, and drinking. She said she was extremely angry when he shaved her pubic hairs. She said he even opened the shower once and urinated on her. She filed for divorce soon after they married, but they reconciled before she went to Kentucky.

Dr. Ernst said her mother died when she was 7 years old. She has two brothers. One of her stepmothers was abusive. She lived with a grandmother until her father remarried the second time. She went to college out of state and married her high-school sweetheart, to whom she was married for over ten years. When they divorced in 1985, she raised her three children and began working on her education. Her ex-husband has not seen the children in three years. She said her ex-husband thinks the children are selfish and believes the children should take the initiative and contact him. He lives in California now and she said her children seem uninterested in visiting him. She said she is not planning to move out of state, which is what Mr. Freeman is concerned about. She said she does not want Mr. Freeman to get custody because he is too severe in his discipline and she thinks he comes from an abusive family. She described herself as flexible with the children and described him as dogmatic.

Charles was interviewed on 8/17/95. He appeared to be a normal child who never said anything negative about either parent.

Evaluation Results
Allison Ernst had a Verbal IQ of 113, Performance IQ of 118, and Full Scale IQ of 117. There is nothing about her ability to be concerned about. Her MMPI scores

were as follows: L = 52, F = 49, K = 61, HS = 43, D = 40, HY = 33, PD = 54, MF = 50, PA = 38, PT = 51, SC = 50, MA = 52, SI = 48. These scores were in the normal range. None of the special clinical scales were elevated. She tried to put her best foot forward, but it was a valid profile.

She had a score of 0 on the Beck Depression Inventory, again emphasizing feelings of well-being and denying depression or anxiety. With a score of 0, there is some minimizing, since she acknowledges she is seeing a therapist and working on personal issues. Any normal person would endorse a few items on the Beck Depression Inventory, but she is attempting to appear perfectly adjusted.

On the MCMI, her only high score was the Compulsive Scale at 95. An elevation on this scale is also related to making a favorable impression, appearing socially appropriate, and conscientious. She said on the Sentences she regretted marrying Jeremy Freeman, her greatest fear is repeating the same type of relationship, and her nerves do not give her any problems. She said she suffers when her children are hurting, marriage "has not been happy for me," and she hates "to be lied to." She wrote that she wishes "my ex would contact the kids and pay support," referring to the father of her older three children.

Jeremy Freeman had a Verbal IQ of 122, Performance IQ of 118, and Full Scale IQ of 124. His intellectual ability is also not an issue, since both of these individuals are bright, professional people. His MMPI scores were L = 66, F = 43, K = 62, HS = 51, D = 42, HY = 48, PD = 50, MF = 43, PA = 56, PT = 46, SC = 51, MA = 45, SI = 47. These scores were in the normal range and nothing was above the level of significance. He also tried to put his best foot forward and attempted to portray social conformity and conscientiousness. None of the special scales on the MMPI were significant.

His MCMI scores were all below the level of significance. Relative to the rest of the profile, he was highest for Histrionic 74, Narcissistic 67, and Compulsive 70. This pattern suggested some emotional reactivity and excitability, but it also suggested passive–aggressive traits.

On the Beck he had a score of only 3, so he also denied feelings of depression. He said on the Sentences he regrets not studying hard in school, he is annoyed by pushy people, and marriage "can be heaven or it can be hell."

Summary and Recommendations
Both Dr. Ernst and Mr. Freeman are bright and sophisticated, so they were able to produce normal test results. I therefore had to rely more heavily on the clinical interviews and background information. In addition, I reviewed Dr. Scott's notes and attempted to make a judgment based on his work. It is important to note that Dr. Ernst does not want to restrict Mr. Freeman's visits in any way and does not believe he is a danger to Charles. She identifies him as basically a good father, but she wants to retain legal custody. Mr. Freeman also states fundamentally that Dr. Ernst is a good mother who has done a good job with her other three children and he has no concern about her ability to parent. Both parents would like to have

legal custody of their son, without implying that the other person is unfit. In discussing their preference to have custody, each comes close to stating that the other is not fit, but when asked directly if they would want visitation to be supervised or blocked in some way, they both back off.

What is reliable and valid are the many incidents in which Mr. Freeman has acted out inappropriately. Both parties present the same set of facts and agree that these events took place, even though Mr. Freeman places a more positive spin on the events and Dr. Ernst believes they show him to be more pathological. It would be foolish to think that all of these incidents are just things Mr. Freeman did and that they have no meaning. To the contrary, all of the incidents taken together clearly point to some problems Mr. Freeman has with impulse control, a history of drinking, some attitude problems toward women, and some feelings of low self-esteem.

Mr. Freeman has high dependency needs and tries desperately to be wanted and to fill the void. He has both anger and deference toward those on whom he is dependent. Mr. Freeman has had difficulty with his self-image and self-esteem over many years and he has never found real happiness in relationships. He experiences life in great bursts of happiness and disappointment. He has a strong desire to seek approval, and yet he finds his behavior often to be repulsive to those to whom he wants to be closest. He is plagued by self-doubt, both in his professional life and in his relationships. The birth of his son was apparently the most important thing in Mr. Freeman's life and there is little question that he deeply loves this child. This child filled a void or emptiness in his life and personality. However, I would not say that he is obsessed or pathological about Charles, and there is no evidence that he would harm this child emotionally or physically.

Dr. Ernst is a strong professional person who has done a good job with her three (and now four) children. One can question her judgment, since she knew there were many problems in the relationship with Mr. Freeman and yet she married him anyway. Her concerns about Mr. Freeman were legitimate, but they had a volatile and dysfunctional relationship for which they share responsibility. Dr. Westin's notes suggested that Dr. Ernst had only adjustment problems related to the marriage and divorce.

Both of these individuals would be capable of raising Charles, and yet I recommend that he continue in the custody of his mother. I think it is in the child's best interest to stay with her, because she provides more assurance of stability. This is not to say that Mr. Freeman could not provide an adequate home, but it is clear that he has a few more emotional problems and seems to have some trouble recognizing boundaries of behavior. This is an issue that tips the scales toward the mother. If the couple got along better, joint custody would be a possibility, but I doubt this would be workable, given their differences.

Mr. Freeman's concerns and motivation for custody are based on his fear that Dr. Ernst will move away or obstruct his visitation. I think these issues could be dealt with separately, apart from awarding custody to Mr. Freeman. Perhaps there would be some way to reassure Mr. Freeman and his attorney that he will have ample visitation and that any relocation of the mother, should it happen, will allow an opportunity for him to present his concerns. Dr. Ernst states she is not going to move and she is going to stay in Arkansas. She plans to work at a local emergency room, which will give her a predictable work schedule.

If Mr. Freeman has some reassurance about the security of his visitation, I think he will ultimately accept this custody arrangement. I think liberal visitation with the father should be considered, since he is willing to devote a great deal of time to his son. Although Dr. Ernst may retain legal custody, there may be some way for Mr. Freeman to have more than usual physical visitation.

Discussion

Custody cases do not always result in a clear choice, with one parent obviously better than the other. There are many times when the parents are both essentially normal in background and on the test results. In many of these cases, the parents are disputing custody, not because they think the other parent is unfit, but simply because both want the child.

In most jurisdictions the law is now sexually neutral, so that the court is obligated to determine custody not based on sex. This is a historical change, since the "Tender Years" doctrine followed in the past usually resulted in custody being awarded to the mother. That doctrine stated that young children need their mother to grow and develop, so that the mother had a basic right to retain custody, especially during the formative years. While statutes in favor of the mother may have disappeared from the books in most jurisdictions, it is obvious that many judges still favor the mother and will only change custody to the father if she has been proven to be unfit in some way. This is an unspoken bias that most lawyers and litigating fathers realize. Still, there are more and more judges making custody determinations solely on the best interests of the child. Because of this shift, more fathers are filing for custody in situations in which there is no evidence that the mother is an unfit parent. In these cases, judges are in a dilemma and have a difficult time determining the best interests of the child, especially if they are trying to adhere to a sexually neutral doctrine. Judges will refer such normal couples for evaluation to assist in their custody determinations.

In cases in which two basically normal adults are filing for custody, determination of the best interest of the child is very difficult with a psychological evaluation. The test results on the MMPI and other instruments are usually normal and intelligence is not an issue. In this case, all the psychological test results were normal and there was no significant pathology in either parent. Both parents were bright, professional people. If there had been nothing else on which to make a determination, I could have come to the conclusion that both parents were fit and that I had no recommendation about placement of the child. However, I try not to do that, because it is frustrating to the judge who ordered the evaluation.

Another possibility in such cases would be a recommendation for joint custody. That recommendation would have to rest on an evaluation of the particular couple's ability to work together. It is important to remember that joint custody is a legal term, meaning that both parents retain their legal guardianship of the child and the right to make decisions for the child. That means that each has the ability to place the child in whatever school he or she wants, to obtain medical or psychological treatment, and to make every other decision related to the child. That can be impossible in a couple who are continuing to fight.

Another possibility in such cases is to comment on both legal and physical custody. Physical custody is actual possession of the child, without regard to legal custody. A couple can have joint legal custody and the noncustodial parent only have normal visitation on weekends. On the other hand, a couple can have shared physical custody, with the child spending 50 percent of his or her time at each parent's home, and one parent still retain legal custody. Shared physical custody, but legal custody maintained by one parent, is often a good option for couples who are not getting along well enough to make legal decisions together about the child. In those cases, one parent needs to be in control, and yet it may be very appropriate to have shared physical custody so that the child sees the noncustodial parent much more than traditional weekends and holidays.

In most cases, however, even when the test results are normal, there will be ample interview and background information, as well as impressions from the clinical interview, to make a recommendation to give custody to one of the parents. No matter how well-adjusted each individual is or how good the test results are, there will always be information provided that will help you decide what is in the best interests of the child. Each parent will make sure that you are aware of anything that is even vaguely negative about the other person that might influence your decision. These cases are determined by fine points and the scales are tipped by the slightest difference, as in every legal decision.

When both parties produce normal test results and neither is actually contending that the other is an unfit parent, it is usually not necessary to evaluate the child. However, it is still necessary to meet the child involved, so that you can assess whether there is any problem with the child that would warrant further evaluation. The more the disputing parents imply that the child has problems or that the child is afraid of the other parent, the greater need there will be to evaluate the child carefully to judge those issues yourself. In the case presented above, neither parent alleged the other was unfit, neither objected to visitation by the other parent, and neither claimed that Charles had any adverse reaction to the other parent.

In this case, I recommended that the mother retain custody, but that the father have liberal visitation. I did not think joint custody would be workable, since the parents were not getting along well and had a history of constant conflict. My decision was based on several factors. First, it was clear that the mother had a better record than the father for child care. She had already raised three children on her own who were all doing very well. Also, even the father admitted that he had engaged in many acts of inappropriate behavior. He seemed to be an impulsive, somewhat immature and insecure man who had very strong dependency needs, coupled with feelings of hostility toward those he loved. The inappropriate, impulsive acts were acknowledged by both parties in this case. He had also had a problem with drinking. These factors were enough to tip the scales in the mother's favor. The father was already involved in another relationship with a new girlfriend who had two children and he seemed to be replacing his wife very quickly. He was someone who felt insecure, and this was not going to change. That underlying insecurity was a fundamental personal attribute not readily measured on psychological tests.

In this case, as in many cases of middle-class couples fighting over custody, the parties had been in marital therapy. This is true in almost every case I see in which the parents are well-educated, middle-class, and have normal test results. Although the mother in this case alleged that the father was bipolar, I did not think that was the case. I reviewed the therapy records, in which the father was diagnosed with depression and the psychiatrist stated that bipolar disorder should be ruled out. Treatment diagnoses in progress notes often have little to do with what you determine the diagnosis to be in a custody evaluation. When a therapist treats a patient, he or she is obligated to come up with a diagnosis. Especially if the person is being seen in a medical setting, the patient will be seen in a pathological role by the treatment provider. In this case, the father was being seen by a psychiatric resident at a medical center. There is much more likelihood that he would receive a psychiatric diagnosis in that setting than if he had been seen in a private office by a nonmedical provider. However, even in a private practice setting, he would receive a diagnosis for insurance purposes. A lot of normal people see therapists to deal with everyday problems in living. They end up with diagnoses, but treatment and diagnoses should not be used against them later. It is only when there is a significant mental disorder that affects the person's functioning and parenting that mental health treatment history becomes significant. Even in cases in which one parent has a verifiable mental illness, such as bipolar disorder, the question is still whether or not the child would be better off with the other parent.

Very often clients in custody cases will say something to let you know that they expect a certain outcome and what their real agenda is. In this case, I believe the father knew he had little chance of obtaining custody of his son. He knew his ex-wife was a good parent and she would probably retain custody. Even though he felt he could be a more full-time custodial parent than his ex-wife, he also said that his primary concern was obstruction of visitation. Legally, he felt compelled to seek full custody to defend his position of wanting unrestricted access to his son.

I have stressed throughout this book the importance of not working as a "hired gun" for either side in doing evaluations. In this case, the mother had already hired a psychiatrist to evaluate herself and her four children. This expert testified that the mother should retain custody and that the father was unfit. Since the judge did not want to make a determination based on testimony by someone the mother hired, I was asked to complete an evaluation of both parties. Although I reached the same ultimate conclusion regarding custody, that the mother should retain legal custody, I did not find the father unfit and I stressed that he should have liberal visitation. The reason the judge disregarded the testimony of the first expert was because it was a one-sided evaluation done by a psychiatrist who had never met the father. This disregard of one-sided testimony will happen more and more as judges realize that they can have access to truly unbiased psychological testimony by referring cases for evaluation themselves.

Case 17

This was a custody dispute in a divorce case in which one parent's mental health was raised as an issue.

Psychological Evaluation Report

Names: Jackson Wade
        Donna Wade
(Required identifying information, date of testing, etc.)

Tests Administered
Both Jackson and Donna:

> Wechsler Adult Intelligence Scale–Revised (WAIS-R)
> Incomplete Sentences Blank
> Minnesota Multiphasic Personality Inventory (MMPI)
> Millon Clinical Multiaxial Inventory (MCMI)
> Beck Depression Inventory (BDI)
> Rorschach

Donna:

> Wide Range Achievement Test–Revision 3 (WRAT-3)

Referral
Donna and Jackson Wade are in the process of divorcing and disputing custody of their two children, Jason, age 6, and Joshua, age 4. Mr. Wade is represented by Carolyn Matteus and Ms. Wade is represented by George Berkman. The two lawyers agreed that both parties would be evaluated. Mr. and Ms. Wade were evaluated separately on June 16, 1995. Mr. Wade completed his tests on June 19. I interviewed Jason and Joshua on June 19. They were brought to the office by the maternal grandmother.

Interview Data
Ms. Wade, who was interviewed first, said she was married to Jackson Wade for seven years. She said she filed for divorce last November because she was "psychologically abused." She said she asked him to leave twice and she finally went through a lawyer to get him to move out. Jackson Wade then filed for custody of their sons, which she believes he did as revenge for the divorce. She said he threatened her

that if she ever left, he would get custody. She realizes that he did not want the divorce.

Ms. Wade was born and raised in Stuttgart. She denied having problems with mental illness as a child or young adult. She was molested by an older cousin when she was 10. She said a friend talked her into taking Valium when she was 12, but she did not consider this an overdose. She has a high school diploma. She said she was a slow reader, had difficulty in college, and did not graduate. She owned a small newspaper which did not do well, causing her to file for bankruptcy.

Ms. Wade said that during the marriage she was depressed and had anxiety attacks for two years. She blamed the marriage for her psychiatric problems. She said her self-image was "destroyed" by her husband. She said she felt worthless, because he criticized her constantly and never encouraged her to do anything. She complained that she had to beg him to get medical care for herself and the children. She said he never took off work for anything, even when the children were sick.

Ms. Wade began psychiatric treatment in 1993 and has continued since then. At present she is seeing Dr. James Sharon, a psychologist at Professional Counseling Centers (PCC). She was hospitalized twice at Baptist Hospital, once in late 1993 and again in January or February of 1994. She was under the care of psychiatrists Manuala Williams and Raymond Treeton. Dr. Williams still prescribes her medication. In July 1994 she said she heard voices. At that time she was taking Xanax, Mellaril, and Prozac, as well as being on antibiotics and pain medication. She said she felt frightened because she had the feeling the devil was after her. She ran away from home two times, leaving the children at home with her husband. She took an overdose of medication twice around that time and both times had her stomach pumped. She says now that she never wanted to kill herself. She said she took the medication overdose because she felt an urge or heard voices telling her that she would hurt the children and she did not want that to happen. She was frightened by her impulses and thought she could make the voices go away by taking the overdose.

Donna Wade said that when she was depressed she would stay in bed and the kids would get up and make a huge mess in the kitchen. She said she slept a lot, was bored, had difficulty making decisions, and had little energy. She said she was sedated at that time. She said her husband was gone a lot, leaving the house at 4:00 A.M., then attending college classes after work. She said she had problems with discipline and was very frustrated with the children. On different occasions, she kicked a hole in the wall and threw things across the room. However, she said she never lost control with the children and did not abuse them. She used "time out" and tried to reward them in positive ways. She thinks Jason has mild attention deficit disorder, but he is not on medication. She said her husband refuses to believe this is true. She is taking the children to counselors of their own at PCC. She said she explained the divorce to Jason by saying that she was not happy and that she and her husband like different things, that is, "Daddy likes it quiet" and she likes company. She felt this explanation was necessary because she thought her husband was talking to Jason about the divorce. She thinks he told Jason that the divorce was about money.

The Wades were separated from January until May of 1993. Ms. Wade took the children with her to North Dakota at that time. She has made the trip to North Dakota on at least two occasions, staying for several months at a time. Her mother has also stayed in Arkansas for months at a time on several different occasions. One of her suicide attempts was in August 1994 when her mother was in Arkansas. She returned to North Dakota with her mother and stayed several months, returning in October. During that time, she discontinued all the medication that had previously been prescribed and began taking Zoloft and lorazepam. By that time she was planning how she could leave her marriage.

Ms. Wade said her husband is accusing her of adultery at this time. She said she has a friend and she has stayed at his home before, but denied they have a sexual relationship. She said she stayed with him because she was afraid to stay at home alone, since she felt Jackson was stalking her. She said he has been following her and taking pictures. She said he is spending time with the children now during visitation, which is every other weekend and one day a week. She said she does not want him to have custody because she thinks he does not provide emotional support. She thinks he is very critical and told Jason he looked like a mama's boy when he had a certain haircut.

Donna Wade denies depression or anxiety at present, saying she feels much better now that she is separated. She currently takes Zoloft, 50 mg daily, and lorazepam as needed. She said she has not had many days when she needed to take the lorazepam. Her last anxiety attack was two months ago. She started working at a new job about a week ago.

After I interviewed Mr. Wade, I questioned Ms. Wade again about some of the information he had presented. For example, she never mentioned being on Social Security Disability. She acknowledged she is getting disability and said she is allowed to receive it for nine months while she works, which is what she is trying to do. She also did not mention $14,000 in back pay she got from Social Security, which she admittedly did not tell her husband about. She said she used it to pay bills and to prepare for her independence. She acknowledged that when she was in North Dakota in 1994 she filed for welfare, even though she was still married. She claimed that her husband was not sending her enough money at that time. During this second conversation, Ms. Wade acknowledged she will probably go to North Dakota with the children if she is awarded custody. She said she has a job there and she wants to be near her mother. If she moves to North Dakota, she believes Jackson can have the children for summers and alternate holidays. She said she does not think her husband is an authority figure for the children and does not discipline them.

During his interview, Mr. Wade said Donna was pregnant when they got married. He said she became depressed two or three years into the marriage. He said her mother stayed with them for extended periods of time. He said he never agreed to her returning to North Dakota as often as she did. He said he never expected the divorce and it was after he bought her a car in November that she announced she was leaving him. He said Donna does not know anything about money and has always put them in financial difficulty by running up their credit cards. He said she knows no restraint when it comes to the telephone, so he had a block put on the long distance service. He complained that she spends too much time watching television. He also believes she cannot handle the stress of raising the children. He mentioned her two suicide attempts and the hospitalizations. He is convinced that she is currently involved with someone. He admitted seeing her car at a man's house. He made a point of mentioning the monthly Social Security Disability benefit his wife is receiving, the large settlement she received from Social Security, the AFDC she filed for in North Dakota, the few times she has worked, and his overall opinion that she knows how to "work the system."

Mr. Wade said he is currently paying the bills while Donna lives in the family house. He is living with his mother in Little Rock until the divorce is settled and he sees what will happen with the house. (Mr. Wade's parents are divorced and his mother lives alone.) He is upset that he is not allowed to see the children unless visitation is scheduled. His wife will not allow him to pick the children up from daycare when he gets off early. If he gets custody of the children, he said he will live with his mother until he can get his own place. He is working at a warehouse, making $27,000 a year. He acknowledged that he is going to school after work, but said he will be finished with college in another year. He said he will spend quality time with the children.

Test Results

Donna Wade had a Verbal IQ of 116, Performance IQ of 114, and Full Scale IQ of 118. This is in the High Average range. The WRAT-3 scores were Reading 112, Spelling 104, and Arithmetic 100. She does not have any academic or intellectual deficits.

She completely denied depression on the Beck Depression Inventory with a score of only 3.

Her MMPI scores were L = 59, F = 61, K = 56, HS = 60, D = 51, HY = 58, PD = 54, MF = 34, PA = 57, PT = 51, SC = 53, MA = 49, SI = 44. None of the scores was significantly high. She was adept at making a good impression and producing a normal profile. She had one significant score on the special scales, which was a score of 77 on the MacAndrew Scale. Elevations on this scale are usually associated with substance abuse. If there is no evidence of substance abuse, the scale is still associated with extroverted, exhibitionistic behavior, and sensation-seeking. She prefers social activity and has a high need for stimulation.

The MCMI scores were elevated for Dependency (79) and Histrionic (82). Everything else was within normal limits, but Compulsiveness and Somatoform both approached significance at 72. She has strong dependency needs and leans on others for a sense of security, identity, and purpose. She is active in reaching out to other persons in order to find someone with whom she can feel secure. She thrives on attention and admiration from others. She has fairly high levels of somatic concerns and histrionic personality traits. On the MCMI she completely denied anxiety, resulting in a score of 58. Her Dysthymia score was only 38. For someone with a significant psychiatric history, it is quite remarkable and unbelievable that her depression and anxiety are so minimal at this point.

On the Sentences she said she would like to be smarter, she wishes she and her husband could get along, and she hates dishonesty. She said she suffers from allergies and her nerves "don't bother me as much as they used to."

The Rorschach responses were very restrained and she gave a small number of responses. She had an unusual response on Card II, seeing bears dancing and their knees bleeding because they bumped. Color responses like that on the Rorschach are suggestive of unrestrained emotionality. This has been a problem for her over the last two or three years. Responses on Card VIII suggested feelings of inferiority. She produced only one response on Card X, showing how controlled she was in responding to the Rorschach.

Jackson Wade had a Verbal IQ of 110, Performance IQ of 110, and Full Scale IQ of 110, which is also High Average at the 75th percentile.

His MMPI scores were L = 69, F = 48, K = 71, HS = 53, D = 46, HY = 60, PD = 52, MF = 52, PA = 56, PT = 50, SC = 53, MA = 40, SI = 47. These scores were very high for defensiveness. He reports feelings of well-being, denies psychological problems, and tends to be rigid and and compulsive. He is a conservative individual, intolerant, non-introspective, and self-righteous. He tends to be inhibited and shy and he has some social anxiety. He prefers a stable, predictable, and unexciting life. He finds life worthwhile and his energy is sufficient to cope with problems. As a person, he is subdued and conventional in almost every respect. He often defers to others and, while he preferred to have the dominant male role in his marriage, in actuality he was easily controlled by his wife. He had a high score on Overcontrolled Hostility, so he attempts to hold in feelings of anger. His MacAndrew Scale was low.

The MCMI scores were high for Dependency (79) and Compulsiveness (100). The Compulsiveness scale reflects his conventional lifestyle and his controlled behavior and thinking. His Dependency score was high, as was Ms. Wade's score on Dependency. Both individuals have close, dependent relationships with their mothers. Mr. Wade had a Beck Depression Inventory score of 0, so he denies any depression. On the Sentences he said he secretly still loves his wife and he suffers when he thinks about what this is doing to the children. He described his nerves as "steady."

He had Rorschach responses that were very concrete and bland, with little emotional content. His Rorschach was much more subdued than Ms. Wade's Rorschach, which reflects his everyday functioning. He does not have a problem losing emotional control.

Jason and Joshua were interviewed and observed. They were seen together and were both well-behaved. When I asked Jason how he was handling the divorce, he got angry and told me that he had already forgotten about it and that I should not have brought it up. Joshua seemed to have no reaction to the divorce, but he is only four. Jason has been diagnosed with a mild case of Attention Deficit Disorder, according to his mother, but he is not on any medication. His behavior was very good and not hyperactive during this particular observation. Overall, both boys appear to be normal 4- and 6-year-old children. They were positive about both parents.

I reviewed medical records on Ms. Wade. For the most part, these records covered the last three years. She has an involved and serious psychiatric history. There were two hospitalizations, two suicide attempts, and two incidents of leaving the home in an emotional state, which the family described as running away. She was on several different medications before settling on her present medicine. She has been diagnosed with Major Depression, Recurrent, and Panic Disorder with Agoraphobia. She has been considered for Dependent Personality and Borderline Personality Disorder. Last year she had auditory hallucinations and appeared to have a psychotic reaction. Included in this episode were unwanted thoughts that she would harm or threaten to harm her children. Her mother wrote in her Social Security evaluation that her daughter was unable to care for herself and her children. She said Donna attempted suicide in the 6th grade by taking an overdose of Valium. She said she tried to cut her hand with a knife, took a bottle of Advil, and disappeared two times. Ms. Wade's mother said her daughter's depression became significant beginning in 1988.

Summary and Recommendations
The assertion that Donna Wade had mental health problems because she was married to Jackson Wade and that she is recovered now because she is away from him is false and not credible. This may be true in cases where someone has an adjustment disorder as the result of a stressful marriage. In this case, Donna Wade has an extensive psychiatric history and her disorder was not caused by Mr. Wade. She has probably experienced some improvement now that the stress of her marriage has ended, but there could very easily be a relapse at any time. Currently she shows a "flight into health," with the psychological tests suggesting she denies any and all psychological problems. Her desire is to return to North Dakota, where she will be very dependent on her mother. If not with her mother, she is likely to transfer her dependence to another relationship in a short time. She is already involved with a man, although she denied that they have a sexual or romantic relationship. Donna Wade is manipulative and quite disingenuous in several areas, not the least of which is her claim for Social Security Disability, while at the same time asserting that she does not have any impairment which would affect her ability to take care of the children.

The evidence is clear that one parent is mentally ill and the other parent is not. Mr. Wade may have personality traits that are compulsive, rigid, and conventional, but this does not constitute a mental illness and would have no bearing on his childrearing ability. In fact, these traits probably make him a responsible and involved father.

I do not think it is in the best interest of the children for Donna Wade to gain custody and move to North Dakota, which is what she wants to do. If she returns to North Dakota, it should be without the children. I recommend that Mr. Wade receive legal custody. If he has custody, I think the children could spend time with their mother in North Dakota for specified lengths of time. At the very least, Mr. Wade should have joint legal and physical custody of these children.

Discussion

This case was between two biological parents, one with a history of mental illness and one without. The attorneys were both taking a chance by agreeing to the evaluation, since they would not be able to suppress the results or pick and choose what entered the record. Psychological evaluations based on objective reports like this are very difficult to overcome if the report favors one side, as it usually does and should.

This mother had a history of significant mental illness, including a history of psychotic symptoms and unwanted obsessive thoughts that she would hurt the children. She was also a dishonest and somewhat psychopathic individual. She had been very deceptive when it came to issues of disability. She wanted it both ways: she wanted to be mentally ill for purposes of Social Security Disability and she wanted to be without mental illness when it came to her husband's concerns and allegations about her ability to parent.

I felt certain that this mother was going to take the children and move across the country with them, resulting in the father having little involvement in their lives. I concluded it was not in the children's best interest for her to get custody or move out of state with them. I recommended that the father either have custody outright or share custody. He was supportive and very much involved with the children, so there would be no traumatic effect on them if he were awarded custody. If he weren't given full custody, it was vital that his role be at least equal to that of his wife in raising the children.

Some people may feel that this evaluation was unfair, because a person with a history of mental illness should not be discriminated against by having her children removed. This was not the case at all. Before I saw these two people, I tried not to have any preconceived idea that it would be better for the children to be with their mother or their father. The only question was who was the better and more stable parent. After looking at all the facts in the case, it was my professional opinion that the father had fewer negatives and would be the more capable parent.

Case 18

This is an example of an evaluation on one person whom the court had concerns about because of a history of mental illness.

Psychological Evaluation Report

Name: Robin Bates
(Required identifying information, date of testing, etc.)

Tests Administered

Wechsler Adult Intelligence Scale–Revised (WAIS-R)
Minnesota Multiphasic Personality Inventory (MMPI)
Millon Clinical Multiaxial Inventory (MCMI)
Incomplete Sentences Blank
Beck Depression Inventory (BDI)
Rorschach Ink Blots

Referral
Robin Bates was referred for a psychological evaluation by the court. At issue is the custody of her two children, who currently reside with their paternal grandparents, Tom and Betsy Colton. Ms. Bates was interviewed and evaluated on June 13, 26, and July 21, 1995. On July 21, I also met with her husband, 29-year-old Kevin Bates. Mr. and Mrs. Colton were interviewed on June 19 and July 10, 1995. During the first session with the Coltons I had the opportunity to meet with Ms. Bates's two children, Susan and Carolyn. I reviewed information from Doctor's Hospital and records from Charles Johnson, MD, Celeste Wilson, LCSW, and Robert Traylor, LPC. I also talked on the telephone with Dr. Johnson, Celeste Wilson, and Robert Traylor.

Background Information
Robin Bates is the mother of two children, Susan and Carolyn, who are in the custody of the paternal grandparents, Tom and Betsy Colton. Their son, John Colton, is the father of the children and also lives with his parents. Ms. Bates has visitation every weekend and is attempting to regain custody of her children. The Coltons do not feel she is capable of having full custody and they wish to retain custody. As far as I know, John Colton is not seeking custody or even unsupervised visitation.

Robert Traylor, LPC, was involved in treating Robin Bates and John Colton when they were married. He also made the referral to Doctor's Hospital, where Ms. Bates was hospitalized in April 1992. Dr. Delia Sanderson was the attending physician. Ms. Bates has been seeing Celeste Wilson, LCSW, at Arkansas Valley Counseling Associates since February 1993. She is not taking any medication at this time. This counseling relationship might not continue, because Ms. Bates does not currently have insurance to pay the cost of counseling. She said she will either terminate the therapy, see Ms. Wilson on an infrequent basis, or change to another provider with a lower fee. Dr. Charles Johnson evaluated Robin Bates in February 1994.

Robert Traylor indicates that Ms. Bates had pressured speech, exercised very poor judgment, and had an unstable mood at the time he saw her, leading to her hospitalization. He acknowledged her husband was psychotic at that time and she was under a great deal of pressure. He has not had an opportunity to evaluate her since she was treated in 1992. In the hospital Dr. Sanderson diagnosed Ms. Bates with bipolar disorder, borderline personality disorder, and substance abuse. Dr. Johnson reported that she was basically clear of these symptoms at the time of his evaluation in 1994. Celeste Wilson does not report symptoms of that proportion at this time.

Ms. Bates said she is not manic depressive and said she is doing well. She said her ex-husband was paranoid schizophrenic and abusive to her. She said she was fearful for her life and that of her oldest daughter at the time she was with him. She said she felt she went into Doctor's Hospital under duress, but she admitted that she did benefit from the hospitalization. She said she finally left the hospital after insisting upon her discharge. She reconciled with her husband after the discharge, but said he stopped taking his medication and again became violent. She left in February 1993 and filed for divorce. She had one child at the time and was three months pregnant. She stayed with friends or her grandmother. Carolyn was born in August. Ms. Bates said that Robert Traylor, who is a friend of the Coltons, helped her receive SSI, even though she did not want it. She claimed that Mr. Traylor coached her on how to apply for disability and the diagnosis from Dr. Sanderson enabled her to receive disability. She said she wants to relinquish these benefits, but the Social Security Administration will not discontinue the benefits until she finally goes to work and reports her employment.

Ms. Bates got her own mobile home in the fall of 1993 and let a married couple move in with her. The man, who was an ex-convict, was abusive and violent, not only with his wife but with Ms. Bates, a fact she acknowledged in her deposition of February 27, 1994. She said she was unable to get him out of her trailer. She acknowledged that the children saw this violence on at least one occasion. It was after one of those episodes, which occurred during the exchange of the children to the Coltons, that Mr. and Mrs. Colton filed for temporary custody. The biological father had supervised visitation all along at his parents' home. Ms. Bates acknowledged that her situation in the trailer was not good and she understands how Mr. and Mrs. Colton were able to gain temporary custody. She said she had gotten the couple out of the house by the time the hearing occurred in February 1994 and custody was transferred to the Coltons.

Ms. Bates's biological parents divorced when she was about 12. She has a younger brother who lives with her father. She had no complaints about her biological father, but said she was sexually abused one time by her stepfather when she was 16. She said it was more of an "advance" at the time, after he accused her of having sex with a boyfriend. She said he tried to unbutton her blouse and tried to fondle her. She said she ran away the next day to her grandmother's house. She did not think her mother supported her when her stepfather made that advance. Her mother is still married to her stepfather. Ms. Bates graduated from high school and went to vocational school. After high school she got a job and moved out with a friend. She began living with her ex-husband after her friend got pregnant.

Ms. Bates had no treatment history prior to seeing Robert Traylor. She said her main problem at that time was her marriage, which she wanted out of. She said she was insecure, had very low self-esteem, and was unable to get out of the marriage, until the time that she did. She said her current husband is loving and supportive and she described their marriage as very stable. During the final session with Ms. Bates, I met her husband, Kevin. He is working full-time. During that last session Ms. Bates said she lost her last job because she was absent so much for therapy, court, evaluation, and other requirements. She said her boss asked her if she was going to continue having court dates and, when she indicated she would need additional time off work, he let her go. Ms. Bates was worried about this and said she would like to get another job. She believes she can be hired at UPS or another delivery service, since she has some experience doing that type of work.

I asked Ms. Bates about some of the concerns the Coltons raised. She denied that she has any trouble being alone with the children. She said her husband's days off rotate, so she often has the children by herself on weekends. She usually has her husband with her when she picks up the children, because she is concerned an incident will occur and she wants her husband or someone else as a witness. She denied that she is depressed or that she cries in front of the children on a regular basis. She acknowledged she is sad when she returns them and her daughter has seen her upset about that. She denied that she breaks down crying on the telephone. She said she has a good relationship with her mother now and both her biological mother and father come to see the children.

Mr. and Mrs. Colton acknowledged their son's mental illness and history of drug abuse. They acknowledged that he does not tolerate stress well and is not able to raise the children alone. They also said Ms. Bates had problems from the first time they met her. Ms. Bates and their son lived with them until their first child was about 6 months old. They claimed Ms. Bates had "attacks" and would scream that she was going to die. They said she would run out of the house screaming without provocation. This was especially true right after the baby was born, something they described as a post-partum reaction. They claimed that Ms. Bates did not hold the baby and had trouble bonding. They said the baby was not fed properly and SCAN was called. They said Ms. Bates hit their son with a hammer while he was asleep, threw a soft drink in his face while he was driving, and once grabbed the steering wheel. They said she was pregnant when she left their son and she moved from one place to another, living with various people. She and both children lived for a time with a man in Sherwood. They felt she was very unstable at that time.

Mr. and Mrs. Colton acknowledged that Ms. Bates is now married and doing well. They acknowledged she has a good relationship with the children, she plays with them, and the children are always excited to see her. The children see her every weekend, plus she has them on Wednesdays, so she has them almost half-time as it is. However, they said she cannot manage the children and has trouble getting them in the car seat when she picks them up. They also said Ms. Bates is depressed and cries a lot, something which Susan reports to them. They are also concerned because Ms. Bates and her husband have two pit bulls in the back yard.

Although most of their concerns are two and three years old, the Coltons fear history will repeat itself. They said Ms. Bates cannot hold a job and has done some shoplifting. Mr. Colton said Ms. Bates accused him of sexually abusing Susan. He thinks she falsely accuses men of sexually abusing her. He thinks Ms. Bates is a very jealous person who does not think anything is wrong with her. He worries that she will be unstable in the future. The Coltons worry that the children will not be safe if Ms. Bates has another divorce. I visited with Susan, who was very positive about her mother. Carolyn was too young to speak with me alone and was fearful.

Evaluation Results
The WAIS-R scaled scores obtained by Robin Bates were as follows:

Verbal Tests		*Performance Tests*	
Information	5	Picture Completion	9
Digit Span	13	Picture Arrangement	8
Vocabulary	7	Block Design	12
Arithmetic	10	Object Assembly	9
Comprehension	8	Digit Symbol	6
Similarities	8		
Verbal IQ	89		
Performance IQ	92		
Full Scale IQ	88		

Her IQ of 88 is in the Low Average range of ability. There are no intellectual deficits which would affect her ability to function as a parent.

The MMPI scores were L = 70, F = 41, K = 68, HS = 52, D = 49, HY = 61, PD = 61, MF = 52, PA = 50, PT = 49, SC = 54, MA = 54, SI = 41. These scores were in the normal range, but the test was also responded to defensively and evasively. She took a full day and part of the next session to complete all of the objective tests. This is an extraordinarily long period of time, which I questioned her about. She said she responded carefully to each item because so much is at stake. She must have obsessed about each and every item several minutes at a time, because it took her more than a day to complete these tests, which are usually done in two or three hours. The scales that were elevated on the MMPI, compared to the rest of her profile, suggested at least mildly hysterical features and difficulty handling stress. Right now she seems well-defended, because the validity scales were so high. At present she is avoiding much self-disclosure and is very concerned about how she appears to others. Naturally much of this is related to the evaluation, which she understands will affect the custody of her children.

The MCMI scores were basically consistent with the MMPI. She had high Histrionic and Narcissistic scores and a high Compulsiveness score. The compulsiveness is not hard to understand, given the test-taking behavior. She has difficulty being alone and she is a dependent individual. This accounts for the elevation on the histrionic scales of both the MMPI and MCMI. While she is doing well now, there are underlying personality traits of dependency, attention-seeking, and insecurity. The irrational and hysterical behavior that has been described during the time she was with her ex-husband seems consistent with these test results. She has difficulty handling adversity and she becomes more irrational as the stress increases. She has always had difficulty with intimacy and trust. She has had periods of insecurity, lack of direction, indecisiveness, and poor judgment.

It is somewhat difficult to separate emotional problems that might be intrinsic to her personality from irrational behavior resulting from abuse and stress, which were clearly present during the time she was married. I think the best explanation is that symptoms displayed during the time she was hospitalized were the result of stress, abuse, and chaos imposed on an individual poorly able to deal with adversity. There was then rapid deterioration and decompensation, resulting in hospitalization. Robert Traylor described her at that time as someone who was experiencing depression, as well as pressured speech and thought, and this is probably true. Whether the diagnosis of bipolar disorder was warranted at that time is debatable, but her emotional instability at that time cannot be disregarded. Since that time there is greater integration and equilibrium. Dr. Johnson evaluated her in February 1994 and found no symptoms of bipolar disorder or decompensation. This continues to be the case, since she simply does not meet the criteria for Bipolar or Manic Depressive Disorder on current evaluation. She continues to benefit from seeing Celeste Wilson, who has functioned as a supportive therapist for her.

Ms. Bates did not acknowledge any feelings of depression on the BDI. If anything, she is overly defensive and trying too hard to make a favorable impression at this time. All people have feelings of depression, yet Ms. Bates did not indicate many areas of concern on the Beck. She needs to acknowledge the normal feelings of stress and vulnerability we all have. She is so defensive at this time that there may be problems not recognizing weaknesses in herself or others.

Her Sentences were mostly concerned with the children and her fears of not regaining custody. She said she needs "the courts to give me another chance to prove myself." She also said she has trouble sometimes "acting on my feelings." She said she would like to write a book about her life.

Even though she has surface feelings of well-being and some narcissism, the Rorschach indicated much deeper feelings of insecurity, vulnerability, and feelings of inferiority and inadequacy. There were also indications of sexual conflict and emotional scars from sexual issues, perhaps the abuse she related. She had a few odd responses, mostly around sexual issues.

Summary And Recommendations
Robin Bates has a Personality Disorder NOS (301.9), which is a mixed personality disorder, including borderline, histrionic, and inadequate traits. I think this personality disorder, which involves problems coping, underlies the emotional prob-

lems she had in 1992 when she was hospitalized. She is most vulnerable at times of greatest stress. A personality disorder such as this is an enduring characteristic, and, when exposed to significant degrees of stress, she is likely to decompensate. She is doing better at this time than she has ever done in her life. The emotional instability that was noted at the time of her hospitalization in 1992 is not present at this time. She had symptoms of major depression and/or bipolar disorder in 1992. The difference between her emotional problems now and a bipolar disorder is that the latter would be a chronic condition requiring medication management. There is no medication that can deal with a personality disorder, except when a patient is in acute distress and requires antidepressant or antianxiety medication for symptom relief. When someone with a personality disorder is doing well, there is no benefit or need for medication.

Mr. and Mrs. Colton concede that Ms. Bates is not displaying the kind of symptoms she did in the past. They are naturally attached to these grandchildren and want to keep them. It would be asking too much of them to be objective about this situation. Their fears about her behavior are based on their experience when she was married to their son. Everyone seems to acknowledge that she was under a great deal of stress at that time and that John Colton was much more seriously ill than she was. At the present time, Ms. Bates is not subject to these stressful conditions and she is married to a reasonably stable person. She is out of a job now, which may suggest a continuing pattern of instability, but I think her reason for losing the job is plausible and she can probably get another job. It is advisable for her to work, because this will increase her self-esteem, provide structure during the day, give the children an opportunity for enrichment at daycare or school, and increase her attentiveness to the children when she returns home each day from work.

I am recommending that Ms. Bates regain custody of her children. It is safe to return these children to her, and there are two adults in the home to care for them. I recommend that Mr. and Mrs. Colton have visitation, which is, in essence, supervised visitation with the father of the children. Since Mr. and Mrs. Colton will continue seeing the children, I believe there are plenty of safeguards in this situation. I am also recommending that Ms. Bates continue in a therapeutic relationship. This can either be done with her current therapist, if she can work out the finances, or with another therapist. Given her underlying personality disorder, a therapeutic relationship is important for her, even if sessions are as infrequent as once a month. I agree with Dr. Johnson that she does not present symptoms at this time requiring medication.

Discussion
The question in this evaluation was whether or not the mother was still substantially mentally ill and unstable, so that she could not assume custody of her two children. The biological father was not at issue, since his history of mental illness was more severe than that of the mother. He would continue to have visitation supervised by his parents. There was also no reason to perform evaluations on the

paternal grandparents. They had been found fit to take care of the two young children and had temporary custody. While they did not have to be tested, they were interviewed to find out their concerns about the mother and to provide information about the background and behavior of the children. Naturally they loved these two children and wanted to keep them. Although they could not be objective about their granddaughters, they were honest enough to say that the children loved their mother and were already spending a substantial amount of time with her. The children were seen simply to verify how they felt about their mother. Since the mother's mental health was in question, medical records were also reviewed. Preparing a report without the benefit of the past medical records would have been inadequate and probably would have been dismissed by the judge.

This mother had a brittle personality and strong feelings of self-consciousness and inadequacy. She also seemed very compulsive and obsessive. However, her previous diagnosis of bipolar disorder was very suspect. (Any time there are hospitalizations in the middle of crisis, marital maladjustment, substance abuse, or other abuse or chaos, the diagnosis of bipolar disorder should be carefully reevaluated later. Bipolar disorder seems to be a popular diagnosis these days. Anyone who is depressed and has any erratic behavior could be given a bipolar diagnosis.) What emerged from the test results was that she had a personality disorder, with emotional instability, inadequacy, and histrionic behavior as primary symptoms, especially when there was chaos in her life. She probably did need to be hospitalized while displaying these symptoms in the middle of her marriage to a schizophrenic husband.

In spite of these personality problems, there was no reason to deprive Ms. Bates of her children or to deprive the children of their mother. She was doing well at the time of the evaluation. She was in a new marriage and was continuing in outpatient therapy. I spoke with several other mental health professionals, who agreed she was not psychotic, she had no symptoms of bipolar disorder, and she was doing much better than in the past. There was everything to gain and very little to lose by reuniting the mother and her two daughters. She had never been physically abusive, so there was no risk that she would harm the children. The worst that would happen was that she might deteriorate and require additional inpatient treatment. Since the grandparents would still have substantial visitation, they would be aware of such a decompensation and could bring an action to the court to regain emergency custody.

If this had been a choice between a biological mother with Ms. Bates's history and a biological father with no history of mental illness, the recommendation might have been entirely different. As long as the choice is between a biological mother and the grandparents, the scale is tipped far to the mother's end. The question to be answered is not whether the mother or the grandparents will make more stable parents for the children; the question is whether the mother meets the minimal standards of parenting and mental health fitness to resume custody of her children. That is the court's standard and should be our standard in evaluating the case of a biological parent and some other intervening party.

Case 19

In this case the mother, who already had custody, was attempting to restrict visitation with the father and the father was seeking custody. Since the father had a history of a head injury, more attention was paid to him in the evaluation.

Psychological Evaluation Report

Names: George Sagen
        Shirley Plante
        Caitlin Sagen
(Required identifying information, date of testing, etc.)

Tests Administered
George Sagen:

> Wechsler Adult Intelligence Scale–Revised (WAIS-R)
> Wide Range Achievement Test–Revised (WRAT-R)
> Wechsler Memory Scale, Form I
> Halstead Category Test
> Aphasia Screening Test
> Wonderlic Personnel Test
> Incomplete Sentences Blank
> Millon Clinical Multiaxial Inventory (MCMI)
> Minnesota Multiphasic Personality Inventory (MMPI)
> Beck Depression Inventory

Shirley Plante:

> Incomplete Sentences Blank
> Beck Depression Inventory
> Minnesota Multiphasic Personality Inventory (MMPI)
> Millon Clinical Multiaxial Inventory (MCMI)

Caitlin Sagen:

> Children's Personality Questionnaire (CPQ)

Background Information
The court ordered all of the parties to undergo a psychological evaluation. As I understand it, Ms. Plante, 44, is seeking to terminate or restrict George Sagen's visitation and Mr. Sagen, 38, is filing for custody of Caitlin, age 9. Ms. Plante is represented by S. W. Engelsman, Mr. Sagen is represented by William Pace, and the attorney *ad litem* for Caitlin is Anne Silver.

George Sagen said he and his ex-wife divorced in 1985. Shortly after that, he received a head injury when he was struck by a two-by-four. He said that when he was in the hospital after his head injury, his ex-wife did not bring Caitlin to see him. He believes she has obstructed visitation for years. He is a CPA, but has not worked since the accident. He lives in Fort Smith on his own. He believes he cannot work because he has been advised by his doctors to avoid stress. He has been receiving Social Security Disability since 1987.

Mr. Sagen said that for two years after his head injury he was not able to pay child support and he rarely saw his child. He said his ex-wife tried to suspend his visitation. Mr. Sagen said he was granted visitation again in December 1987. At first this visitation was at his mother's house. His ex-wife remarried and moved to Oklahoma in 1989. He said that after that he would visit his child in Oklahoma City on weekends. In July 1992, he said he was accused of molesting Caitlin and visitation was again supervised. He received unsupervised visitation in December 1992 and that has continued until this year. The last visitation was scheduled in September. Caitlin refused to go with him when they made the exchange in Oklahoma. This resulted in the police being called and Mr. Sagen coming back to Arkansas without Caitlin.

Mr. Sagen denied emotional problems. He said he has headaches and eye pressure. He is not on any medication at this time. He admitted marijuana use before and after his head injury. He was on probation in February 1988 for possession of methamphetamine. In July 1989 he had another drug arrest and was convicted. He went to the Department of Corrections and spent six months at the Diagnostic Unit, five months at Cummings, and then some time at the Varner Unit. Mr. Sagen admitted he used marijuana, saying he needed it to reduce pressure to the optic nerve. He believes he had a legal right to use marijuana as a medicine. He said he stopped using the drug during the last two years and has been drug-tested for the last six months.

Mr. Sagen feels Ms. Plante is unfit as a mother. He said she wants to stay gone all the time, either working or going to bars. He believes she has an alcohol problem, smokes excessively in front of Caitlin, and was a terrible mother to her older daughter. He said the older daughter has raised Caitlin. He is also concerned about her husband, Ray Plante, who he said was violent to him during one of the exchanges. He believes Shirley has been married to seven different men. He believes Caitlin is under pressure from her mother and is negatively influenced against him.

Ms. Plante said she was concerned about Mr. Sagen's drug abuse, both during the marriage and after the divorce. She said Caitlin has seen her father using marijuana. She said Caitlin described on one occasion seeing marijuana and drug paraphernalia in a tobacco can. Ms. Plante said she took Caitlin to a drug education program and she identified the drug she saw at Mr. Sagen's house as marijuana. Ms. Plante also alleged that Caitlin was dirty and was not cared for or encouraged to bathe while at her father's house. She believes Caitlin was exposed to strangers and, on one occasion, witnessed an altercation between a man and woman who were apparently Mr. Sagen's neighbors. She said her ex-husband has little girls over at his house all the time. (Mr. Sagen said he watches his friend's children.) She acknowledged that there was no sexual abuse, even though she thinks her ex-husband inappropriately touched Caitlin on the "stomach or chest." Ms. Plante described this as "poor judgment."

Ms. Plante said Caitlin suffers from allergies, especially when in Arkansas. When I asked Ms. Plante if she smoked in the home and in front of Caitlin, she said, "I don't see what that has to do with it." She believes Caitlin has allergies, but does not believe exposure to cigarette smoke has anything to do with her condition. Ms. Plante believes Caitlin came home sick from visitation several times. Ms. Plante thinks the visitation was very stressful for Caitlin because she had to ride in the car for several hours to Arkansas on Friday nights, only to repeat the long trip on Sunday. She said Caitlin was lucky to get in bed by 9:00 or 10:00 P.M. on Sunday evenings. This occurred every other weekend.

Ms. Plante admitted she wanted Mr. Sagen's visitation with Caitlin limited almost from the beginning. She said that between 1988 and 1992 he did not ask for visitation. Part of that time he was in prison. She said she petitioned the court in Arkansas to suspend the visitation because she was concerned about Caitlin's medical health, her exposure to drugs, and Mr. Sagen's association with people she did not approve of. Ms. Plante said the September attempt at visitation was a disaster, because Caitlin refused to go with her father. She said Mr. Sagen grabbed Caitlin and held her in the back seat of his vehicle. She said he finally opened the door to let Caitlin out and Caitlin ran to her. Ms. Plante said her ex-husband was screaming to Caitlin that God demanded that she obey him. She said Mr. Sagen cannot be reasoned with when upset.

Caitlin apparently refers to Mr. Sagen as George, rather than as her father. Ms. Plante said Caitlin "is scared to death of him now. I don't blame her for not wanting to go." She said that Caitlin knows that her father is "forcing the issue." Ms. Plante said Caitlin is very close to her and she sees herself as a stable parent. She said Caitlin would be traumatized if taken away from her, saying, "I'm her parent." She said Caitlin is seeing a psychologist in Oklahoma.

Ms. Plante said her mother was somewhat abusive, although she describes their relationship now as good. She was married for a short time at 17 to a man who had a violent temper. She was married the second time for three years. She said her second husband was not violent. Her third husband was the father of her first child. She was married to him for 4½ years. Her fourth marriage, which lasted about eighteen months, was to an abusive alcoholic. Her fifth husband was Mr. Sagen and this marriage lasted about three years. Her sixth marriage lasted for two or three years. Problems included the fact that her husband wouldn't work and was abusive.

Ms. Plante was married for the seventh time last November to Ray, age 34. She denied that she uses alcohol or drugs or that she ever had a problem with alcohol. She denied that Ray uses drugs or alcohol. She did acknowledge that he had a battery charge, but she did not know if it was a felony conviction. She said he has not been in prison and denied that she had a prison record herself. She described Ray as a "househusband." She said she earns a good income and they have an arrangement for him to stay home. She said she had one psychiatric admission, but she was very defensive about this, saying it was only counseling on a more "intensive level."

Caitlin is a 9-year-old fourth-grader. During the interview, she reported most of the same information her mother did. She said she saw a man and woman fighting when she was visiting with her dad. Her father explained that this was an altercation between neighbors that he had no control over. Caitlin also told me she saw her father and a friend smoke what she later believed was marijuana. She said she had taken a drug awareness class. She said "George" has had girlfriends and he visits other people while she is there. She described in a very calculating way how she decided not to go on the last visit with her father. She told her mother ahead of time not to leave the area and told her father that she did not want to go with him. She said she knows her mother does not want her to visit her father. I asked her if her mother's smoking bothered her, since she has allergies, and she said no.

Evaluation Results
George Sagen had a Verbal IQ of 109, Performance IQ of 126, and Full Scale IQ of 119. This is compared to an IQ score of 83 obtained on him by Dr. James Mason in March 1987. His Full Scale IQ of 119 is at the 90th percentile and is in the High Average classification.

His WRAT-R scores were as follows:

	Standard Score	Percentile	Grade Equivalent
Reading	97	42	>12
Spelling	103	58	>12
Arithmetic	124	95	>12

These scores are all more than adequate for average daily functioning.

He had a Wechsler Memory quotient of 135, which is in the superior range, compared to the 1987 report which described him as "severely impaired" on the Wechsler Memory Scale. He had only 12 errors on the Halstead Category Test, which is also superior. He quickly understood the abstract concepts from subtest to subtest on the Category Test. On the previous Category Test he was "totally confused and unable to get re-oriented" (Mason 1987).

He had no errors on the Aphasia Screening Test. On the Wonderlic he had a score of 44, which is at the 99th percentile. At this level on the Wonderlic, he would be able to gather and synthesize information easily. He can infer information and conclusions and his ability is equivalent to other college graduates. There are no neuropsychological or intellectual deficits at present.

The MCMI was slightly elevated for Dependency and Somatoform. He had no significant elevations on the MMPI. All of the drug and alcohol scales on the MMPI and MCMI were not significant.

On the Sentences, he said he regrets not spending more time with Caitlin and said he feels lucky to be alive. He said his nerves can handle stress, he hates lies, his father is a good man, and he loves his daughter very much.

He had a score of 8 on the Beck Depression Inventory. He did not indicate significant depression, but at least he acknowledged normal human frailties, such as feeling sad, having difficulty making decisions, and crying occasionally.

Shirley Plante had a Beck Depression Inventory of 0. This indicates a significant amount of defensiveness. She is not acknowledging even the slightest weakness. She was defensive during the interview and on all the tests.

She responded to the MMPI evasively and defensively. She had an F minus K score of 20, which is an extremely defensive profile. She attempted to minimize and deny problems of a personal and social nature. According to her, she is socially extroverted and enterprising. She tends to be happy, successful, and attracted to lively, exciting people. She has been married seven times and several of those marriages were to abusive and dysfunctional men, but she brushed this off as "bad judgment."

She had an elevation on the Compulsive scale on the MCMI. This indicates her effort on the test to appear very self-disciplined, proper, and moral. She approached significance on Narcissism. She tends to be rigid and bureaucratic in her approach toward life. She is authoritarian in her outlook and overly concerned with status.

On the Sentences she said she wants to know "why my family has to be subjected to the stress of a custody case filed by a mentally disabled drug user." She said that what pains her "is the stress and anxiety my child is going through because he filed for custody" and that her greatest worry "is Caitlin being with her father."

On the CPQ, Caitlin came across as a bright child, emotionally stable, and very calm and composed. She tends to be undemonstrative, deliberate, and placid. She is usually obedient, accommodating, and conforming. She is socially precise, controlled, and somewhat compulsive. She is sober, restrained, and generally unafraid. She had low scores on anxiety, showing that she is not a child who is overwrought, depressed, or anxious.

Summary And Recommendations
Mr. Sagen qualified for Social Security Disability by having marked difficulty in maintaining social functioning and frequent deficiencies in concentration, persistence, and pace, resulting in failure to complete tasks. Neither of these is a legitimate limitation at this time. This is a person with high-average to superior ability in all areas. The previous psychological report was two years after his head injury.

Maximum improvement should have taken place by that time. I can only conclude that he was seeking compensation at the time and deliberately depressed his scores.

A mental status evaluation conducted for Social Security in 1986 by Dr. Ernest Johns, a psychiatrist, found Mr. Sagen to have an excellent memory, quick ability to calculate, good ability to handle proverbs, and adequate judgment. At the same time, Dr. Johns saw him to be tangential and somewhat expansive in his personality. This evaluation was prior to Dr. Mason's report, so there is evidence that his neuropsychological functioning was adequate at that time.

Dr. Johns diagnosed him with a personality disorder, which I think is correct. Mr. Sagen had a preexisting personality disorder that involved drug abuse. Dr. Mason also noted the premorbid problems in personality. The closed head injury probably exacerbated his personality disorder and added some traits and characteristics that were not there previously. For example, Mr. Sagen is often rambling in his explanations. This was apparent in his deposition, as well as during our interview. He will continue talking after he has answered the question and he has trouble switching from one topic to the next. This perseveration was not apparent on the testing, because he can shift from one topic to another if the items are neutral. He shifted from one item to the next very easily on the intellectual and neuropsychological instruments. However, when the material is personally relevant to him, he becomes obsessed and somewhat pressured to give his side of the story. This could be very frustrating to other people trying to solve problems with him.

By the end of our long evaluation, Mr. Sagen was able to do a little more self-examination and listen to input. In the end, he does value the input of Dr. Mason and others who attempt to give him an alternative viewpoint. In my view, Mr. Sagen has a Mild Organic Personality Disorder (310.10) with no significant impairment in intellectual, social, or occupational functioning. The pre-existing disorder was Personality Disorder NOS (301.90).

In my opinion, Shirley Plante also has a character disorder (Personality Disorder NOS, 301.90). She is very high-functioning, shrewd, and able to make a good impression. She dismissed her own psychiatric history and possible problems with alcohol in the past. She was reluctant to say anything about her husband, Ray, who will be spending a lot of time with Caitlin. Ray is an unknown factor and his character should also be evaluated in assessing this case.

I think Ms. Plante has contributed a significant amount to this crisis. She genuinely believes that Caitlin does not need to see her father and that it would be just as well for him to disappear. She is reinforcing Caitlin's reluctance to visit her father, saying "Caitlin has rights." I think she nurtured false allegations about sexual abuse and heightened Caitlin's concern about drug abuse by taking her to a drug awareness program at the police station. Allegations that the child is in poor health when she is with her father are a very common complaint in custody disputes. However, some of Ms. Plante's complaints are legitimate because she said "there is no reasoning" with Mr. Sagen, which is a problem. However, I think Caitlin's problem with Mr. Sagen has more to do with Ms. Plante than it does with Mr. Sagen's behavior.

Because the child is bonded to her mother and has seen her father only sporadically for visitation, I am recommending that custody remain with the mother. It would be traumatic at this time for custody to be changed. At the same time, I am recommending that Mr. Sagen resume normal visitation with Caitlin. In my opinion, this visitation does not need to be supervised. It would be easier for Caitlin if the parties could reach some agreement on scheduling of visitation. It would be difficult for any child to travel all day Friday and all day Sunday every other weekend for just one full day of visitation on Saturday. Perhaps a more effective schedule can be worked out.

By the end of our evaluation, Mr. Sagen did admit that he needs some guidance regarding parenting and how to better help Caitlin. Because of his personality disorder, exacerbated by organic factors, Mr. Sagen tends to be argumentative and very rigid. He therefore approaches Caitlin in a self-defeating way. I think this can be modified with parent counseling and therapy. He should attend an organized parenting class and should also continue his therapeutic relationship with Dr. Mason.

Discussion

Because of the previous head injury, drug problem, and incarceration, there was a great deal of emphasis placed on the father's fitness in this case. This was another case in which an individual was disabled for purposes of Social Security benefits but, in his view, perfectly fine and without mental illness when it came to the issue of custody. This case dramatizes how malingering can occur where disability is concerned. His IQ of 119 at the time of my testing was compared to an IQ of 83 he obtained when applying for Social Security benefits. That IQ of 83 was not obtained immediately after his head injury, but two years later. There should have been as much compensation and reorganization of the brain then as there was at the time of my evaluation, yet the difference in IQ scores was very significant. In this evaluation he obtained a Memory Quotient of 135 on the Wechsler Memory Scale, the same Memory Scale on which he had what was described as "a severe impairment in memory" in 1987, two years after his injury. If you think a neuropsychological evaluation cannot be faked, then compare his 12 errors on the Category Test at the time of the custody testing with his total inability to do that test in 1987. When I asked Mr. Sagen why he was on disability and why he could not work, even he had difficulty telling me.

The 9-year-old daughter in this case was clearly coached by her mother to be negative and to avoid her father. This child was very manipulative, which her mother was encouraging. The father had a personality disorder and there was no way that he should be granted custody. At the same, the mother, who was on her seventh marriage and had a personality disorder herself, was interfering with the father's visitation. Even though the father was stealing disability money, in my view, and had a history of drug abuse, there was no credibility to the allegation that he had ever abused or harmed his daughter. I recommended that custody remain with the mother and that she stop interfering with his visitation. Since they were in different states, I recommended that this child not have to make the long trip every other weekend for visitation, but that some other arrangement be worked out which would be less stressful on the child.

This case went to court and the court ordered a disposition consistent with the test results. I later heard from both the mother and father that they were very unhappy with my evaluation. They both threatened a lawsuit and a complaint to the State Board of Examiners, but neither followed through on it. Since they were both so unhappy, I felt I had probably done a good job in the report.

This case is a good example of the need to evaluate all parties in custody matters. Once we interview and evaluate everyone involved, we can clearly see the personality profiles of both parents and whether the child would be traumatized by changing custody. In other words, when we do have access to all parties, the data will do the work for us.

Case 20

In this case, the request for evaluation came from the Department of Human Services after the children had been removed because of the mother's drug problem.

Psychological Evaluation Report

Name: Janice Stanley
(Required identifying information, date of testing, etc.)

Tests Administered

> Wechsler Adult Intelligence Scale–Revised (WAIS-R)
> Minnesota Multiphasic Personality Inventory (MMPI)
> Millon Clinical Multiaxial Inventory (MCMI)
> Incomplete Sentences Blank
> Beck Depression Inventory

Clinical Interview
Janice Stanley is a 27-year-old black female referred by the court for a psychological evaluation. Her children were removed from her care in November 1993. The children are Marcus Waring, DOB 9/25/92, and Meredith Waring, DOB 7/3/93. They are currently in foster care. Ms. Stanley resides at Gyst House, a residential drug treatment program. She has visitation with the children on weekends at that facility.

Ms. Stanley was an only child and said she had no complaints when her mother was alive. Her mother was killed when she was 9 years old and she went to live with her grandmother in Arkansas. At 13 she started having problems with her grandmother and started using drugs. By 14 she was using IV drugs and her drug use has been extensive. Although she has abused alcohol and many other drugs, her drug of choice seems to be cocaine. She was in the Job Corps at 18. She did not do well after that and returned to Michigan, where she said she was selling drugs and working as a prostitute. At that time she was a heroin addict. She said she stopped using all drugs when she got pregnant. She said she does not have the HIV virus.

Ms. Stanley said her children were removed in November 1993, shortly after she moved from Michigan to Arkansas. They were removed after she left them with an adult female on a Thursday and did not return to pick them up. They were placed in DCFS custody on Saturday. She said this was the first time she left the children with anyone. She was somewhat resentful that the person did not keep her children until she returned. Ms. Stanley said she continued to use drugs after her children were removed. She had an initial admission to Gyst House in February 1994, but she was asked to leave after a short time. She also had an admission to the Benton Rehabilitation Center. She has now lived at Gyst House for seven months and says she has not used any drugs during that time. She said the Department of Human Services does drug testing and she had a clean drug screen in December.

Ms. Stanley hopes to get an apartment next month and get her children back. She has a job as a nursing assistant at a nursing home, a job she just started this week. She is working the day shift from 7:00 A.M. to 3:30 P.M. Before that, she worked three weeks at another nursing home, but she was fired after she had an altercation with another employee. She said she would like to begin LPN training. This would be a one-year program.

Test Results
The WAIS-R scaled scores were as follows:

Verbal Tests		Performance Tests	
Information	4	Picture Completion	7
Digit Span	4	Picture Arrangement	4
Vocabulary	5	Block Design	6
Arithmetic	6	Object Assembly	3
Comprehension	5	Digit Symbol	11
Similarities	6		

Verbal IQ	72
Performance IQ	76
Full Scale IQ	73

Her IQ of 73 is in the Borderline range of intellectual functioning. The scores are judged to be reliable and valid, because Ms. Stanley tried her best. She is at the fourth percentile level and is low functioning. The highest score was on Digit Symbol. She may have considerable difficulty passing an LPN program. Her highest level of performance may be as a nursing assistant.

Her MMPI scores were L = 50, F = 114, K = 35, HS = 52, D = 45, HY = 31, PD = 59, MF = 52, PA = 73, PT = 65, SC = 76, MA = 66, SI = 55. The soundness of the profile is debatable. She is an unstable individual and she attempted to emphasize a need for treatment by exaggerating her symptoms. She probably had difficulty understanding some of the items. She tends to be full of ideas and overly ambitious. She is apt to be ineffective and easily thwarted in the pursuit of poorly chosen goals. She is tense, restless, impulsive, and hyperactive in both thought and behavior. She is easily agitated and blows up with very slight provocation. She has strange and unusual thoughts and feelings. She has defective inhibition over loss of control. She probably has mood swings and has a very high need for excitement, risk taking, and activity. She may complain about concentration difficulty. The indications of drug abuse, which were obvious from the history, were also very strong on the MMPI. Her substance abuse has played an important part in her life, almost as a self-medication.

The MCMI scores were very extreme in several areas, including delusional thinking, drug use, paranoia, and narcissism. There was also an extreme tendency to exaggerate problems. I think she was determined to acknowledge almost every psychological problem, in an attempt to be overly compliant and cooperative. She was also very honest about her history during the interview. To her credit, she does not deny any past behavior and she accepts responsibility for her actions.

On the Beck Depression Inventory she does not appear to be suffering from significant depression at this time. She denied feeling sad or despondent. She blames herself for what has happened and she is not as irritated by events as she was in the past. Just one week ago, though, she acknowledged losing her temper and losing a job.

The Sentences were also completed in an honest and forthright way. She said her nerves were bad when she was on drugs and that she suffers without her mother. She wants to go to school to be an LPN and she acknowledges that she is an addict. She displays all of the language, expressions, and philosophy one learns at a drug treatment program. Some of her responses on the Sentences were difficult to understand and had meaning only to her.

Summary And Recommendations
Ms. Stanley has the following diagnoses:

Axis I	Polysubstance Dependence (304.90)
Axis II	Borderline Intellectual Functioning (V40.00)
	Personality Disorder, NOS (301.90)
Axis III	None
Axis IV	Moderate (3)
Axis V	Current GAF 50

I saw no evidence in the evaluation or other reports that Ms. Stanley was ever physically abusive to her children. As a mother, she had her first child for fifteen months and her second child for only four months. It is difficult to say what her level of care was during the time in Michigan, when she was using drugs. She is not a risk to her children at present, as she was in November 1993. To her credit, she has been in the Gyst House program for seven months and has apparently been drug-free for that period of time. I would encourage verifying her progress with Gyst House personnel. If she is able to establish a residence and maintain employment, I can recommend return of her two children.

As a group, heroin- and cocaine-addicted individuals have a very high relapse rate. Ms. Stanley will continue to be a very high risk for relapse into drug use. She will need continued outpatient involvement and her children will need services and daycare. Recommendations are for continued drug testing and supervision. In addition to Narcotics Anonymous and group therapy, she should have an individual therapist. Ms. Stanley has low intellectual functioning and few cognitive resources to solve problems. It is imperative that she receive supervision for at least a year after the children are returned.

At this time Ms. Stanley is very honest, making a good effort, and appears to be sincere in her attempt to recover. While she faces difficult odds for success in her addiction, I think she has at least minimally acceptable ability to parent while in a recovered drug-free state.

Discussion

This type of case is usually referred by the court or a state agency. It was not in chancery or circuit court, as most civil custody actions are, but in juvenile court. Most states have a policy of reunifying families in these circumstances if at all possible. The court wanted to know whether the mother was receptive to rehabilitation, whether she was capable of parenting, or whether termination of parental rights should be considered.

In this case, the children were in foster care and the mother was in a drug treatment program. Although she had been neglectful to the children, there was no evidence she had ever been abusive. Since this was the first time her children had been removed, since the case was not complicated by physical abuse of the children or mental illness, and since the test results were positive, the court was advised to continue with its reunification efforts. If she had already had her children removed three or four times, my recommendation might have been different.

There was every indication that the court and the Department of Human Services (DHS) should continue working with this mother and give her another try. I stated in the report that there is always a high risk of relapse for drug-addicted individuals. The court and DHS would hopefully monitor this patient for at least two years, since young children were involved.

In another somewhat similar case, I tested a parent from a juvenile court referral who had a 65 IQ and a chronic history of cocaine abuse. She also had repeated interventions by DHS over a several-year period and her children had been repeatedly removed. In that case, my recommendation was that parental rights be terminated. With her IQ and her chronic history of drug abuse, I saw no potential for rehabilitation. In cases that bad, we should not shrink from our responsibility to make some prediction, even if it is negative and parental rights should be terminated.

6

EVALUATING SEXUAL ALLEGATIONS

Cases alleging sexual abuse are referred because the court has great difficulty sorting out the truth of the allegations. In these evaluations, the psychologist must make a judgment regarding whether the abuse occurred. This type of forensic practice is not for the timid, tentative, or cautious professional. Some psychologists are so intimidated and threatened by these cases that their reports are very tentative and fail to reach reasonable conclusions. Those reports are not helpful to the court. Everyone knows that the psychologist does not know for certain whether sexual abuse occurred, but the court wants an opinion on that question. The psychologist is asked to reach a conclusion based on a reasonable evaluation of the facts and the parties involved in the case. Even when you do reach definite conclusions and recommendations, those recommendations may not be followed, since the judge is the ultimate fact-finder and is responsible for the ultimate decision.

These evaluations can be very troubling, whichever way you find, because you never know for sure whether you are allowing a sexual abuser to resume contact with the child or whether you are preventing an innocent father from having a relationship with his child. If the evidence is not very compelling, I usually err on the side of recommending reintroduction of the father into the child's life, usually on a supervised basis. At times, the allegations seem to be blatantly false and I will recommend that the father either regain custody or have unsupervised access and visitation. (When performing these evaluations, it is important to stay open to the possibility that sexual abuse did not occur. False allegations do happen, especially in the context of custody disputes.) In some cases, the psychological evidence pointing toward the abuse is very compelling, even in the absence of physical evidence, which is often not present, and even in the face of a denial by the child that sexual abuse has taken place. In other cases, there is medical evidence, such as gonorrhea or other evidence of sexual trauma, that almost negates the necessity of a psychological evaluation.

All the cases presented here are complex. Allegations of sexual abuse do not occur in a vacuum, so family dynamics are also evaluated. In this way, many sexual abuse evaluations are very closely related to ordinary custody evaluations. Referrals come from a variety of sources, including the Department of Human Services, Child Welfare, the courts, or private attorneys. Sexual abuse is often not the only issue and may not even be the most important issue.

Case 21

This shows one typical pattern in incestuous families, that of a passive-dependent wife, sometimes abused herself, and a domineering, jealous, and irrational husband who controls everything in the family. In this case the father was mentally retarded, which increases the likelihood that sexual abuse is occurring.

Psychological Evaluation Report

Names: Henry James
        Diane James
        Patty James
(Required identifying information, date of testing, etc.)

Tests Administered

> Wechsler Adult Intelligence Scale–Revised (WAIS-R)
> Minnesota Multiphasic Personality Inventory (MMPI)
> Millon Clinical Multiaxial Inventory (MCMI)
> Incomplete Sentences Blank
> Beck Depression Inventory
> Clinical Interview

Background And Clinical Interview
A psychological evaluation was ordered by the Hon. Judge Winston Bailey. He ordered evaluations on Mr. and Mrs. James and their 17-year, 10-month-old daughter Patty. Patty and her two sisters, Deidre and Josephine, are named in the dependency neglect case. Lana is an 18-year-old daughter who was allegedly sexually abused, but she is no longer a minor and was not named in the juvenile case. Mr. and Mrs. James have twelve children, ranging in age from 6 months to 18 years of age.

On or about November 1, 1994, DCFS received a report about possible abuse of several children in the James home. The children reported their father hit them because they would not sleep in their nightclothes instead of the street clothes they apparently wear to bed. Lana reported her father "played with her breasts." The children were interviewed in school the next day. All the children stated their father spanked them with a belt or extension cord. There were no marks on any of the children. Deidre, Josephine, and Patty all stated they were punished for not sleeping in their nightshirts without bras and panties. Patty and Josephine reported their father climbed in bed with them and touched them, or tried to. Deidre reported seeing her father get in bed with Lana, Josephine, and Patty. Josephine reported that "he feels me on my back." Patty reported seeing her father playing with Lana's breast about a month ago. Mr. James allegedly makes the girls undress and put on their nightshirts in front of him. Mr. James is currently out of the home. The children have all been returned to the custody of their mother, Diane James.

Mr. James is the father of all twelve children. He drives a truck for a living and works the midnight shift. He has worked all of his life and supported the family. Mrs. James wants to stay with him and does not contemplate divorce. She said she has thought about divorce, but she said the children are "crazy about their dad." Mrs. James was very open about what happens in her house and, during her interview alone, she expressed concern about her husband's behavior. She admitted that he gets angry, pushes the kids, and whips the children hard with a belt or extension cord. She has called the police before.

On the night of the alleged abuse, Mr. James woke up four of the children shortly before he went to work at 1:00 A.M. and spanked them. Patty was apparently on the telephone and others were in bed with their clothes on at the time. He was angry about a variety of things, including the fact that he felt they had not done their chores. When I talked to Mr. James, he admitted waking his daughters up that late at night and giving four of them four licks. It does not seem to matter that the older girls are 17 and 18, because Mr. James feels free to spank them with a belt or extension cord. He stated that he believes this is his right and responsibility. Mrs. James saw this occur and asked him why he was doing it. It is clear she has very little power and exercises little authority to intervene. Mrs. James said her husband complains that she is too easy on the children. She believes the girls are too old for whipping, but he disagrees. However, he says he will not whip them if the court tells him not to.

When I asked Mrs. James about possible sexual abuse, she said, "I really don't know." She has heard her husband insist that the children sleep in nightclothes, rather than in cut-offs, and said she does not understand why he makes a big deal out of what they sleep in. It could be that they consider their father a threat and they are more comfortable in regular clothing. Mrs. James admitted she saw her husband attempting to pull Patty's clothes off in 1990. She saw this through the window and called the police. A DHS case was opened and Mr. James was out of the home for a time. Part of the resolution in that case was that he had to see Clifford Thomas in Little Rock for counseling.

Mrs. James said Patty is "slow" and at 17 is still in the ninth grade. Mrs. James thinks Patty has been sexually active since age 13 and she apparently had a sexually transmitted disease at one time. Patty also has a 2-year-old child. At eight months pregnant, Patty did not believe she was pregnant, which gives an indication of how backward she is.

When I talked to Mr. James, he was very angry about being out of the home and defended his right to whip the children. Although he denied abusing the children, he said he did not mind going to counseling before and would go again. Although he complied with counseling in the past, he stated that he did not consider himself to have a problem. No matter how I asked him, he denied any sexual abuse, although he had no problem admitting the spankings.

When I interviewed Patty, she said her father has asked her to take her clothes off in front of him, but she told him no. This occurred when her mother was not present. She said he touched her when she was asleep, causing her to wake up. She was not able to describe what he was doing at the time. She said she saw him touch her older sister's breast one time. She said that once last year her father cut her pants off when she was asleep. She told her mother about this. This allegedly was for sleeping with her clothes on instead of a nightgown. She said her father said, "Sleep in them again and I'll cut them off again." She remembered the incident several years ago in which he tried to pull her clothes off. Patty does not want her father to return home and said there has been no trouble at home since he has been gone.

Test Results

Mr. James has a Verbal IQ of 69, a Performance IQ of 67, and a Full Scale IQ of 67. He is in the mild range of mental retardation at only the one percentile level. His mental retardation was consistent across all areas of functioning. It is difficult to reason with Mr. James and his IQ partly explains this. He is very rigid, dogmatic, and authoritarian. The MMPI was high on Scale 6, so he blames others for his problems and feels he is being treated unfairly. He is also quick to anger. On the MCMI he had a high score on Somatoform, which was also true on the MMPI, so he has psychosomatic symptoms. He said on the Sentences that he likes to read and hates to get sick. He had little ability to spell on the Sentences, but this is expected, based on his intelligence.

Mrs. James has a Verbal IQ of 82, a Performance IQ of 80, and a Full Scale IQ of 80. She is higher-functioning than her husband and this was apparent during the interview. On the MMPI she had high levels of defensiveness and did not readily acknowledge psychological problems. The MCMI suggested she is withdrawn, schizoid, and nonassertive. She is a passive-dependent individual with low self-esteem who is unable to stand up for her rights. She was positive about her children and I think she is probably a good mother, although she is dominated by her husband.

Patty had a Verbal IQ of 82, a Performance IQ of 75, and a Full Scale IQ of 78. This is not as low as I thought it might be, since Patty appears to be low-functioning and perhaps retarded. Her scores indicate she is not retarded, but has borderline intellectual functioning. There is credibility in her report of abuse and inappropriate touching by her father. The other striking thing about Patty's psychological evaluation, especially on the Sentences, is that she loves her father and blames herself. This is a very passive-dependent 17-year-old who has low self-esteem and is easily controlled. She is shy and backward, which is why she appears to be lower functioning than she actually is. She worries about getting into trouble, regrets talking back to her parents, and feels she is a bad person. She internalizes everything that happens, including any inappropriate sexual behavior by her father. She will tolerate a great deal and she is an easy target for abuse, not only by family members, but possibly by boyfriends. It is not surprising that she has been sexually active, since she would be easily used by males. She showed a great deal of distress on the MCMI with high scores on anxiety and depression. She is a sad and unhappy individual, withdrawn and schizoid.

Summary and Recommendations
Patty has borderline intellectual functioning and is not able to defend herself. She is low-functioning, not only in intelligence but even more so emotionally. She is a reliable informant and I think her father has been inappropriate in a number of ways with her and the other children. There is no evidence that he had intercourse with any of the children, but I think he has at least fondled Patty and two or three of the other girls. He does not acknowledge this. He also defends his right to whip the children. Mrs. James has a great deal of difficulty standing up for herself and the children, but she has called the police in the past. With support, I think she can do better.

I am not sure Mr. James will stop whipping the children. It is also quite possible that he will continue fondling the children, if not the older ones, then the younger ones, when they increase in age. Patty could be a target of abuse again, because she is so withdrawn and inadequate. This is a very difficult situation, because Mr. James has apparently been a good provider for his children. However, considering all the facts, the father should stay out of the house. If he is allowed back in the home, I recommend a great deal of therapy and services for this family. The prognosis for improvement is poor, since Mr. James is so low in intellectual functioning. He also did not gain much from previous therapy. If he is permitted to reenter the home at some point, he should be ordered not to spank these children or dictate what they wear to bed. This will require a great deal of supervision and monitoring by SCAN and Social Services. Unfortunately, if Mr. James is allowed back in the home, there will be additional incidents of corporal punishment and probably more fondling and molesting.

Discussion
This was a child abuse case in juvenile court in which the judge ordered evaluations of the parents and the 17-year-old daughter. Reports were received from the Department of Human Services indicating that three daughters were alleging sexual

abuse. These reports are often vital to reach conclusions. Even though reports were available on the other girls, the judge only ordered one of the daughters to be evaluated.

It is very typical for evaluating psychologists to see children who are victims only after they have been interviewed by several different health-care profession als. Our job as forensic psychologists is usually not to do the initial investigation or make the initial determinations of abuse, but to perform more comprehensive evaluations. These are done after preliminary information has been gathered and usually after there have been several court hearings.

We do not always get everything we want when performing evaluations on families and not everyone is evaluated in every case. If the judge in this case had ordered only the father or the mother to be evaluated, any written report would have pointed out the incomplete, inadequate nature of the evaluation and its limi tations and qualifications. We should always try to evaluate the key individuals in a family, including the alleged perpetrator and his wife, especially if the wife is the one making the allegations, which was not the case here. We also consider infor mation available to us from other sources. The court hears different viewpoints and fragmented information, so the task of the psychological evaluation is often to pull all this information together, as well as to provide new information based on the evaluation itself.

In this evaluation, the evidence was very compelling that sexual abuse, as well as other abuse, was occurring. The mother was credible. The children and the 17-year-old interviewed in this case were credible. The father had a 67 IQ, which is another trait to be concerned about. In my clinical experience, there is a greater likelihood of deviant behavior, especially incest, among retarded individu als. In this case, Mr. James was not only mentally retarded but he was rigid and authoritarian and exerted total control over the family. The mother was brighter, but she was defensive, withdrawn, schizoid, and nonassertive. The daughter, Patty, had an IQ of 78 and was low-functioning socially. She is just the kind of teenager to be sexually abused, since she was shy, backward, and low functioning. I con cluded in the report that the father was fondling the children as well as abusing them physically and mentally. I recommended that he stay out of the home. There was a price to pay for this recommendation, because this man was the breadwin ner and raised twelve children. His wife was dependent upon him and still wanted him in the home.

In cases such as this, when the mother is not the primary person making the allegation, there is a greater likelihood of substantiation of the allegations. Sub stantiation is also more likely if the child is the first one reporting sexual abuse to a party outside the home. In this case, the mother was not the first one to report the sexual abuse, since the children were interviewed in school. The mother was a passive individual, uncertain about what was going on. She also wanted to stay with her husband and was not contemplating divorce. This mother was very typi cal of mothers in incestuous families who are unable to protect the children. This is very different from accusing mothers who make the charge of sexual abuse against a hated or estranged husband when child custody is the primary issue. That situation is much more likely to be consistent with false allegations.

This family had a very typical incestuous profile, with a passive-dependent wife and a domineering, jealous, and irrational husband. In other abusing families, the incestuous father is passive and inadequate with a domineering wife and mother. These polar opposites seem to typify incestuous circumstances. In one extreme, the father dominates and does so sexually. In the other extreme, the father is a passive, emasculated individual who seeks comfort and refuge in a wife-surrogate, who may be his daughter or stepdaughter.

Unlike what many mental health professionals seem to believe, the incestuous, abusive father is usually not a well-adjusted normal father in all areas except the incest. Anyone who has a few years' clinical experience and has evaluated a number of these cases knows better. The incestuous fathers usually fall into the two polar opposites described above. These are not absolute guidelines, but they are markers to at least begin evaluating family dynamics.

This type of direct recommendation is what the court wants. Why would the court refer cases for evaluation if it didn't want firm recommendations such as I made in this case? The court is more likely to make decisions that will protect the children if recommendations are as straightforward as they were in this report. I could be wrong about Mr. James, of course, but it is ethical and within our charge and responsibility to make recommendations based on our best clinical judgment.

As in most cases, I do not know how this matter was resolved. Chances are good that Mr. James was allowed to reenter the home. It is a common practice in almost every jurisdiction for the courts to reconcile families, or at least to attempt reunification. I recommended against this, but, if it did occur, I said there would be a need for ongoing supervision and case management. I also said there would be future incidents of corporal punishment, fondling, and molesting, so it is the court's responsibility if this occurs again.

Case 22

This case shows the second prevalent pattern in sexual abuse cases: an inadequate, passive, dominated husband who turns to the child or children to meet his emotional needs. In this case the father was mentally retarded and the mother was volatile and explosive. Sexual abuse was just one part of a pattern of abuse and neglect of the children.

Psychological Evaluation Report

Names: Rachel Bundt
        David Bundt
        Crystal Bundt, 7
        Loren Bundt, 6

Darla Bundt, 4
Beverly Bundt, 1
(Required identifying information, date of testing, etc.)

Referral
The Bundt family was referred for psychological evaluation by the Chancery Court of Garrison County and the Department of Human Services. Rachel and David Bundt, the parents, were interviewed together for about two hours. They were then interviewed separately for approximately one hour each. Rachel Bundt was administered the Incomplete Sentences Blank, Thematic Apperception Test (TAT), Beck Depression Inventory, Hand Test, Minnesota Multiphasic Personality Inventory (MMPI), and the Millon Clinical Multiaxial Inventory (MCMI). David Bundt was administered the Hand Test, Wide Range Achievement Test–Revised (WRAT-R), Wechsler Adult Intelligence Scale–Revised (WAIS-R), and the Thematic Apperception Test (TAT). Crystal, Loren, and Darla were interviewed separately. All of the children, including Beverly, age 1, were observed visiting with their parents.

Background Information
The four Bundt children have been in foster care since being removed from their parents five months ago. At that time, the Department of Human Services received a police report that three children were playing in the street with no supervision and were not dressed appropriately for the weather. Crystal, Loren, and Darla were found on Sixth Street and stated that their parents were not at home. Crystal directed the police to their apartment, which was two miles from where the children were found. The children stated they got themselves up, dressed, and ready for school. They stated they had not eaten and had not seen their parents all morning. All three children were cold and hungry. Crystal had red marks on the top and back part of her legs. She said this was from when she called her mother "a fucking bitch."

At approximately 1:00 P.M. that day, a DHS worker and a patrol officer entered the Bundt house. The parents were sleeping in their bedroom and the baby, Beverly, was also in the room. The condition of the house was dirty and unsafe. The house was cold and the heat had apparently been shut off. The parents were unaware that the children had left the home. Mrs. Bundt said she was up all night with the baby because she was sick. Mr. and Mrs. Bundt proceeded to yell at Crystal for leaving the home. At that point the children were temporarily left with their parents, until a decision could be made as to disposition. When it was determined that the children would be removed and the DHS worker and officer returned, Crystal was crying, saying she had been spanked for "getting Mommy and Daddy in trouble." Pictures were taken of the home, which showed knives and medicine lying out easily accessible to the children. Guns and ammunition in the parents' bedroom were also easily accessible. Clothes covered all of the floor surfaces in the bedrooms. Roaches and dirt were found in all rooms.

The Bundts have had a protective service case since at least 1991. The children have received services at Children's Safe Place run by Western Guidance Center (WGC). WGC wrote a letter in December 1993 expressing their concern that the children continued to be at risk for abuse or neglect. Mrs. Bundt was exhibiting significant anger toward the agency and she was seen as noncompliant, which affected the prognosis. She was belligerent and had stated on numerous occasions she was not willing to work in counseling on family problems.

The record is voluminous and contains many examples of abuse, neglect, and inappropriate parenting. The high level of anger Mrs. Bundt exhibited toward the children was a significant concern. Many incidents of threats of violence were reported by the children to the Children's Safe Place staff. On a date in October 1993 Mrs. Bundt whipped Crystal with a belt and the bruises were reported by treatment staff. The same day Mrs. Bundt did not allow the children to have their snacks when she picked them up at Children's Safe Place. When the teacher asked Mrs. Bundt if the kids could take the snacks with them, Mrs. Bundt responded, "Don't tell me what to do. I'll hit you."

The children were noted to model the mother's angry outbursts. Kate Hensley of the WGC, who worked with Crystal and Loren, documented the language and acting-out that the children displayed. In play therapy Crystal regularly played the mother who was angry and blaming her children. She would tell the therapist, who was in the child's role, that she did not love her and did not want her. Crystal called the therapist/child a "fuck bitch." She was physically aggressive with the therapist and with objects in the room. She attempted to spank the therapist with a wooden stick. On another occasion she said, "Shut up or I'll hit you in the face again." Loren was also reported to act out and to curse using the same kind of language. Overall, Loren exhibited violence and aggression and he was seen as anxious and angry. Both children invited the therapist to play cards, but then attempted to punish the therapist for "touching their things." Loren and Crystal ran into an adjacent room and Loren was observed pulling his pants down and shaking his penis at the therapist. He was stimulating himself and inviting Crystal to sit on his lap. Crystal said someone put a knife in her "pee-pee," but she could not say who did it because she would get in trouble. The children were seen to give each other "the finger." Loren referred to his private parts as his "dick and balls" and to Crystal's private area as her "dick ass." In an interview shortly after the WGC report, Mr. Bundt said he caught Loren with his pants down attempting to put his penis in the face of Darla, who was 2 at the time. Mr. Bundt also told the police that the apartment was haunted and you could hear footsteps at night. It was revealed that the children were exposed to horror films.

After the children were placed in foster care, Crystal especially demonstrated disturbed behavior. She called the foster mother "fucking bitch" and she tried to run away once. She began making sexual allegations. She told the foster parent that her daddy is a vampire and makes her bleed in her private parts. She allegedly told the foster mother that "Daddy kisses Beverly on her privates." She was noted to play with Barbie dolls, acting out sex between her and her father. She also stated that her mother takes pictures of these activities. Crystal asked a stranger if he "jerked his mare." She was noted to wet the bed frequently. Her behavior in foster care included a strip tease, in which she removed her clothes while humming music.

Following these severe problems in foster care and the disclosure to the foster parents that she and her siblings had been sexually abused, Crystal was admitted to Charter Hospital in January 1995. An extensive battery of tests was administered to her by Dr. Florence Chase. The testing revealed a Full Scale IQ of 56. Crystal gave several responses on the projective testing which suggested sexual abuse within the home. Dr. Chase diagnosed her with Post-Traumatic Stress Disorder, Enuresis, Adjustment Disorder with Mixed Disturbance of Conduct and Mood, and Mild Mental Retardation. Throughout the hospitalization Crystal expressed fearfulness and anger toward her biological parents and more positive attachment toward her foster parents. Her final diagnoses were Post-Traumatic Stress Disorder, Mental Retardation, and Attention Deficit–Hyperactivity Disorder. She was discharged on 5 mg of Ritalin. Dr. Langston, the attending psychiatrist, recommended against return to the biological parents, since he believed there was evidence of chronic physical and sexual abuse and neglect by the biological parents.

Evaluation Results
During the interview with Mr. and Mrs. Bundt together, the relationship between them emerged very clearly. Mrs. Bundt was clearly dominant. She was frequently annoyed or irritated with her husband and often criticized him. Mr. Bundt was a much more passive and seemingly cooperative individual who deferred to his wife. Mrs. Bundt admitted she has a problem "cussing people out." They both said they had whipped the children in the past, but denied doing it after the court told them to stop. They claimed that all the recent bruises the children had were the result of mistreatment at the Children's Safe Place, since they had not whipped the children in two years. This was not a believable statement, especially from Mrs. Bundt, who could not maintain control even during the interview. The Bundts acknowledged swearing at the children in the past, but said they do not do it anymore. When they were asked about the children getting out of the house and ending up two miles away, they said they had been up all night with the baby and did not realize their children left the house that morning. David Bundt said he believed someone opened the door that morning so the children could get out of the house. He said this was a plot to take the children from him and his wife. Both parents complained about the children's treatment in foster care, although they were unable to be specific about how the children might not be treated well.

When questioned about the allegations of sexual abuse, Mrs. Bundt said the children, especially Crystal, just want attention. She denied that any sexual abuse of the children had occurred, stating that if a parent did that, they should be shot. She believed Crystal came up with that story after hearing her talk about her own sexual abuse when she was younger. She thinks Crystal should be hypnotized to get the truth. Mr. Bundt believes Crystal made up the story about the sexual abuse because she was jealous of Mrs. Bundt breastfeeding Beverly. He said he does not need to sexually abuse his children, because he has his wife. He also believes other children in the neighborhood grab the children by the genitals and engage in both sexualized language and behavior. He said he is afraid to pick his children up because of the allegations. (However, he hugged the children during this visit.) The Bundts acknowledged that the children "accidentally" saw them having sex on more than one occasion. The Bundts believe Loren and Crystal were coached by DHS staff to allege the sexual abuse. They were both critical of the Charter hospitalization, saying they believe Crystal was hospitalized only to get the sexual abuse charges. Mrs. Bundt said Crystal told her once that she was molested at Children's Safe Place.

Both Mr. and Mrs. Bundt said several times that they were afraid of criminal charges and that they were not "going to the pen." In fact, one motivation for wanting the children back is to avoid criminal prosecution. In their minds, removal of the children is automatically associated with initiation of criminal charges regarding sexual abuse. They claim the children want to come home and that they tell them this during the visitation. Mrs. Bundt said Crystal now "apologizes" and wants to come home and get out of foster care. Both parents mistakenly believe that because the children are positive to them during the visitation, this proves there has been no sexual abuse or other kind of abuse. The children hear discussions about the entire conflict with the state every time they have a visit with their parents.

Mrs. Bundt said, "I love my children, but I can't take this pain." Several times she made the assertion that the children should either be taken away permanently or returned. Once she commented, "Why am I here? We're not going to get the kids back." At another point in the interview, the Bundts stated that if they do not get the children back, they will have more children.

Even though the Bundts currently have a residence, the apartment has been described as not suitable. The Bundts said they have no ability to move, especially now, because they do not have the children's Social Security checks to rely on. Both Mr. and Mrs. Bundt are receiving SSI. When they had all four children, their cash income was between $1,600 and $1,800 a month. They claim that the residence in which they have lived for the last five years is now clean, but that they would still like to relocate because of the neighborhood. They also said they got rid of the gun they had in the home. They both said they have been going to counseling and have learned a lot, so they believe they are able to take care of the children.

During Mr. Bundt's separate interview, he said he was born and raised in Arkansas. He has two brothers and one sister; his parents are divorced. He was in and out of foster care from an early age himself. He said he was abused by his mother and he once saw her break a broomstick over his brother's head. He said she whipped him and slapped him out of a chair one time. He said his father would "kick me in the ass." Mr. Bundt seemed to justify all the abuse in his childhood, saying, "I'm still living." He denies he was ever sexually abused. He said, "I would remember that."

David Bundt was in special education classes and quit school in the seventh grade. He denied any arrest record. He worked off and on and lived with his mother until he was about 23. After his mother died in 1983, he went to the rehabilitation center in Hot Springs, completing a one-year program in housekeeping. This is where he met Rachel. He said he was about 24 years old at the time. Rachel returned to Fort Smith with him and they resided with his sister. He said he worked a short time, but "couldn't get along with the bosses." He said he was fired from a chicken plant.

When he and Rachel married and had their first child, they moved to the Fayetteville area. They stayed at the Salvation Army and then moved to a hotel. He had a few jobs in the Fayetteville area until he received disability. Prior to that, they were living on Mrs. Bundt's Social Security income. Mr. Bundt said he and his wife only had one physical fight in their marriage and the children were not present. He did acknowledge that she curses him almost every day. He said he reacts by laughing at her and "it pisses her off." He said he has to "call her down with the kids" because she screams at them. He acknowledged that she cursed at the children and then said, "we both would." He said his wife is easily frustrated and, for example, will turn to him and say, "Why the fuck are you looking at me?" Mr. Bundt said he will not let the children outside because the neighborhood kids curse and grab each other in the genital area. He said he never observed sexual activity between his children, but Crystal wanted to be in Loren's bed. He acknowledged that his wife let Loren urinate outside the home on several occasions in the past. He said a 17-year-old nephew is living with him and his wife at this time.

David Bundt had a Verbal IQ of 67, Performance IQ of 75, and Full Scale IQ of 69. This is in the mild range of mental retardation.

The WRAT-R scores were as follows:

	Standard Score	Percentile	Grade Equivalent
Reading	<46	.03	<3
Spelling	52	.09	<3
Arithmetic	56	.4	3E

David is functionally illiterate and functions at less than the third grade level.

On the TAT, many of his responses reflect the dynamics in his relationships. He saw one card in which the wife wanted attention and the male figure did not want to give it to her. He saw a male who was being tortured and, in another card, he saw a female who was crying about something. He had an unusual response to a card which is almost never seen as a mother–son card. He said the mother was lying in bed and the son walked into the room and saw her breasts exposed. The son turned his head. He saw another mother–son card in which they were mad at one another. He saw another TAT card in which the male figure was "wanting to choke her or take her out." Some of these responses may reflect his relationship with his mother, who was abusive toward him. He is also married to a woman who is just as verbally abusive as his mother and probably more explosive. He tends to be passive and inadequate with low self-esteem. This is simply reinforced and increased in his marital relationship. He has a great deal of hostility for his wife, but he usually does not express it. I think he feels bullied by his wife and has a difficult time standing up to her.

David Bundt probably turns to the children for affection and, when angry, is likely to take his anger out on the children instead of his wife. During the observation of the visitation, I observed David hugging Crystal for a long period of time. His eyes were closed and he seemed lost in the warmth that he derived from the child. I think he gets a great deal of emotional support and physical contact with Crystal that he may not experience with Mrs. Bundt. This increases the possibility that either sexual abuse or at least an inappropriate relationship exists with Crystal.

His Hand Test had an acting-out ratio which was high, which suggests a propensity for acting-out or fantasies of doing so. There were two aggressive responses, one on a card which is not usually associated with an aggressive act.

During Rachel Bundt's individual interview, she said she was born in Jacksonville and raised in the Searcy area. She has two brothers and one sister. She said all the children were beaten by both parents. She said she ran away from home once because her father raped her. Her parents are still together and she remembers her mother telling her that she was lying about the sexual abuse. She said her parents called her and the other children bitches, bastards, whores, and other names. She said she was sexually active by the time she was 10 or 12 years old. She said she went to the twelfth grade and graduated. After high school she said she stayed home a while and "put up with it." She said she left at 19 and stayed with her older brother. She then went to Hot Springs Rehabilitation, where she stayed only one week before leaving with David.

Mrs. Bundt said when she first had Crystal they lived in hotels for about a year and a half. Darla, who was born several years later, was removed from the home for a period of about a year because she was not gaining weight and was thought to be a failure-to-thrive child. She said Beverly is normal weight and they did not have the same problem with Beverly that they did with Darla. She said she hardly ever talks to her husband now and their relationship is poor. She admitted feeling depressed and nervous and said, "Wouldn't you be?" She said David's nephew, 17, is currently living with them. She said she does not want him to live there, but she acted powerless to change this, since "David wants him to stay." She also mentioned another single man from her church who stays at her house. She admits that people are in and out of her house.

Mrs. Bundt denied hitting her children in the last two years. Before that, she admitted spanking, cursing, and whipping the children because "I thought it was the way to do it." She acknowledged letting the children go to Oklahoma for up to a week or so to stay with friends who have a retarded son. She admitted that the home in Oklahoma is filthy and that there are animals in the house. She said the woman whipped Crystal, and the retarded son who lives next to his mother bathed the children. Mrs. Bundt thinks this man could have molested Crystal or the other children, but she said she was powerless not to let the children go when the woman asked to see them. Mrs. Bundt said, "I don't want to hurt the kids' feelings" and "If I say no, they'll get mad." She let the children stay with these people several times after she was concerned about the possible abuse. She said the children wanted to see cockfights in Oklahoma and she saw no problem with this.

Mrs. Bundt said she visits her parents with the children and her mother gave Crystal a bath and hurt her. She could not explain why she let this happen. Mrs. Bundt finally said, "I need a mother, okay?" Mrs. Bundt sees the alleged sexual abuse as the only issue, rather than her total care of the children. She said she used to allow Loren to urinate outside and she saw no problem with it. She said she has trouble with the children, because they do not want to mind. She denied any drug or alcohol history.

On testing done at the rehabilitation facility in Hot Springs, Rachel Bundt obtained a Verbal IQ of 72, a Performance IQ of 69, and a Full Scale IQ of 70. The reports from Hot Springs were very negative. She was openly displaying sexual affection at the facility, apparently with David. She was loud and disruptive and she bragged to other students that she was taking drugs.

Mrs. Bundt is extremely labile and unstable. During the course of the evaluation, she changed from cooperative to tearful to angry and abusive. Her MCMI scores were high for anxiety and dysthymia. These scores should actually have been even higher, since she showed an extreme tendency on the test to deny problems and to attempt to present herself as well-adjusted.

The MMPI scores were L = 102, F = 94, K = 65, HS = 94, D = 79, HY = 92, PD = 61, MF = 57, PA = 53, PT = 71, SC = 74, MA = 57, SI = 52. These test results suggest a defensive and ambivalent person. She acknowledges numerous stresses, while at the same time making a naive attempt to foster an image of healthy adjustment. She reports a wide range of physical complaints, which probably coincide with emotional problems. These include weakness, tiredness, dizziness, and other symptoms which exacerbate during stressful times. She is tense, anxious, and angry. She relates poorly to others and the test indicates a history of abuse. On the Beck Depression Inventory, she denied depression and her insight was very poor. Thus, on one instrument she indicated that she is depressed and anxious and on another test she endorsed items like, "I do not feel sad"; "I do not feel like a failure"; and "I don't feel I am being punished."

She said on the Sentences that she wants to get her children back and she attributes all of her emotional problems to the loss of her children. She said she is mad because her children are not with her and her greatest fear is losing her children for good. She said she hates other people and what pains her are people. Her responses on the Hand Test were extremely neutral and defensive. Mostly, her responses were simply descriptions of the hand.

On the TAT, she saw an abnormal image, just as her husband did. She said, "Looks like he's mad, the old lady don't give him much, worried about something, don't want to go to school." Neither she nor her husband saw projections of a healthy male–female relationship. On another card on the TAT she said a mother was mad "because the kids won't clean up the room." When she viewed a mother–

daughter card, she said, "Looks like she wants Mother to play doll with her, she said no." On yet another TAT card, she said the child was telling the mother she was going to school, but "Mom don't care." She obviously has a great deal of difficulty providing nurturing.

When the children were interviewed, Crystal was initially very reluctant to go to the testing room. In fact, she was nearly impossible to evaluate and test, since she was initially very fearful and, at times, refused to participate. Part of the McCarthy Scale was administered in an effort to establish rapport. Her performance on the McCarthy was consistent with mental retardation. Her mother then entered the room, knowing, I believe, that I was in the office with Crystal. After that, Crystal refused to cooperate and became extremely angry. She wanted to visit her mother, which had been arranged for later in the afternoon. Crystal appeared to be extremely insecure, and vacillates between that insecurity and hostility. She told me she wanted to stay both with her foster mother and with her mother and father. She was observed to be very clingy to her foster mother. She is inappropriate for a 7-year-old: she told me she hated me and, toward the end of the session, she was screaming at the top of her voice. Her emotional disturbance is obvious and has been well-documented in the record. She changes emotions rapidly and is just as labile as her mother. She refused to discuss anything regarding possible sexual allegations.

During the evaluation with Loren, he acknowledged that he was spanked with the belt and with his parents' hands. He was fairly hyperactive during the interview, refusing to do most of the testing and drawings. Most of our time was spent in interview and observation. However, he was less volatile and friendlier than his sister. Loren, without question, said, "Dad did something to Crystal. I seen the pictures." He would not say anything else, and said he wanted to go home.

Darla was very fearful and Crystal volunteered to come back with her. Crystal had apparently changed her mood by then, so this is what we did. Crystal tried to be very supportive of Darla and showed her some of the test materials on the McCarthy. At this time, Crystal was shown a few pictures from the Children's Apperception Test which she was familiar with from Dr. Chase's evaluation. She seemed totally uninterested in the cards.

During the observation of the entire Bundt family, the baby seemed to be in good condition and the parents both spent time holding her. At various points during the visit, the parents threatened all the children with putting them in "time out." Crystal entered the room and pointed to me and said to her mother, "I hate him." During the visit, she tended to be manipulative and whining. Loren was oppositional and difficult to control. At times he was very angry and disobeyed both parents. Darla walked in and said to her mother, "No, bitch." For most of the 45 minutes of visitation, Darla sat alone and was completely detached from her parents.

A couple times her parents asked her to come over and she stood by their side for a few minutes. It was obvious that she would have nothing to do with them. Once when Mrs. Bundt tried to engage Darla, Darla fought her and said, "No, no." At other times Darla hit her mother. One of the most telling moments was when Kate Thomas, a DHS social worker, entered the room. Darla lit up, saying "Kate!" and ran to her. She showed excitement and animation at seeing her that was completely opposite from her depressed appearance before Ms. Thomas entered the room. During the visit, Mrs. Bundt asked the children, "Are you ready to come home? Your cousin's home." Later she asked, "Do you want to come home? Yes or no, you have to tell the truth."

I talked with both foster parents, Judy Brown and Sue Fraser. Ms. Brown said Darla was very fearful at first about taking a bath. She would scream and have nightmares. Now, however, she is much improved. Ms. Fraser said Loren is also afraid of the bathroom. She commented that Loren is positive about his father. However, after visits with his parents, he has nightmares. Ms. Fraser said Loren made comments such as, "If Dad does that to Crystal, I will call the cops." He also said to Ms. Fraser, "When he gets into bed and makes her scream, then Mom comes with the camera and makes pictures." The foster parents said Crystal does well in foster care until there is a visit with the parents. These visits happen twice a week, which they complain is extremely disruptive for the children.

Summary and Recommendations
Crystal, Loren, and Darla are all developmentally delayed and emotionally disturbed. Crystal certainly has the most serious emotional disturbance. She is extremely labile and oppositional. Loren is also oppositional and developmentally delayed. Darla is detached from her parents, depressed, and isolated. I observed that she functions much better with her foster mother. The parents demonstrate a long history of inadequate childrearing practices. The children have been exposed to verbal abuse and harsh physical discipline. The children model a variety of abusive behavior and language.

The sexual abuse is very difficult to evaluate because the children have been exposed to so much inappropriate sexual language, violent images, observation of their parents having sex, and possibly other children in the neighborhood displaying inappropriate language and sexual behavior. In spite of all of these other influences, I think Crystal has been sexually abused. Her mother mentions that Crystal may have been sexually abused, given the number of places she has been left and the number of people who have had opportunity.

I am not able to rule out the possibility that Mr. Bundt sexually abused Crystal. This abuse is a distinct possibility based on a number of factors. Mr. Bundt is mentally retarded and married to a very abusive and hostile wife. He is a passive individual who finds that he has little power in the relationship. He has the same kind of relationship with his wife that he did with his mother, who was abusive and domineering. He therefore turns to his children for love, support, and nourishing. I think there is a good possibility that he derives sexual and emotional gratification from his relationship with Crystal. Loren clearly verbalized to me that his father was engaging in sexual activity with Crystal. Even more important, I believe this risk will increase as Crystal becomes older and Mr. Bundt relies on her even more. His relationship with his wife will continue to be chaotic and pathological and Crystal will become more of a comfort to him. He also displaces some of his hostility onto the children, because he is unable to deal with his wife.

In my opinion, Rachel Bundt is not able to parent her children and will not be able to make the necessary changes to do so. This is a woman who simply cannot cope. She makes changes on a very short-term basis, but she is so emotionally disturbed and labile that her moods are unpredictable and volatile. She is extremely hostile and, within minutes, she changes from affectionate with the children to angry and rejecting.

Children are naturally going to say and feel that they want to be with their parents. However, the visitations are extremely difficult and disruptive for the children. At present they see the parents twice weekly and the parents provide fuel for their anxiety, anger, and depression. I do not see how the children will ever adjust as long as visitation continues in its present form. I cannot recommend that the children be returned to the parents. If they are, the Department of Human Services should be prepared for indefinite supervision and monitoring of this case.

Discussion
This case had some similarity to the previous case. It was also a very dysfunctional family being investigated by the Department of Human Services or Child Welfare. There were global concerns about the fitness of the parents and sexual abuse was just one symptom of the abuse and neglect that were taking place. My job was not primarily to determine facts about the sexual abuse, since others already reported symptoms and statements of the children suggesting sexual abuse. The court wanted an evaluation of the entire family, tying together all the data available and making recommendations. In addition to the interviews and testing, I had access to reports by several other mental health professionals and had the opportunity to observe the family during one of their visitations. Thus, the data base was very rich and complete.

In this case there seemed to be clear evidence that two of the children had been sexually abused. They could have been abused in a variety of settings, since the parents permitted them to be with people capable of abusing the children sexually. They were also exposed to sexually explicit material and they probably witnessed sexual intercourse between the parents on a frequent basis. Whether the father sexually abused the daughters is almost irrelevant, given the amount of evidence suggesting that they were both inadequate as parents. However, given the facts here, it was thought likely that the father did take refuge and comfort sexually with one or more of the children. This risk was judged to increase as the children grew older. The parents were also from abusive backgrounds themselves, a marker and indication for continuing abuse to another generation.

In this case I recommended that the four children, ages 1 through 7, not be returned to either parent. I said the visitation should not continue, and, if the children were returned to the home, DHS and the court should be prepared for long-term supervision and monitoring. These recommendations were similar to those made in the earlier case, except that here both the mother and father were judged to be unfit. This was one case in which I did receive feedback: parental rights were finally terminated. I did not feel guilty, nor did I feel any sense of accomplishment, about that outcome. I believe it is vital not to be an advocate for anyone or to persecute those parents who are neglectful or abusive. For our own mental health, it is important to be detached and objective. Objectivity is also vital for the sake of quality and accuracy, as well as credibility with the court.

Case 23

This case shows a father with above-average intelligence whose objective test results showed little basis for concern. His sexual perversion was only uncovered during projective testing.

Psychological Evaluation Report

Names: Larry Carlson
        Stephanie Schorer
        James Carlson
(Required identifying information, date of testing, etc.)

Tests Administered
Larry Carlson and Stephanie Schorer:

Wechsler Adult Intelligence Scale–Revised
Wide Range Achievement Test–Revision 3 (WRAT-3)
Minnesota Multiphasic Personality Inventory (MMPI)
Incomplete Sentences Blank
Millon Clinical Multiaxial Inventory (MCMI)
Beck Depression Inventory (BDI)
Rorschach Ink Blots [Larry only]
Hand Test [Larry only]

James Carlson:

Wechsler Intelligence Scale for Children–Third Revision (WISC-III)
Peabody Picture Vocabulary Test–Revised (PPVT-R)

Wide Range Achievement Test–Revision 3 (WRAT-3)
Bender Gestalt Drawings
House–Tree–Person Drawings (HTP)
Thematic Apperception Test (TAT)

Background Information
Stephanie Schorer, Larry Carlson, and James Carlson were referred for a psychological evaluation by Hon. Judge Melanie Johnson. James is in the custody of Ms. Schorer, but is a DHS protective service case. James's father Larry Carlson is seeking visitation with James. Allegations were made that Larry Carlson sexually abused James and he has not seen his son in over a year.

Stephanie Schorer is a 37-year-old white female. She said she is trying to prevent visitation between Larry Carlson, 44, and her son James, who is 6 years, 5 months in age. Ms. Schorer said that when she and Mr. Carlson were together, she walked into the bedroom where James and his father regularly slept together and observed Mr. Carlson close against the back of her son while they lay on the bed. She said she observed a pelvic movement and Mr. Carlson immediately relocated himself in the bed. In four days she moved out and never returned. Soon after and since that time, James has made sexual comments and displayed sexual behavior to his mother. Once when he was "hunching" a pillow, he said he was "pee in the butt." She said he demonstrated this by showing his finger going to the rectum. He told his mother that it was something he and his daddy did. She said James tried to have sex with a cat and, when asked about it, said, "I'm fucking the cat." She said James pretends to have oral sex, or it looks like that to her, especially when he is drinking from a bottle. Ms. Schorer said James still talks about his father. She believes he loves his father and wants to see him. James is attending Springdale Public Schools. His mother said she sometimes has trouble with his behavior.

Ms. Schorer said she left Mr. Carlson in June 1994 and went to the battered women's shelter, where she stayed until October 1994. She stayed in another shelter until April 1995 and was then able to secure her present apartment. She said this is Section Eight housing, which is clean and safe. In July 1995 Mr. Carlson was awarded visitation, but Ms. Schorer was able to get DHS to assume protective custody, although she kept physical custody. Ms. Schorer reports that James has stated some of the sexual information to mental health professionals and caseworkers who have interviewed him.

Stephanie Schorer grew up with both parents and one brother. She said her father was physically abusive, especially to her brother. She denied any history of sexual abuse. She met and was involved with Mr. Carlson beginning in 1977, but they never married. They lived together on and off until James was born in 1989 and then lived together continuously until they broke up in 1994. She said he had numerous girlfriends and affairs during those years, especially when they were separated. When they lived together, she said she usually slept on the couch while he slept with his son. She said she felt like the outsider in the home, because Mr. Carlson insisted that he sleep with James.

Ms. Schorer said that Larry Carlson was physically abusive, slapping and hitting her, and that he threatened to kill her in the past. She accused him of abusing alcohol, smoking marijuana, and using methamphetamine. She admitted she also had a drinking and drug problem. Through the 1980's she abused marijuana and alcohol. She went to a rehabilitation center in 1988. She said she was free from drugs for two months prior to her pregnancy and she has not used drugs since then. She continued to drink beer after that and also started using over-the-counter wake-up pills. She said she is not using anything at this time, although she sometimes drinks "near beer." Ms. Schorer said she has a history of many health problems and she even lost her hair while living with Mr. Carlson. She had surgery on her ears and her hearing is now much improved. She also had gastrointestinal problems and she has a problem with obesity. She is receiving AFDC, Section Eight housing, and food stamps.

Larry Carlson grew up in Arkansas. After his father died in 1963, his mother lived with an abusive man she has now gotten away from. He has an older brother and two brothers who are deceased. He denied any criminal record. He has a year and a half of college. Mr. Carlson works as a trapper for a large paper company. He is under contract to them and has three employees. He has never been married.

Mr. Carlson reinterated much of the same history Ms. Schorer had reported regarding their relationship. He said Ms. Schorer had a child before James who was given up for adoption. He believes that child may have been his. When I asked Mr. Carlson if he ever hit Ms. Schorer, he acknowledged that he slapped her on "a few occasions" before and after James was born. He denied ever physically abusing James. He acknowledged that he had girlfriends during his frequent separations from Ms. Schorer.

In his interview, Mr. Carlson denied molesting James. He said he did sleep with James, but denied doing anything inappropriate. He does not remember the incident in which he was accused of sexually abusing James. He said he slept with James because Ms. Schorer would stay up late and play the television loud because she could not hear. He said she has a problem with drug abuse. He has not had contact with James since the summer of 1994 and he wants visitation with his son. He denied ever knowing that he could see James at the DHS office. He said he would have taken advantage of that if he had known. He said Ms. Schorer was upset because his mother threatened to get custody of James, since the trailer was dirty.

Test Results
James Carlson had the following WISC-III scaled scores:

Verbal Tests		*Performance Tests*	
Information	7	Picture Completion	8
Similarities	5	Coding	6
Arithmetic	2	Picture Arrangement	5
Vocabulary	8	Block Design	9
Comprehension	9	Object Assembly	10

Verbal IQ	79
Performance IQ	84
Full Scale IQ	80

James had a Full Scale IQ of 80, which is in the Borderline range of intellectual functioning. The PPVT-R score was better and was in the average range with a standard score of 99.

His WRAT-3 scores were as follows:

	Standard Score	Percentile	Grade Equivalent
Reading	95	37	K
Spelling	98	45	K
Arithmetic	63	1	Pre

James's academic ability is commensurate with kindergarten placement, except for arithmetic and number comprehension. Actually, his WRAT-3 scores and the PPVT-R were good compared to the IQ of 80. The Bender Gestalt Drawings were poorly done at less than the five-year level. James has a speech defect, so there is little doubt that he is behind in language and general intelligence. On the positive side, he is able to communicate well. He can be considered a slow learner and he will need help and remediation.

James's HTP drawings were consistent with his age level, but on the drawings of a family he drew only himself and his mother. The TAT responses were typical for a boy his age. There were no sexual responses on the TAT. When asked for three wishes, he said he wished that he would go to heaven, that his mother would have a car, and that it would snow.

James was very well-behaved and did not appear to be hyperactive during the evaluation. He had excellent endurance for a child his age, since he was in the office so long. He talked about living in the battered women's shelter. He also mentioned that his father hit his mother. When I asked him fairly directly about whether his dad hurt him or did anything bad to him, he said, "He didn't do nothing bad to me." He said he misses his father. It should be remembered that this is only a 6-year, 5-month-old child who has not seen his father in about fifteen months. Fifteen months is a long time for a child this age. His father is an idea at this point, even though he would have some memory of his dad. I asked him why he does not see his dad and he said, "because my mom is scared of him." I asked him about seeing the social worker for sessions and he said, "I love it."

Stephanie Schorer had the following WAIS-R scaled scores:

Verbal Tests		Performance Tests	
Information	8	Picture Completion	10
Digit Span	9	Picture Arrangement	10
Vocabulary	10	Block Design	9
Arithmetic	7	Object Assembly	9

Comprehension	9	Digit Symbol	8
Similarities	11		

Verbal IQ	95		
Performance IQ	99		
Full Scale IQ	96		

She has average intelligence and the 96 IQ causes no concern.
Her WRAT-3 scores were as follows:

	Standard Score	Percentile	Grade Equivalent
Reading	100	50	PHS
Spelling	100	50	HS
Arithmetic	88	21	8

These are also average scores. She is a bright enough person to take care of herself and her child.

Her MMPI scores were F = 70, L = 72, K = 62, HS = 75, D = 73, HY = 80, PD = 84, MF = 46, PA = 64, PT = 76, SC = 67, MA = 70, SI = 51. These scores had at least moderate elevations for Scales 1, 2, 3, 4, and 7, indicating anxiety, depression, somatic complaints, feelings of distress, and a long history of poor adjustment. She was also high on the MacAndrew scale, consistent with her history of substance abuse. She had lower MCMI scores with nothing above the level of significance of 75. On the BDI she had a score of 15, so she has mild feelings of depression. This is lifelong throughout her adulthood. She has always felt somewhat sad, unhappy, and poorly adjusted.

She indicated on the Sentences that she can't please her mother or quit worrying about it, but she feels "better about my life than I have in years." She makes no secret of her poor adjustment and the pathological relationship she had with Mr. Carlson for so many years. She also said on the Sentences that she failed her son and she takes a good deal of the responsibility for what happened. She said she feels lonely and she is very "confused about child abuse," particularly the conflicting statements her son has made. She knows that recently James is denying sexual abuse, and yet she knows what she saw and what James did and said after July 1994. She also knows that he talked about sexual incidents with the DHS caseworker and social worker.

Larry Carlson had the following WAIS-R scaled scores:

Verbal Tests		Performance Tests	
Information	16	Picture Completion	10
Digit Span	12	Picture Arrangement	13
Vocabulary	11	Block Design	9
Arithmetic	10	Object Assembly	5
Comprehension	13	Digit Symbol	10
Similarities	13		

Verbal IQ   118
Performance IQ   100
Full Scale IQ   110

His Full Scale IQ of 110 is in the Bright Average range.
His WRAT-3 scores were as follows:

	Standard Score	Percentile	Grade Equivalent
Reading	104	58	PHS
Spelling	105	63	HS
Arithmetic	96	39	HS

These are also average and slightly above. There is no problem with his intellectual or academic ability.

His MMPI scores were F = 47, L = 47, K = 53, HS = 51, D = 67, HY = 50, PD = 60, MF = 60, PA = 67, PT = 58, SC = 53, MA = 26, SI = 61. He was guarded and none of the scores were above the level of significance.

The MCMI scores were high only for dependency (85). He tends to be passive and noncompetitive. On the Beck, he had a score of only 4, so he denies feelings of depression. He said on the Sentences that he likes "to be with his friend," he is annoyed "by injustice," and he cannot "communicate with others" as well as he would like to. He said life "is sometimes sad," he hates "man's inhumanity to man," and he is "colorblind" when it comes to mankind. The profile based on the objective tests and the Sentences suggests a rather passive, withdrawn individual, somewhat isolated from others. He gave many socially approved answers.

It was not until the administration of the Rorschach and the Hand Test that his significant psychopathology emerged. The Rorschach protocol was extremely pathological and indicates the likelihood of sexual acting out. He had a total of 74 responses, which is almost twice the number given by the average subject. He has an almost unrestrained fantasy life and little impulse control. Of the 74 responses, 33 (44 percent) were sexual responses. On the average Rorschach protocol, a normal patient will usually not make any sexual response at all. One or two responses out of 30 or 40 Rorschach responses might cause concern. Mr. Carlson's profile, on the other hand, is more pathological than anyone could even pretend to make. It was as though Mr. Carlson heard the Rorschach instructions as, "Tell me as many responses you can think of and make sure most of them are sexual responses." Of course, no such instructions were given and these responses are Mr. Carlson's deepest thoughts and perceptions.

The sexual responses given by Mr. Carlson included the following perceptions: "a woman's breast, an erect penis here, a penis sticking up the rear end and the penis sticking up the vagina entrance here, a body laying back and a large penis, a nose so long it could be a penis also, could be a vagina, looks like a penis here sticking up, an erect penis, a woman's breast, could be the head of a penis, two women's legs and hips, could be a breast, the slit is a vagina, looks like a woman's rear end." These responses show Mr. Carlson's all-encompassing sexual obsession.

Sex takes up his entire thought process, both waking and sleeping. His sexual hunger seems to be all-possessing and consuming. Sex dominates his personality. The other responses he gave were mostly animals and anatomy responses. Anatomy responses come close to sexual responses, but they are acceptable. The other animal responses are entirely normal, given his occupation as an animal trapper.

What is even more astounding about Mr. Carlson's Rorschach protocol is that it was given by a bright man who was being evaluated as an accused sexual perpetrator. He was either extremely uninsightful or completely unable to control his underlying sexual disorder. He was able to do fairly well in suppressing his responses on the MMPI and other objective tests, but the Rorschach is an indirect and largely unconscious instrument on which he was unable to control his responses.

The Hand Test was also pathological, which confirms that the Rorschach was not an isolated finding. He had 58 Hand Test responses, also a very large number, since most subjects do less than half as many. He continued to give sexual responses on the Hand Test, although not as many as on the Rorschach. His response on Card 6 was that the hand was masturbating. On Card 9 he said the hand was massaging a woman's vagina. On Card 10, a blank card, he said the imagined hand was masturbating and touching a woman's vagina. He again could not control his responses and his all-consuming sexual perversion.

Summary and Recommendations
Stephanie Schorer has had her problems, and her drug history and rehabilitation are well known. She continues to have difficulty with feelings of depression and anxiety, but she is doing better now than she has at any time in the past.

Based on the test results, Larry Carlson is a sexual risk to James and should not have any contact with his son. He would not be able to control his sexual behavior with his son and, given the opportunity, he will molest this boy. I cannot endorse even supervised visitation, since someone with so little restraint could abuse James even during a supervised visit.

Discussion
This case was referred for evaluation by the juvenile court judge, rather than a chancery court judge. The case was in juvenile court because the mother filed a protective service case with the Department of Human Services attempting to prevent visitation by the biological father because of alleged sexual abuse. There is a great deal of overlap between juvenile and chancery court. Sometimes the juvenile judge will decide a case is actually a custody case and refer it to chancery court. Other times the judge will determine there is a legitimate child protection issue and hear the case, as was done here.

In all sexual abuse or incest cases, it is important to evaluate the mother, the child, and the perpetrator. The mother is evaluated to judge her credibility. The child is seen to determine if there are any obvious signs of sexual abuse. The perpetrator is evaluated to assess the likelihood that the abuse occurred.

The mother in this case looked fairly good. She did not seem to have a vendetta against the father and she freely acknowledged her own substance abuse problems and her long-term marginal adjustment. She never tried to portray herself as perfect or without problems, as is often the case in a falsely accusing mother. She reported a history of being physically abused, a history that the father admitted. Her test results, especially the MMPI, revealed a great deal of distress, anxiety, and depression.

When I interviewed the son, he denied that his father sexually abused him. It is not my practice to go into great detail when evaluating a child who is a possible victim. My job in interviewing the child is not to be an investigator, using dolls or other play therapy techniques to make another determination regarding the sexual abuse. My job is to do an overall evaluation of the situation and the relationship between these individuals. By the time I receive a family like this for evaluation, the child has been through therapy and has been interviewed many times about the sexual abuse by caseworkers, therapists, and investigators. It has usually been a long time since the alleged incident occurred. All of these conditions were true in this case. This child had revealed verbal and behavioral information to his mother and several case workers, even though he was now denying the abuse to me. There were at least two therapists and caseworkers who were going to testify about statements of abuse the child made to them over a long period of time.

I think it is sufficient for the kind of evaluation we are performing to interview the child, ask a few questions, and see what happens. Many times the child will not open up in an initial session with yet another investigator. Sometimes the child will reluctantly open up and reveal details about the abuse that are very credible. Other times the child will give a rehearsed recall of the abuse that is very suspect. Still other times the child will deny sexual abuse, as this child did. Given the history he reported to others, it was difficult to say how he was coping and what the purpose of the denial was. He was doing well in other ways, although he was somewhat low in intellectual functioning and had a speech articulation defect. Otherwise, he seemed to be a happy and very engaging child, especially considering the chaos in which he lived when his mother and father were together.

The father in this case looked fine during the interview. He was a bright man who denied all the allegations and pointed to his ex-girlfriend's mental problems and drug-abusing past. He said he was a victim, not seeing his son in fifteen months. All of that seemed entirely feasible. He denied any problems and the MMPI, MCMI, Beck, and Sentences all looked normal. There was some suggestion of social withdrawal and dependency, fitting with his occupation of trapping for a living. That caused a little concern, because incestuous men sometimes fit a profile of inadequacy, social withdrawal, poor social skills, poor sexual adjustment, dependency, and somewhat schizoid functioning. These men had a lack of nurturing in their own childhood and have a propensity to derive comfort and emotional support from their children. The mother in this case was also similar to mothers seen in some incestuous families: inadequate and a victim herself.

Although there were a few indicators like that in the present case, I probably would have recommended supervised visitation, perhaps progressing to unsupervised visitation, if I had not administered projective tests. Fortunately, I did do projective testing and the father fell apart. He began giving one sexual perception after another on the Rorschach and he appeared quite serious when he gave those responses. He concentrated and focused on each card, not a bit embarrassed, and seemed to have no awareness that what he was doing was suicidal and inappropriate. In fact, he almost seemed to be in a trance as he was describing his Rorschach perceptions. The sexual anatomy responses were frequently Dd responses, so there was a compulsive quality to his sexual responses.

One or two sexual anatomy responses might have been explained away, but this father's Rorschach protocol was severely pathological by anyone's standards. He continued the same pattern on the Hand Test, giving four more sexual responses, including masturbating and touching a woman's vagina. What was even more disconcerting was that two of the sexual responses were on the blank card, on which there is no stimuli at all. Thus, in projective testing he showed himself to be an individual completely consumed by sexual content, with little or no ability to control his impulses.

Based on Mr. Carlson's test results, I had absolutely no choice but to say that he had a serious sexual perversion and would be a risk to his son. I recommended against any visitation at all, including supervised visitation. Supervised visitation can be dangerous if a man is determined to molest his child. I remember one case in which a man with supervised visitation molested his son in the DHS bathroom. A recommendation for no visitation is an extreme and harsh recommendation, but the child had not seen his father in fifteen months, he seemed to be doing fairly well, and it would not have been in his best interest to reintroduce his father into his life. There was a very low probability that they would ever have a normal relationship, given the test results. The father denied that there had been any abuse and showed no desire for treatment, so his prognosis was poor.

I went to court on this case and the father's attorney made the ridiculous assertion that, since he was being evaluated for possible sexual abuse, he believed he should give sexual responses on the Rorschach. I believe she took this line of attack from my report, since I commented that he seemed to be responding to his own test instructions. Putting that line in the report was probably a mistake, because the lawyer was able to use it in the father's defense. Clearly, this man understood the instructions and was responding with his own perceptions. Attorneys for the state and the attorney *ad litem* were able to ask questions on redirect to elicit my reaction to these assertions.

While the findings in this case were powerful and probably influenced the judge, there was no assurance that the judge would follow my recommendations. Judges are very reluctant to terminate parental rights and chances are high, even with these kinds of results, that the judge would allow some kind of supervised visitation. In a sense, this puts our work in perspective and takes some of the burden off us. The psychological evaluation report containing our recommendation is only one piece of evidence provided to the court. The judge will hear all the evidence prior to making a decision about the allegations and any future visitation.

The next two cases are representative of those in which the sexual abuse allegations were determined to be false. Following are some of the variables that cause suspicion:

1) The accusing mother is anxious, overwrought, insecure, and not over her own feelings of victimization from the ex-husband.

2) The mother has strong dependency needs transferred to the child and demands total dependence upon her. She is threatened that any relationship with the father will undermine her own relationship with the child.

3) The child who is reportedly abused is almost always a very young child, usually under the age of 4. This enables the mother to make suggestions of sexual abuse, so the child has recall of sexual abuse as if it were his own memory.

4) The mother is the first one who discovers and pursues the sexual abuse allegations. She is not satisfied with the outcome of any investigating agency until she finds a therapist or child care worker who is totally aligned with her abuse allegations. Often the mothers are successful in finding such people.

5) Grandparents and anyone else supporting the alleged perpetrator are incorporated into the belief system, which might be described as delusional.

6) The description of the sexual allegations and the nature of the abuse knows no bounds for perversity or for sexual acts.

7) The alleged perpetrator usually is baffled by the sexual allegations. The ex-husband is rarely enraged or extremely defensive. While there may have been acknowledged marital conflict, the ex-husband does not usually have a history of psychiatric disturbance, low IQ, or psychopathic deviancy.

8) By definition, there is no evidence of venereal disease or other profound medical evidence of abuse. (Even substantiated sexual abuse is often without physical correlates.)

9) There is never a satisfactory ending until the father is totally driven from the child's life. In extreme cases, the mother will flee or go underground to avoid visitation.

In these cases, the accusing mothers are fundamentally neurotic and histrionic. They are sick individuals and, in the long run, they are actually abusing their children.

Case 24

This case, in which the mother was attempting to restrict visitation, was referred by a court-appointed social worker.

Psychological Evaluation Report

Names: Karen Hamilton
        Paul Taft

Referral

Ms. Hamilton and Mr. Taft were referred for a psychological evaluation by Lisa Dougherty, a social worker appointed by the court to oversee and coordinate the services provided to the parties and the minor child. Ms. Hamilton and Mr. Taft were evaluated on January 27 and February 7, 1995, respectively. They were both administered the Wechsler Adult Intelligence Scale–Revised (WAIS-R), Minnesota Multiphasic Personality Inventory (MMPI), Millon Clinical Multiaxial Inventory (MCMI), Incomplete Sentences Blank, and Beck Depression Inventory. Each was interviewed for about two hours.

Background Information

Karen Hamilton is a 31-year-old white female; Mr. Taft is a 28-year-old white male. They have a 4-year-old child, Layton Taft. Ms. Hamilton does not want Mr. Taft to have unsupervised visitation with Layton, since she said he was neglectful and abusive toward Layton. She said that after Mr. Taft had Layton for visitation, he came home with severe diaper rashes. She also believes Mr. Taft sexually abused Layton. She said he came home on more than one occasion with a red, raw, and abraded penis.

Ms. Hamilton and Mr. Taft were married for two and a half years, separating when Layton was about 13 months old. Ms. Hamilton said she had ulcers and was affected by the stress of the marriage. She said Mr. Taft was emotionally abusive to her, but she denied any physical abuse. She said he was always jealous and interrogated her whenever she left the home. She said he did not trust her and constantly threatened her. She believes Mr. Taft's father was also abusive and interfered with their marriage. She said his father has total control over him and that he exercised this during the marriage, trying to control such decisions as how many children they would have. She said her ex-husband was always on the phone with his father, consulting him about everything. She does not think her father-in-law ever liked her. During the marriage, Ms. Hamilton said Mr. Taft played with Layton for only short periods of time. He never got up at night with him. He allegedly told the baby to shut up. She could not name any other abusive incident that she witnessed or suspected while they were together. Ms. Hamilton said that when Mr. Taft was 17 he had a "sex charge" involving a 10-year-old girl. Ms. Hamilton found this girl. She told Ms. Hamilton that Mr. Taft locked her in his home and tried to take her coat off. She screamed and ran away.

Ms. Hamilton said she served Mr. Taft with divorce papers while he was at work. She put all his possessions on the porch and changed the locks. She refused any phone calls and would not talk to him after she placed him out of the home. She said he cried and tried to get her to take him back. She said he did not care that she was sick and she divorced him soon after she was released from the hospital with ulcers. The divorce took place within 45 days after their separation.

Mr. Taft got his own place after the divorce and started having visitation. Ms. Hamilton alleged there were pornographic magazines in the home and clippings of young children that appeared to be from clothing and underwear catalogs. I asked Mr. Taft about this and he denied the magazines were anything other than what can be purchased at any convenience store in Arkansas. He denied having any pictures of children or young girls and he said if there were pictures of children with the magazines they were placed there by someone.

Soon after the separation, Ms. Hamilton denied Mr. Taft visitation because she learned of the magazines. The police were called during one attempt by Mr. Taft to exercise his visitation. A couple of months later she discovered the diaper rash after one of the weekends. She also saw the red, raw penis. She alleged that Layton made comments to her and to Ms. Dougherty that "Daddy eats penis." Ms. Hamilton said the penis was healed by the time she took Layton to the doctor. She said it occurred a second and final time, but she again did not take Layton to the doctor quickly. She contacted Social Services, but she said she had to continue sending Layton for visitation. Layton came home one weekend with a bruise on his eye and she took pictures of it and called Social Services. I asked her if she thought Mr. Taft put the mark on Layton's eye and she said, "It was something to get an investigation started." She admitted she did not believe Mr. Taft inflicted that injury and that she filed an abuse report anyway. Ms. Hamilton said she has had four lawyers, but now believes she has "a good one." In 1994 she represented herself for a short time.

Ms. Hamilton filed for supervised visitation after she filed on the black eye. Thereafter, Mr. Taft's parents had to supervise the visitation. Layton was about 2 years old at the time. Ms. Hamilton was not satisfied with that, because she believed Mr. Taft's father abuses the entire family. She also believed the grandparents were not taking the supervision seriously and were allowing Mr. Taft to be alone with the child. She said Mr. Taft was sleeping with Layton at either his parents' home or at his own home. She said that Layton continued having nightmares and screaming at night. She said Layton was scared of her when he returned home from visitation. She took him to see Ms. Dougherty and Layton has continued regular visits with her. In October 1994 overnight visits were suspended after Ms. Hamilton alleged the supervision was not proper because Mr. Taft slept with Layton. Ms. Hamilton said she wants a third party, someone other than his parents, to supervise Mr. Taft. She believes her ex-husband performed oral sex on Layton, although no charges were ever filed against Mr. Taft for the alleged sexual abuse. She denied that he was ever sexually abusive to her.

Ms. Hamilton does not work and is disabled. She has a long medical history involving problems with her feet. She acknowledged she was addicted to prescription medication for pain for a six-year period. She went to the eleventh grade and got a GED. She lives in a house owned by her parents and, in fact, the homes are on the same block. She and her ex-husband lived in this house during their marriage. This is as far as she has ever lived from her parents. Her parents are still together, but she said they do not get along and they "play tug-of-war with me." They apparently still get her to take sides. When I asked her if she were ever sexually abused, she said she had been "sexually harrassed" by an uncle and grandfather, her mother's stepuncle and stepfather. Her marriage to Mr. Taft was her first and only marriage.

Mr. Taft said he and Ms. Hamilton dated for about six months before they got married. They did not have sex before they were married. He said she was molested as a child by a step-grandfather and uncle. He believes it was more than "sexual harassment." He acknowledged that during the marriage he was overprotective of his wife, partly because of her fragile medical condition. He also believes that her uncle continued making sexual advances toward her. This is the reason he gave for being possessive. He thinks Ms. Hamilton has an unusually close and special relationship with her father. When asked about the incident at age 17 that Ms. Hamilton referred to, he said a 10-year-old girl accused him of trying to jerk her coat off. He thinks the family was after money. He said this charge was dismissed in court. He has no other arrests or convictions. He said he was never molested or abused.

Mr. Taft was in the military for a few months, but was discharged because of medical problems. He said he had the option of staying in, but he chose to be discharged. He said he and his ex-wife lived near her parents and this did not go well. He thought her father treated him poorly and put him down. He also noted that her parents did not get along with one another. Her mother was at their house constantly. He wanted to move away from her parents, but he said his ex-wife always found an excuse not to move. Mr. Taft said he called his father during the marriage, but he denied that his father was running his life. He described his father as domineering, but not abusive. He denied any drug or alcohol abuse. He denied he ever told Layton to shut up. He said his wife breastfed Layton, which is one reason why he did not get up with the baby at night.

Mr. Taft said he and his ex-wife argued a great deal about both her parents and his parents. They also did not agree about politics or any other topic. However, he said the divorce was a total surprise to him. He said he was served with papers while he was at work and he was never allowed back in the house. He said he did not want the divorce, but his ex-wife would never agree to marriage counseling. He said he was unable to see her, talk to her, or discuss the separation in any way. He spent only two months with his parents after the separation before getting his own place. He is living in Jonesboro and working full time, earning about $25,000 per year.

Mr. Taft said he had visitation with Layton soon after the separation. He said he filed for custody a few months after the divorce, and only then Ms. Hamilton made allegations about abuse. Mr. Taft said he thinks it would be better for Layton if he had custody. He believes he could do more with his son than his ex-wife, especially since she is handicapped. He said he has been to parenting class. For a time he saw a counselor at a local mental health center.

Mr. Taft denied sexual abuse of any kind toward Layton. He said the diaper rash was already present when he got his son for visitation. He said Layton had a problem with diaper rashes even when they were married. Mr. Taft believes his ex-wife is coaching Layton to say that he was sexually abused. He acknowledged Layton slept with him off and on, but he said the child was only 2 or 3 years old at the time. He said his son is happy to see him for visitation. Mr. Taft does not think his ex-wife gets along with anyone. He said she accused one of the judges in this case of taking bribes and she has gone through several attorneys. He believes she is trying to take Layton away from him and will use any excuse to do so.

Evaluation Results
Paul Taft had a Verbal IQ of 96, Performance IQ of 113, and Full Scale IQ of 102. This is in the Average range of ability.

His MMPI scores were L = 70, F = 50, K = 51, HS = 48, D = 48, HY = 46, PD = 46, MF = 47, PA = 57, PT = 44, SC = 42, MA = 48, SI = 41. These scores are in the normal range, but he had a tendency to answer in a socially approved manner. There was no elevation on the Psychopathic Deviant scale. He had a slight elevation on Scale 6, which suggests anger and suspiciousness. He believes he is being treated unfairly and is misunderstood. This slight elevation in Scale 6 is probably related to the current circumstances regarding the sexual allegations. The high MacAndrew Scale indicated he is an extroverted individual who tends to be uninhibited socially. High scores on the MacAndrew Scale are sometimes associated with substance abuse, but he denied any history of substance abuse.

On the MCMI, he scored high on the Narcissism and Histrionic scales. This is a self-confident individual who emphasizes his strengths, which elevated the Narcissistic scale. He tends to be active and easily bored. Again, the possibility of substance or drug use was indicated on the MCMI. I have no evidence that he uses or abuses drugs, but the MMPI and the MCMI suggested he may have the kind of personality which predisposes him to substance abuse. This may never actually be manifested, if he finds other ways of coping with stress or disappointment. I do not see him as the inhibited, maladjusted, socially alienated, or confused person often associated with incest. He is not a weak or dependent individual. All indications of schizoid, avoidant, and dependent personality were very low on all of the tests. Incest offenders often have extremely poor ego development and low self-esteem, which does not appear to be the case with Mr. Taft.

He denied significant depression on the Beck Depression Inventory. At the same time, his score of 11 suggests that he has been disappointed with himself. This was a realistic self-appraisal, rather than denying any weaknesses. He said on the Sentences that he failed in his marriage and he made several references to his ex-wife and his troubles over visitation. The Sentences gave some indication why he appeared suspicious on the MMPI and MCMI. For example, he said what annoys him "is my ex-wife trying to destroy me and my family." There was no suggestion of suspiciousness or blaming others for his problems, outside the context of this particular conflict. Mr. Taft was in good contact with reality and there was no evidence of major mental illness. He denied depression or anxiety, other than that related to his current circumstances.

Karen Hamilton had a Verbal IQ of 94, a Performance IQ of 104, and a Full Scale IQ of 97. This is in the Average range of ability.

On the MCMI she had a significant elevation on Compulsive Personality and Anxiety. She approached significance on Dysthymia. Her symptoms of anxiety include worry, tension, and irritability. She has stress-related problems, including psychosomatic and psychophysiological illness. She has mild to moderate levels of depression and ongoing feelings of discouragement. She expressed a great number of somatic complaints. She has an unusually strong need to conform with social norms, rules, and regulations and to restrain herself from actions that seem unacceptable. She presents as strict and moralistic. She lacks flexibility and she is afraid of criticism, embarrassment, and disapproval. She is judgmental, irritable, and disparaging toward others. There is little diversity in her life and an absence of spontaneity and pleasure. She had strong compulsive personality traits and overuse of self-control.

The MMPI scores were L = 44, F = 53, K = 56, HS = 80, D = 51, HY = 62, PD = 52, MF = 55, PA = 60, PT = 56, SC = 61, MA = 49, SI = 42. She had a significant score on Scale 1, Hypochondriasis. She left 42 items unanswered, which is too many to be acceptable. She had exaggerated caution and defensiveness and this probably contributed to not answering. She also may have been so compulsive that she had difficulty choosing. The items that she did complete suggest a great deal of somatic and psychosomatic preoccupation.

On the Beck Depression Inventory, she had a score of only 7, so she denied most depression, although she said she feels sad and she is discouraged about the future. She said on the Sentences that marriage "scares me" and her father "made a lot of goofs raising me, but I know he loves me." She said she suffers from pain and she described herself as "bull-headed." She said a mother "needs to give her children plenty of hugs." She also said she wants to know "what was said in that November 1992 hearing." During the interview she had a number of complaints about the way her case has been handled and she believes decisions have been made behind her back.

Summary and Recommendations

From the interview and test data, it does not seem very likely that Paul Taft is a sexual offender. I did not see the kind of weak ego and maladjusted personality consistent with incest. At the same time, Karen Hamilton is an overwrought, anxious, and compulsive individual who seems to have strong personal motivation to exclude Mr. Taft from her son's life. Her family life has been conflicted, she is dependent on her parents, and the idea of marriage was frightening to her. She never made an adequate adjustment when she was married. Instead of working it out or seeking counseling for their problems, she took the most definitive action she could, erasing Mr. Taft from her life in one day. She is adamant about this current matter and perhaps, in her own mind and heart, she does believe Mr. Taft abused Layton. I simply do not see the psychological evidence that this occurred. If a very young child, like Layton, has been coached either intentionally or indirectly, he can develop and have memories as if they were his own. Ms. Dougherty has been working with Layton and she will be able to report on her impressions. The statements of a 4-year-old about events that took place one or two years ago, in the context of this conflicted adversarial situation, should be carefully evaluated.

If other evidence does not contradict the findings of this evaluation, I think steps should be taken to normalize the relationship between Paul Taft and his son. If there are no other counterindications, the supervised visitation should be lifted. Both parties should be instructed not to discuss this matter any further with Layton. Finally, I think there is a high probability that Karen Hamilton believes in and is encouraging Layton to accept false sexual allegations. I have to conclude, based on my evaluation, that Paul Taft is not a threat to the child.

Discussion

The referral in this case was a little different from most of the evaluations emanating from the court or the Department of Human Services. This case was assigned to a very competent social worker who has an excellent reputation working with the court. She was appointed to work with the child, to evaluate the sexual abuse allegations, and to make recommendations regarding visitation. She sought a psychological evaluation of the parents to assist in her evaluation, because she was unsure about the validity of the sexual allegations and wanted to investigate both the alleged perpetrator and the ex-wife making the allegations. While she heard vague sexual complaints from the 4-year-old child, she was not able to substantiate clearly that Mr. Taft had engaged in the behavior he was accused of by his ex-wife.

In requesting the evaluation, the social worker realized that my report would assist her in her overall report to the court, but that my report would also stand independently. Once a case is before the court, any document generated is subject to discovery and can be admitted for use in that particular case. My report was sent to both attorneys and the judge, as well as to the social worker requesting the evaluation. Like myself, the social worker had no preconceived idea about how the evaluation would turn out, so there was no pressure to coincide with her findings. In this way, the evaluation of the child and parents became a team effort, seeking truth rather than justifying any particular preconceived position.

In this case, the mother wanted restricted visitation (and really no visitation at all). She believed the father was abusive, neglectful, and sexually abused her son. As in most cases of false allegations, the mother alleged that she was also physically, sexually, and emotionally abused by the estranged, divorced husband. The mother was the one who initiated the sexual abuse charges and pursued them vigorously. She even paid the travel expenses of a woman who alleged that Mr. Taft attempted to sexually abuse her when she was 10 years old. The judge refused to hear the testimony of this woman and it appeared to have no substance.

Typical of cases of false allegations, the mother denied and obstructed visitation soon after separation. No one ever saw the injuries that she alleged her son suffered. She never took him to the doctor to look at the "raw penis" until it was healed. She even acknowledged that she falsely accused her ex-husband of putting a mark on her son's eye because it was "something to get an investigation started." She changed lawyers, filed complaints against every expert, judge, or lawyer who did not believe her story, and threatened to file an action against me and the social worker after the report was completed.

This mother instilled fear and false allegations into her son's perceptions, so that whatever the 4-year-old reported was a reiteration of his mother's perceptions. This is why children can make allegations and statements about sexual abuse that are perfectly untrue, and yet the child reports suggestive material as if it is real and represents a true memory. In this case, I chose not to evaluate the 4-year-old child, since the social worker had seen the child over a long period of time and established a relationship with him. The social worker was perfectly capable of reporting what the child said about sexual abuse.

This mother was dependent on her parents, fearful of men, and never comfortable in marriage. She was insecure and sexually anxious. She attempted to wipe her ex-husband from her life and from her son's life. At best, she believed the sexual allegations she was making, and at worst it was a totally conscious fabrication. My judgment was that this anxious, angry woman believed her son was sexually abused and I think this is usually the case. The father did not appear to be someone who would molest his child, based on the interview and the test results.

My recommendation in this case was to normalize visitation and the court did that, allowing the father to see his child unsupervised. The mother continued pursuing her allegations long after the evaluation and the court disposition.

Case 25

This is another case of unsubstantiated allegations in a case in which custody and visitation of a young child were at issue.

Psychological Evaluation Report

Names:　Daniel Jones, 26
　　　　　William Jones, 60
　　　　　Carla Jones, 55
　　　　　Sam Huddleston, 27
　　　　　Heather Huddleston, 23
　　　　　Mark Jones, 5

Referral Information
Daniel Jones was interviewed and tested on July 12, 1994, and reevaluated on December 5, 1994. He was administered the Wechsler Adult Intelligence Scale–Revised (WAIS-R), Minnesota Multiphasic Personality Inventory (MMPI), Millon Clinical Multiaxial Inventory (MCMI), Incomplete Sentences Blank, and Beck Depression Inventory. William and Carla Jones were evaluated on July 15 and December 5, 1994. They were both administered the same battery of tests as Daniel Jones. Sam and Patricia Huddleston were evaluated on December 5, 1994, and administered the MMPI, MCMI, Beck Depression Inventory, and Incomplete Sentences Blank. Mark was interviewed on December 5, 1994, and administered the Hand Test and Children's Apperception Test (CAT).

The Huddlestons are represented by Robert J. Smith. William and Carla Jones are represented by Jacob Laws. Daniel Jones is represented by Patricia Nelson. Initially I evaluated William, Carla, and Daniel Jones. I told the lawyers the evaluation would remain incomplete unless I had the opportunity to evaluate Mr. and Mrs. Huddleston and also talk to Mark, which was finally arranged.

Background Information
I first talked with Carla and William Jones, Mark's grandparents. They did not have formal visitation rights, but had Mark during Daniel's visitation. When Mark was with his father in Arkansas, Mr. and Mrs. Jones were just as involved with Mark as Daniel was. Mark was with them six weeks during the summer, two weeks at a time, and about a week out of every month during the rest of the year. They said they returned Mark to his mother, Patricia Huddleston, after a normal visitation in June 1993. That was the last time they had visitation. After that, they said, their phone calls were not returned, letters were not answered, the phone number was changed, and eventually the address was not the same. Basically, they said Daniel's visitation with Mark was terminated unilaterally.

Daniel Jones filed contempt charges in July 1993, but Ms. Huddleston was not served until December. In the fall the Huddlestons moved from Tennessee to Kentucky. By December, Mr. and Mrs. Jones and Daniel Jones became aware that there were sexual allegations against them. A court date was set for February 1994. Daniel Jones was able to see Mark for two hours at that time in a supervised setting. There was another more extensive hearing on June 28, 1994, in which a local social worker testified, as well as a social worker and therapist from either Kentucky or Tennessee.

The allegation was that William Jones had anal intercourse with Mark while Carla Jones watched. There was an allegation that Daniel Jones did the same thing and also that Carla Jones exposed herself to Mark. The accusation from Mark was that his grandfather and father "put tookie in my bootie." The allegation about Carla Jones was that Mark sat "on her hairy bush and played with his mamaw's booties." William Jones was accused of wearing a colored condom. The Joneses said the stepmother Roberta Jones was accused of putting a goldfish in Mark's bottom. When I asked Patricia Huddleston about this, she denied there were any charges against Roberta, other than Roberta locking Mark in his room. Mark alleged that his father, Daniel Jones, was using cocaine, but he identified it as something else. (I think he said it was salt.) Mr. and Mrs. Jones said Sam Huddleston also accused his ex-wife and her family of sexual abuse.

The interesting thing about the initial interview with Mr. and Mrs. Jones and Daniel Jones was that the information they provided, especially about the allegations, was not very different from the allegations I heard from Mrs. Huddleston during her interview. In other words, both Mr. and Mrs. Jones and Daniel Jones related the allegations in full detail with no embarrassment or defensiveness. Mr. and Mrs. Jones said they thought Mark was taken for a medical examination, but no physical trauma was reported. Over time, Mark has become more negative over the telephone, especially to his father. He now tells his father that he does not want to talk to him. Mark now calls his father "Daddy Daniel" and calls Mr. Huddleston "Daddy." Daniel Jones is apparently suing for custody, as well as for visitation. Mr. and Mrs. Jones want visitation, but they agreed that if their son had either custody or visitation, they would be able to see Mark through him.

Mr. and Mrs. Jones have been married 32 years and have two sons. This is Mr. Jones's second marriage and his wife's only marriage. William Jones had three children by his first marriage. He left the marriage after his daughter was born. He said his first wife was very bitter about his leaving and he was not able to see his children except when he visited Nebraska, where his ex-wife lived. He has a good relationship with his adult sons, but he and his daughter are estranged. Patricia Huddleston was aware of this and even called Mr. Jones's first wife. Even by her report, she was not told that Mr. Jones was abusive or that he was denied the opportunity to see his children because of abuse. She was told he was denied visitation because they lived in different states and he was not paying child support. Mr. Jones said he paid child support on all three children. He acknowledged that this was a failed relationship with his first three children, at least until the sons became adults. However, there is no evidence that he was abusive to these children or his ex-wife.

William and Carla Jones had a separation of about six months when their youngest child was a baby. Mr. Jones was seeing someone else during that time. Although he initially wanted to divorce Carla, he said he decided against it because they had two young children. They reconciled and have been together ever since. This seemed to be a repeat of the withdrawal he made from his first wife when they had young children and suggests a problem with commitment. Carla Jones denied that Mr. Jones was ever abusive to her. He has no history of alcohol or drug problems. Carla and William Jones do not have a history of mental health treatment. Mr. Jones has worked at the same company for twenty years. Mrs. Jones keeps children in her home. They said they always had a special relationship with Mark. They said their son and Patricia lived with them for several months, perhaps a year. Mrs. Jones said she had a close relationship with Patricia and she was like a daughter.

Both times Daniel Jones was interviewed he related much of the same information. He thinks Patricia is a hypochondriac and sees Mark as sick, too. He said

Patricia accused him of physically and sexually abusing her, but he denied this. (He did say that Patricia's father had "a pile of pornographic tapes" and had shown one of them to him and Patricia.) Daniel Jones said the allegation against him was that he put his penis in Mark and, when it would not fit, he used a vibrator. He denied doing any of this. Daniel Jones related the other sexual allegation charges that he was aware of. These did not deviate from the report made by his parents.

Daniel Jones admitted having drug and alcohol problems in the past, but said they were over by the time he married Patricia. He said he has not used drugs since before he married. He said he drinks socially, but this is never a problem and he never gets intoxicated. He admitted that he was "a little wild" as a juvenile, but he has no criminal record as an adult. He admitted that he was possessive and jealous during the marriage, especially at first, but said he is over that and is very trusting toward his wife, Roberta. He is working for a local electric utility company. Before that, he worked for Systematics. He has a baby about 15 months old from his present marriage.

Patricia Huddleston said she originally stopped dating Daniel because of his drug problem and his lifestyle. She said about six months later she heard he was doing better, so she agreed to date him again. She said he was very possessive and threatened to kill himself when she rejected him. She felt pressured to marry Daniel after she became pregnant with Mark. She claimed that during the marriage Daniel was sexually abusive to her and demanded sex. She believes she was raped by him on several occasions. She said she had to do everything around the house, including the child care. She said when she left Daniel in October 1991, he threatened to take Mark. The divorce was final in June 1992 and she married a few days later. She said she had flashbacks of the sexual abuse and she sought counseling at a rape crisis service in Kentucky. She has a 21-month-old child from her marriage to Sam Huddleston.

According to Patricia Huddleston, Daniel had visitation for one week a month and a total of six weeks during the summer. She said Mark would come home from visitation and scream for his grandparents and not want to stay with her. She was upset that Mark would tell her that she did not care for him and seemed to have a preference for his grandmother. She felt the grandparents were saying inappropriate things against her. She also said Mark came home constipated and had a raw bottom. She and Sam Huddleston said Mark needed a light on at night and also had night terrors in which he became hysterical. She said she wanted to find out what was going on and even to explore the possibility of supervised visitation. She said when her lawyer made an initial contact with Daniel Jones's lawyer, they agreed to supervised visitation. She said this all took place before any sexual allegations were made.

Patricia Huddleston scheduled an appointment with the Department of Human Services (DHS) office in Tennessee to explore the concerns she had and also to see if the visitation should be changed. She said Mark revealed the sexual abuse to her before the appointment took place and revealed the same abuse at that first DHS appointment. Mark has seen a therapist ever since these allegations.

He also attends a therapeutic daycare program. He was taken to Children's Hospital for an evaluation. Patricia Huddleston said Mark once retracted the allegations, after Daniel Jones had a visitation in February, but now he is continuing to make the allegations. When I explored the allegations further with her, she seemed to think there was oral sex involved as well. Mr. and Mrs. Jones and Daniel Jones were never prosecuted. A detective interviewed Mr. and Mrs. Jones, but apparently nothing came of that.

Mrs. Huddleston said Mark has behavior problems and is easily out of control. She also said he does not feel any pain and seems to enjoy being hurt. She said Mark does not want to see his father and she believes he should have this choice. She said, "It's his body" and he has the right to see or not see his father. She said she wants the visitation terminated.

Sam Huddleston had a first marriage and a child who is 5 years old. He does not have any visitation with his child. He said his ex-wife obstructed visitation from the beginning. Once, when he picked his son up, he noticed his son had a black eye. He took the child to Children's Hospital. At that time he also alleged possible sexual abuse, because his son knew too much sexual terminology. The child was turned over to DHS custody for a couple days and then returned to the mother. He again had difficulty seeing his child and decided it would be best for the child if he withdrew from his child's life.

Test Results
Daniel Jones had a Verbal IQ of 93, Performance IQ of 112, and Full Scale IQ of 100. William Jones had a Verbal IQ of 100, Performance IQ of 93, and Full Scale IQ of 96. Carla Jones had a Verbal IQ of 95, Performance IQ of 114, and Full Scale IQ of 101. These are all in the Average range. Mr. and Mrs. Huddleston did not receive IQ tests because of the late date of testing. Their intelligence was easily judged to be average.

All four individuals had normal MMPI and MCMI profiles. Clearly, the least defensive protocols were those of Carla and William Jones. They were the most open and least defensive. All of the adults deny depression or mental health problems. They are all smart enough to perform well on objective tests, such as the MMPI and MCMI. After examining the Incomplete Sentences Blanks of the four adults, it was clear that Mrs. Huddleston is the most overwrought person. Almost all of her responses concerned the alleged abuse.

I found Daniel Jones to be forthright during the interview. He made good eye contact. He acknowledged the allegations about drug abuse prior to his marriage and his possessiveness during the first part of the marriage. He did not have the angry, hostile, and defensive attitude often found in incest perpetrators who deny the allegations. Daniel Jones never expressed any hate for Patricia. He did not criticize her as a mother. The most negative thing he said about her was that she was overly concerned about Mark's health. Other than denying her accusations, he never said anything slanderous about his ex-wife.

Mr. and Mrs. Jones were also not particularly hostile toward their ex-daughter-in-law. They were baffled by the accusations and at times related their belief that the charges were so ridiculous as to be laughable. They never said anything terribly negative about Patricia, other than to defend themselves and to say they did not engage in the behavior. Mrs. Jones was very positive about Patricia and how she loved her as a daughter. Mr. and Mrs. Jones and Daniel Jones never were embarrassed by the charges. Mrs. Huddleston's interview did not add anything substantial to what all three Joneses related during their interviews. This is quite strange, because usually there are vastly different reports and the accused party often leaves out very important information that has to be obtained from the aggrieved party. In short, William, Carla, and Daniel Jones did not act like perpetrators and their test results did not look like the profiles of perpetrators.

During the interview Patricia Huddleston was anxious and tearful. She was the only person who had inconsistent test results. Her defensiveness on the tests was more significant than the other three adults. She was the one adult out of the four who displayed the most clinical anxiety and yet turned in a normal profile. Mrs. Huddleston reported a history of rape in her marriage to Daniel Jones, posttraumatic stress, anxiety about her child, and yet she cut off these emotions on the test results.

During Mark's interview, he said, like a robot, that he does not like his grandfather and he put "his tookie in my bootie." About his grandparents and father, he said, "I hate them, they're mean, they do bad stuff." He said he does not like his father and does not want to see him. He said he does not like the telephone calls "because he did bad stuff, 'cause he's mean." He said his grandmother "made me sit on her fuzzy hair." He said Roberta Jones locked him in his room. He said all of this without any change in affect. Throughout the interview he had the same intensity, no matter what he was reporting. There was no difference in intensity if he said his father was raping him or if he said that Roberta Jones would not let him come out of his room. He referred to Sam Huddleston as his daddy. He said he is talking to a counselor.

On the Hand Test, Mark had a lot of "touching" responses. He then had a very unusual response. He said the hand was "pointing to my mom, gonna get a truck and roll over my mom." This is from a child who is making allegations about his father and grandparents. This was a completely unconscious response and, after he made it, he seemed a little taken aback. When he responded to Card 10, which was a blank card, he said, "somebody touching private parts." This child has discussed private parts and touching so much that these responses are automatic. When he was asked to make three wishes, he said, "not to see Daddy, to get a Volkswagen, and to get some green blocks." On the CAT he saw another response which indicated hostility toward maternal figures. He saw a little boy trying to run over a lady who was about to fall. He saw a card in which he described a child without a mother or father. He saw another card in which a baby was in a bed by himself with no mom or dad.

Summary and Recommendations

I think Mark and Mrs. Huddleston have come to believe false allegations of sexual abuse without consciously fabricating them. Mrs. Huddleston had emerging and evolving concerns about her son, which at first did not include sexual abuse. She was anxious and overwrought that her son seemed to be rejecting her or, at least, was too attached to his grandparents. She thought about and proceeded to do something about the visitation prior to her knowledge of sexual abuse. Within a short time she reported sexual allegations from Mark. She was also frustrated by her attorney at that time, who did not believe much could be done. She subsequently changed attorneys. She reports that three people were involved in perverse sexual abuse of a 3-year-old, possibly engaging in this behavior at the same time. There is no indication of psychological disturbance in these three people to even approximate the alleged conduct. The improbability of the alleged conduct increases with the bizarreness of the report.

Sam Huddleston lost a son the same age as Mark after making similar sexual allegations about the mother and her family. The argument that he has simply replaced his own son with Mark is a strong one. Mrs. Huddleston reports that she was raped by Daniel and I think she is projecting that same fear onto her son and identifying Daniel as a perpetrator. Sexually abused children at 2, 3, and 4 usually do not hate the perpetrator. They also do not talk about the abuse the way that Mark did. He behaves in a very atypical way and is displaying, more than anything else, hatred for his grandparents and father that is rehearsed and reinforced over a long period of time. Again, I do not think Mrs. Huddleston committed a conspiracy, but that she believes the allegations are true and has sought therapy for her son which served to verify the allegations. She has alienated the child from his father and grandparents. At best she did this unknowingly, but she reinforces it at every turn. She makes comments that Mark does better when he does not have phone calls from his father. In a daily way at every opportunity, this issue comes up and she is convinced and has convinced Mark that he is better off without his paternal family. The projective testing on Mark suggested he may be recoiling from this hypercritical attitude toward his paternal family. This came out in hostile responses on the projective tests regarding his mother.

Various psychotherapists have joined Mrs. Huddleston as sympathetic allies. These therapists were inducted into a perniciously triangulated relationship. Mrs. Huddleston found therapists who never evaluated the grandparents or father and yet endorsed her assessment of who the villain was. They probably defined the mother as a victim, as well as the child. This reinforced the mother's beliefs, as well as Mark's, and by now the beliefs are impenetrable. Therapists who get involved in sexual abuse cases without evaluation of all parties abandon even the pretense of objectivity and appoint themselves as advocates for the custodial parent.

Now that Mark is so aligned with his mother and fearful of his father, a change in custody would adversely affect his mental health. However, I think visitation should resume with Daniel Jones and it can be unsupervised. I do not think the grandparents need separate visitation rights, since they will have access to Mark when Daniel has his normal visitation. The therapeutic approach in which Mark is involved should be reevaluated. The entire premise of his current treatment is that he was sexually abused by his father and grandparents. If my recommendations are accepted, this kind of therapeutic orientation is now inappropriate. As a postscript, I will note that over the last few years I have more often than not substantiated abuse allegations. However, each case must be evaluated objectively with no predetermined bias in either direction.

Discussion

It would be difficult to find a better example of false sexual allegations than this case. This is another case in which the mother actually believed the sexual allegations. She had feelings of anxiety and was preoccupied with her own victimization that she perceived was perpetuated by her ex-husband. She was also upset that her son seemed to be too attached to the paternal grandparents. Even before the sexual allegations, she shopped around in her home state for a state agency to take action. She was later able to solicit support from an army of therapists in her own state, one of whom actually came to court with her on two different occasions.

When I testified in this case, it was very clear that the judge was extremely skeptical, especially during and after my testimony. When the Huddlestons saw how the judge was leaning, they attempted to change the venue back to their home state, which the judge denied. In this case, I did receive feedback on the decision. The judge dismissed the sexual allegations and reinstated regular and normal visitation with the father. It would have been very difficult to actually change custody of the child, however, since the child was so fearful of his father. The best a father can usually hope for in such cases is to restore visitation. However, the prognosis is often poor, because the accusing mother will continue her crusade and sometimes fathers just give up.

After receiving an unfavorable decision in this case, the mother refiled in her local district, again seeking to obstruct visitation with her ex-husband. This is very typical, because women like Mrs. Huddleston never stop fighting in their quest to shut the father out of their child's life and to affirm the imagined sexual abuse. In addition, the Huddlestons also filed an action with the state Board of Examiners in Psychology, which I had to defend.

The therapist who testified for the Huddlestons, a doctoral student, was an excellent example of therapy misapplied to forensic psychology. She testified that the child was sexually abused, even though she never met the grandparents or father who allegedly performed this abuse. She made the most outrageous allegations, including ritualistic abuse by the grandmother, grandfather, and the father. She said that at times the grandparents had abused the child together. Ritualistic or cultlike sexual abuse does occur, but the unusual and bizarre nature of the allegations should have raised the level of skepticism and the burden of proof.

This therapist had no business in the courtroom, since she had absolutely no objectivity and did not evaluate the case in any way other than to be the child's therapist and to accept whatever the mother had to say. She looked foolish on the stand when the father's attorney asked if she even met the alleged perpetrator or the grandparents who were accused of performing cultlike sexual abuse on a 3-year-old boy. She responded that she hadn't met them, but that the child told her this occurred. The fact that a 3- or 4-year-old boy told her this means nothing. She showed complete naivete and a lack of understanding of human memory, cognition, development, and suggestibility by taking the position she did.

This represents a big problem in our profession. If you tell a therapist that your child was sexually abused, and you are a believable victim yourself, it would be insensitive for the therapist not to believe the sexual abuse occurred. Some therapists will actually say they don't care what the truth is—their job is just to help their patients. If they want to take this position and support their clients without regard to the truth, they should do it in the therapy room and stay out of the courtroom. When innocent people are going to be prosecuted, denied visitation, labeled sexual abusers, have their relationships destroyed, and perhaps lose their jobs, discerning the truth of the allegations is extremely important.

In this chapter, the first cases were clear-cut examples of sexual abuse and other types of abuse. The last two were examples of sexual abuse fabrications. When lawyers and judges in your community see that you can find in either direction, you will receive the greatest respect as a professional.

Even when there is substantiated sexual abuse, you should forget about trying to save the victims. You should simply report your findings and let others, including the courts, child protective agencies, and other therapists, provide the remediation and treatment. It is almost impossible to conduct a forensic assessment practice and be deeply involved in therapeutic issues, especially with the same client.

7

SOCIAL SECURITY DISABILITY DETERMINATION

Throughout the country there are many opportunities to perform Social Security evaluations. The Social Security Administration (SSA) administers two programs that provide disability benefits. One is the Social Security Disability Insurance Program, Title II, which provides benefits for those individuals who contributed to the Social Security system through their earnings. The other is Supplemental Security Income Program, Title XVI, known as SSI. These are disability benefits for those individuals, including children, who are disabled and qualify for income.

The law defines disability as the inability to engage in any substantial gainful activity by reason of a medically determinable physical or mental impairment which has lasted, or can be expected to last, a continuous period of no less than twelve months. SSI disability can be awarded to children under the age of 18 if they have a medically determinable impairment that limits their ability to function independently, appropriately, and effectively in an age-appropriate manner.

To file for disability benefits, claimants first make application to the local Social Security Administration (SSA) office. It is then the responsibility of the SSA field office or the state Disability Determination Service (DDS) office to make a determination regarding the application. The federal government funds an office in each state known as the Disability Determination Service (DDS). Its job is to develop medical evidence and to render an initial determination on whether or not the claimant is disabled. DDS initially attempts to make this determination through medical information already available from the treating professional or other sources. The treating physician or mental health professional may be asked to provide records or to write a letter summarizing the treatment.

If that evidence is not sufficient, DDS will arrange for a consultative examination (CE) to obtain additional information. DDS contracts with doctoral-level psychologists to perform mental status examinations and intellectual testing as part of the CE process. Psychiatrists may also be asked to perform CEs for mental disorders. Licensed master's level professionals trained in psychology may perform intellectual testing. Physicians of all specialities will be asked to perform CEs for medical complaints. CEs are always contracted with psychologists and physicians who were not the treating professional.

The DDS office has a panel of experts in a particular geographical area and rotates CE examinations among the members of that panel. However, psychologists who perform thorough, comprehensive, timely evaluations will simply be more available for appointments, resulting in a larger number of referrals. Psychologists on the panel who specialize in forensic evaluations will find that they receive many more requests for CE evaluations, mainly because they are meeting the needs of the DDS office.

After the DDS office calls to schedule the appointment, the psychologist will be mailed a packet of information, including medical reports, background information from treatment sources, schools, and so on, and a purchase order. The purchase order is to be signed and returned for payment, so no additional billing is necessary. Fees for CE exams are set by the state and may vary from state to state. Once the examination is completed, DDS requires that reports be submitted promptly. Claimants or their attorneys will often ask for a copy of their report, but they are always referred to the DDS office to obtain these copies.

Once the psychologist submits a CE report, the DDS office will make the determination as to whether benefits will be awarded. This is done by evaluation of the written reports by the DDS experts, psychologists and physicians on contract or employed by the state office to make the determinations. This is another opportunity for psychologists to work for the DDS office. However, while working for DDS, the psychologist cannot do CE evaluations, which is certainly the bulk of the work. The psychologist may not do both, since this would be a conflict of interest. If the claimant is turned down for disability, he or she may reapply and the state DDS office will reevaluate the claim using a different team of evaluators within the state office.

If that second application is unsuccessful, the applicant may appeal to an administrative law judge in the Social Security Administration Office of Hearing and Appeals, which is completely separate from the DDS office. This process is very different from the DDS determination, since the law judge has an opportunity to actually see and question the claimant. The claimant's lawyer is also able to question his client and provide any witnesses or additional information desired. This is another point in the process when psychologists may perform evaluations, since the administrative law judge can decide that he wants additional information and can order additional testing. In those cases, the law judge sends the order for a CE back to the DDS office, which makes an appointment with one of the regularly available panel of consultants in the community. The law judge then takes the information from the CE report and makes a determination. On rare occasions, the law judge may call the psychologist directly after the CE is completed or even ask him to appear to answer additional questions.

Many law judges develop a panel of medical experts to testify and assist them in these determinations. This is another way for a CE psychologist to serve an administrative law judge. Psychologists performing regular CE evaluations for the DDS office may also serve as medical experts at this point in the process. However, psychologists serving as psychological consultants for the DDS office would be prohibited from serving as medical experts before the law judge on the same case.

When called in as a medical expert, the psychologist will be asked to review the medical record and testify on a claimant he or she has never seen. At the hearing, the psychologist will be asked in a straightforward way to determine whether the claimant meets the criteria for disability and what the degree of limitation is. At these hearings, the psychologist may have an opportunity to ask the claimant questions. However, any opinion rendered should be based primarily on the review of the record and not on a one-time meeting in a non-clinical setting with the claimant at the hearing. In some jurisdictions, the percentage of claims approved by administrative law judges is as high as 80 or 90 percent. This is their prerogative, since they are not bound by any decision made by the DDS office.

There is a huge difference between performing CEs for law judges and acting in the role of a medical expert and testifying on claimants you have not evaluated. In the CE evaluation, you are not asked to make definitive statements regarding disability. As a medical expert for a claimant you have not evaluated, the law judge may ask more direct questions. The best standard of practice, as always, is to answer the questions that are asked by the referring source. Sometimes law judges want the medical expert to rate the four criteria on paragraph B (functional limitation) and other times they do not. You will secure your position as a medical expert by providing your referral source with the information he or she needs.

Should the claimant fail in his appeal to the administrative law judge, he or she has the right to make a final appeal to federal court. Since the administrative law judge approval rate is so high, the federal appeals option is rarely exercised. Psychologists are rarely asked to testify in these matters in federal court.

STANDARDS FOR DISABILITY

For adults, "mental disorder" is one of thirteen disabling conditions recognized by the Social Security Administration. The others are disabilities of the musculoskeletal system, special senses and speech, respiratory system, cardiovascular system, digestive system, and most other medical systems. For children, "mental disorder" is one of fourteen listings for disability. Some of the other listings involve the immune system, neurological system, multiple body systems, endocrine systems, digestive systems, respiratory system, and musculoskeletal system.

A vast number of evaluations you will be doing will be on individuals who have applied for benefits on the basis of one of these medical impairments. They will not be alleging mental or emotional impairments as their primary allegation. The reason they are referred for CEs is because they have some history of psychiatric involvement. They might have stated on the application that they are nervous or depressed or they might have listed a history of counseling or psychiatric treatment. Once psychiatric symptoms are listed on the SSA application, DDS has an obligation to check out these allegations.

Another reason medical claimants are referred for a psychological CE is to evaluate possible malingering or somatization. Administrative law judges are especially prone to obtain psychological CEs on medical applicants to get some sense of whether they are exaggerating or malingering or if they have a somatization disorder. Many claimants, especially those with back pain, have very vague symptoms and non-medically verifiable symptoms of pain. Fibromyalgia is a good example and is very difficult to disprove. The law judge also wants to know what the claimant's intellectual ability is, whether there is potential for vocational rehabilitation, whether the patient is able to read and write, what the daily activities of the claimant are, and whether there is impairment in social functioning. The law judge uses all this information in an effort to determine if the claimant meets the criteria for disability. Psychological CEs are also ordered when claimants have applied for disability on the basis of a neurological deficit.

There are eight categories of mental disorder under which applicants may qualify for disability. These disorders must impose impairments on the individual's ability to work that are expected to last for a continuous period of at least twelve months. These eight categories are: organic mental disorders (12.02), schizophrenic, paranoid, or other psychotic disorders (12.03), affective disorders (12.04), mental retardation and autism (12.05), anxiety-related disorders (12.06), somatoform disorders (12.07), personality disorders (12.08), and substance addiction disorders (12.09).

For each category of disorders, except mental retardation and addiction disorders, a set of clinical findings, that is, paragraph A criteria, must be met. The determination of these diagnosed mental disorders under paragraph A is straightforward and consistent with the DSM-IV. Test results are usually vital in making these determinations. The test-taking ability of the claimant is also important diagnostic information.

If paragraph A criteria are met, then the assessment of severity must be made. Two or three functional restrictions listed in paragraph B must be met for disability to be awarded. The test-taking ability of the claimant is important diagnostic information in considering the degree of functional impairment under paragraph B. Sometimes there are additional considerations listed in paragraph C. To make matters more complicated, individuals who do not meet the criteria for a mental disorder under paragraph A may still have severe deficits in residual functional capacity and be eligible for disability, even without meeting the criteria for one of the mental disorders. This finding will more likely be made during a review by an administrative law judge rather than in the original determination by DDS.

The functional areas considered under paragraph B are (1) restrictions of activities of daily living, (2) social functioning, (3) concentration, persistence, and pace, and (4) deterioration or decompensation in work or work-like setting. Ratings in each area are: none, slight, moderate, marked, and extreme. An individual who is severely impaired by the paragraph B or C criteria as a result of a listing in paragraph A is presumed unable to work. The ratings of "marked" or "extreme" are used as the standard for measuring impairment in functional capacity.

For the first functional category, activities of daily living, a "marked" impairment is not determined by the number of activities which are impaired or restricted, but by an overall assessment of the level of impairment. This is impairment in adaptive functioning, such as shopping, cooking, doing the laundry, personal hygiene and care, making appointments, going outside, going to the grocery store, driving, or using public transportation. The listings do not actually say what a "marked" impairment is, but, as consultants, it is our job to assess whether claimants are suffering with "marked" or "extreme" deficits in their ability to carry out daily activities.

The second category, social functioning, refers to an individual's ability to communicate, get along with other people, and relate to family, neighbors, and ordinary people in the environment, such as clerks, secretaries, waiters, and so forth. Impaired social functioning might include fighting, avoidance, argumentativeness, paranoia, lack of cooperation, or antagonism to authority. Again, a "marked" impairment is the standard for disability and this judgment is based on an assessment of the overall impairment in social functioning.

The third category of functional impairment, concentration, persistence and pace, refers to the ability to sustain attention, complete tasks, and perform the usual duties found in a work setting. Concentration, persistence, and pace can be assessed partially, although not completely, by psychological tests. The ability to perform mental capacity items is a good indication of the ability to pay attention. Tests of intelligence, memory, neuropsychological functioning, and academic achievement all measure this domain. "Marked" impairment would refer to people who are so unable to follow instructions that they will probably not perform successfully on even an unskilled job.

Deterioration or decompensation in work or work-like settings, the fourth category, refers to repeated failures to deal with stressful circumstances. This might be indicated by an individual working two or three days on several jobs over the past year. For example, the claimant may have left a job in anger or in fear after just a day or two, because he or she could not adjust to the demands or the stress of the work environment.

Criteria under paragraph C were added to listings 12.03 and 12.06, schizophrenia and anxiety-related disorders. For these two diagnostic categories, the patient may not have marked impairment in two or more paragraph B areas, only because symptoms are controlled or attenuated by psychosocial factors, such as placement in a highly structured setting or medication. However, the person's ability to function outside of a structured environment or without medication may be poor and would lead to two or more "marked" failures in paragraph B criteria without this support.

The listing for mental retardation and autism refers to sub-average general intelligence and deficits in adaptive behavior manifested before age 22. Autism is described as a pervasive developmental disorder characterized by social and communication deficits originating in early development. The listing for mental retardation lists four categories, A through D, any of which may be satisfied for the claimant to qualify for benefits. A is mental incapacity established through dependence on others for personal needs, including toileting, eating, dressing, or bathing, and the inability to follow directions. People in this category are so impaired that an IQ test cannot be administered. B is an IQ of 59 or less. With an IQ in that range, no other criteria need to be met for disability determination. C is an IQ of 60–70 and an associated or collateral physical or mental impairment imposing additional and significant work-related limitations. D is an IQ of 60–70 or autism, along with marked deficits in two of the four paragraph B functions.

For substance abuse, the diagnosis of addiction is not sufficient for disability to be awarded. Other mental or physical disorders are used to evaluate the damage resulting from addictive substance abuse. Secondary to addiction disorder, the claimant must meet the criteria for one of the following: organic mental disorder, depressive syndrome, anxiety disorder, personality disorder, peripheral neuropathies, liver damage, gastritis, pancreatitis, or seizures. In addition, the claimant has to have functional restrictions associated with one or more of those disorders.

Although the psychologist will be aware of the criteria for awarding benefits, it is never appropriate for the psychologist to make statements in CE evaluations that a claimant is or is not disabled. In CE reports, you should avoid any statements or opinions regarding eligibility, but you should address limitations under paragraph B. Statements related to functional limitations are integrated into the psychological report.

Even when you are testifying as a medical expert before an administrative law judge, you do not make the statement that a client is or is not disabled. In fact, you should never be asked that question. When testifying as a medical expert, you will be asked whether the claimant has "marked" impairments in two or more functional areas. The psychologist should certainly give an opinion on specific impairments, but this is very different from saying that the claimant is or is not disabled.

CONSULTATIVE EXAMINATIONS

The original consultative examinations ordered by psychological consultants for DDS will usually involve mental status examinations and IQ tests. CEs ordered later in the process by administrative law judges are usually broader in scope and may require complete batteries of tests, including MMPIs, other personality testing, and/or neuropsychological testing.

Mental Status Examinations

These can be performed by doctoral-level psychologists or psychiatrists. The format will vary, but the DDS office will typically provide a form they want followed in performing the examination. The report can be written on the DDS form or the headings can be used in a separate report, so there are no constrictions of space in addressing the relevant issues.

Objective and specific information should be included in the report, information which will allow an independent reviewer to reach diagnoses and conclusions regarding the claimant's disability. Statements that the claimant is psychotic, depressed, or delusional are not sufficient by themselves, but must be accompanied by specific examples or direct quotes, so that the psychological or medical consultant can see how functional capacity is affected.

The mental status examination format used by one DDS office is shown in Table 7–1.

As you can see, the questions to be covered by a mental status examination are rather voluminous. If you tried to answer each question in detail, the reports could run to excessive length, so this is not done. All that needs to be done is to answer the basic questions under each heading, at least briefly. You want to give enough information so that the medical or psychological consultant at DDS will be able to judge the level of impairment of the claimant. The psychological consultant wants more than a page, but probably doesn't want a ten-page report. They just want to know how the person functions, whether there is a mental disorder, and how badly impaired the person is in daily activities, social functioning, concentration, and behavior in work or work-like settings.

The testing psychologist must also realize that DDS is not concerned with minor symptoms. DDS just wants to know if the person can show up for work and perform unskilled work in the labor market. If the claimant is a nuclear scientist who, because of an aneurysm, is now only capable of teaching math in public school, he or she will not qualify for disability benefits, even though there might be very significant brain damage compared to premorbid functioning. A drop of 50 IQ points from 150 to 100 from a head injury certainly indicates brain damage, but the question still remains how the person is functioning now and whether he or she has marked impairment in the four areas relevant to work activities. The determination of disability rests on whether the claimant can function reasonably well in the local job market, not whether he or she can function in the occupation that was previously held.

Although DDS may order additional testing after getting your report, it is not appropriate in the mental status examination report to list additional tests or procedures that you think the claimant should have. The psychological consultant at DDS is a psychiatrist or psychologist, just like you, and they can decide what tests are needed. If you estimate a person's IQ to be 69 or 70, the consultant will know what additional testing should be done. If you have concerns about the

Table 7–1. Evaluation for Mental Disorders

PATIENT'S
NAME:_____SSN:_____

Note: The evidence needed to evaluate this patient's disability application must be objective and as specific as possible. It should be sufficiently complete to allow an independent reviewer to reach diagnosis as well as a conclusion regarding the patient's disability. Specific examples of the patient's behavior and functioning are necessary to make these determinations. Objective data, signs, and examples are better than inferences, e.g., direct quotes and anecdotes rather than "patient is delusional or paranoid." This is not a questionnaire but a guide for report writing. Typed reports required.

I.   **GENERAL OBSERVATIONS:** Did the patient come alone or accompanied? Please give as specific a description as possible of grooming, posture, gait, mannerisms, clothing, hygiene, dress, general appearance, ability to relate, abnormal behavioral patterns, etc.

II. **PRESENT ILLNESS:** What are the patient's complaints and symptoms? How and when did they begin? What effect have these symptoms had on the claimant's ability to work? What effect do they have on present illness?

III. **PAST HISTORY OF MENTAL DISORDER:** List any hospitalizations with duration, as well as outpatient, medications, etc.

IV. **FAMILY, SOCIAL, AND ENVIRONMENTAL HISTORY:** Discuss the following areas, if relevant: family, education, marriage, divorce, work, sickness, alcohol, drug abuse, prison, etc.

V.   **MENTAL STATUS EXAMINATION:** For each of the items listed below, we need enough descriptive details to allow us to independently confirm your conclusions.

   A. **ATTITUDE AND BEHAVIOR:** Please describe the patient's general attitude, e.g. pleasant, hostile, relaxed, fearful, etc. and any noteworthy behaviors, e.g. tearfulness, motor activity, explosive behavior, etc.

   B. **STREAM OF MENTAL ACTIVITY:** Spontaneous, inhibited blocked, illogical, odd, vague pressure of speech, slowed, circumstantial, well organized. Give examples.

C. THOUGHT CONTROL: Hallucinations, delusions, persecutions, thoughts controlled by other people, obsessions, unusual power, suicidal ideas, worthlessness, homicidal, etc. Give examples of content of hallucinations or delusions. Are they occurring currently or in the past?

D. AFFECT: Describe the affect and mood observed both in quality and intensity.

E. DESCRIPTION OF AFFECT DISTURBANCE: The development of depression/mania. Describe symptoms of affective disorder: suicidal/homicidal ideation, change in appetite/weight loss or gain, insomnia, sleep disturbances, changes in social relations, energy level and interests, self concept. If there are cyclical patterns note frequency, duration and precipitating events.

VI. **INTELLECTUAL FUNCTIONING/SENSORIUM:**

A. Orientation: time, person, place; contact with reality presently.

B. Memory: Immediate: How many numbers repeated:

	5-8-2		2-4
Forward_____	6-4-3-9	Digit Backward_____	6-2-9
	4-2-7-3-1		3-2-7-9
	6-1-9-4-7-3		1-5-2-8-6
	5-9-1-7-4-2-8		

Past: Date of Birth, recent presidents, phone number, address, current events, etc.

Recall of 3 objects in 5 minutes (Name, Number & Color)

C. Information: Name 5 large cities, current personages & events, etc.

D. Calculation: Subtract 3's from 100, count 20 down to 1 backwards, add, subtract, multiple, and divide single digits, etc.

E. Abstract Thinking: What do these sayings mean: "The grass is greener on the other side of the fence," "Don't cry over spilled milk," etc.?

Table 7-1. (*continued*)

___

F. Similarities and Differences: How are a bush and tree alike/different; a midget and a child; a lie and a mistake, etc.?

G. Judgment: What should you do if you found a stamped, addressed envelope? If you discovered a fire in a theater?

H. Estimated IQ: 69 or Lower_____, 70–79_____, 80 or Greater_____

I. Organic Involvement: In instances in which there are specific questions about the presence of organicity, special attention should be focused in the exam on the patient's short and immediate memory recall. In evaluating functional limitations relate affect, behavioral or cognitive problems occuring in organic mental disorders. Other issues include lability, mental confusion, disorientation, judgment, word finding skills, etc. Comments by family or friends accompanying can be very helpful. Identify as descriptive history or clinical objective observations.

J. If the patient alleges pain, are the allegations consistent with your clinical observations of patient? (Evidence of repositioning frequently, moaning, grimacing, etc.)

K. If patient abuses alcohol/drugs does this cause functional restrictions?

VII. **CURRENT LEVEL OF FUNCTIONING:**

A. Address how the patient's clinical condition restricts or is incompatible with the ability to work. One's activities of daily living help to assess this area (e.g., cleaning, cooking, self care, shopping, paying bills, socializing, etc.). Adaptive activities may be further judged by the patient's independence, appropriateness, and effectiveness. Lastly, consider the ability to initiate and participate in activities independent of supervision or direction.

B. Ability to Relate: Describe how patient gets along with and communicates with family members, neighbors, friends, etc. In what way has this changed as a result of the patient's condition?

VIII. **CURRENT MEDICATION:** (IF ANY) & DOSAGE.

IX. **DIAGNOSES:** (Must meet *DSM III-R* Criteria Classification System and supported by data in body of this report.)

X. **PROGNOSIS:** (Is the pt's condition expected to improve significantly within the next 12 months?)

XI. Is this patient competent to manage funds without assistance? YES_____
NO_____

XII. Do you feel the patient has been open and honest in providing information for the mental status and activities of daily living? Is there evidence of exaggeration or malingering?

XIII. **ADDITIONAL COMMENTS:** Please supply additional information which you feel would be of assistance regarding this patient's application for disability benefits.

_____	_____	_____
	Signature (No Stamp)	Title (Degree)
_____	_____	_____
Name & Address	Telephone	Date of Examination
(Typed and Printed)		

claimant's organic functioning and you state the symptoms that are present, whether aphasia, poor abstraction, loss of memory, confusion, disorientation, poor judgment, word finding problems, or other organic symptoms, the psychological consultant will decide what to do from there. The consultant can order additional testing or can decide the patient is so impaired organically that he or she already qualifies for benefits. On the other hand, if you suggest additional testing in your mental status exam reports, the psychological consultant at DDS will be obligated to order those examinations. If DDS does not order the tests, that will be grounds for appeal and the law judge will end up ordering the additional tests on appeal.

Following are some mental status examination reports, so that the reader can see how these various questions are addressed.

Case 26

In this case the patient was malingering and feigning psychotic symptoms.

Mental Status Examination Report

Name: Monique Paine
(Required identifying information, date of testing, etc.)

General Observations
Ms. Paine is a 26-year-old black female who is 160 pounds and 5 feet, 2 inches tall. She came with her sister, and carried her cigarettes. She engaged in a malingering act from the beginning to the end of the session.

Present Illness
She has been treated before at the state hospital and the Little Rock Community Mental Health Center. She was diagnosed before with depression, but they seemed to settle on the diagnosis of a personality disorder.

Ms. Paine said she is bothered by a man who keeps her up all day and all night. She said he attacks her with little pink monkeys and she cannot get any rest. She said he was right there in the office with us. During the evaluation she said the monkeys were attacking her and she started to cry, saying, "Doctor, get them off." She said she cannot get along with anyone and that people make fun of her. She said she feels nervous and cannot be still. She said her husband keeps her locked up. She thinks she was hospitalized briefly in 1987 at the state hospital. She said she goes to the outpatient clinic at the state hospital, but I am not sure she is keeping appointments at this time. She is not taking medication.

Family, Social, and Environmental History
Ms. Paine is living with her husband, James. She thinks she has been married for two years to her present husband and this is her first marriage. She said she has four children and "somebody stole three." She has one child with her who is a year old. Later she said she has not been seeing the three kids that live with her mother. She was very angry with her mother and referred to her as "that woman."

Ms. Paine said she is unable to go anywhere by herself and her sister takes care of her. She said she has no friends. She said she was not good in school and she has never worked. She denied any drug or alcohol use. Overall, she was a very poor historian.

Mental Status Examination
Attitude and Behavior: Ms. Paine persisted throughout the evaluation in her statements that there was a little man in the room with monkeys. It was difficult to get

any other information from her. She talked in a very childlike and whiny voice that was extremely affected.

Stream of Mental Activity: She was poorly organized in her speech and not able to stay on the topic. Everything was in the context of the malingering (or whatever she was trying to accomplish), so it was difficult to get accurate information.

Thought Control: She claimed auditory and visual hallucinations and also claimed that she was visually hallucinating in the office. This was not credible. I do not think that she is psychotic.

Affect: Historically her affect has been anxious. She was somewhat angry when she talked about her mother and other family members.

Intellectual Functioning/Sensorium
Orientation: She was oriented to time, place, and person and, in my view, had good contact with reality. The other mental capacity items could not be administered, since she said "don't know" to every item.

I administered the first 20 items from both the Peabody Picture Vocabulary Test-Revised, Forms M and L. The first 20 items for each of the forms can be completed by a 3-year-old child. Even by chance alone, she would be able to get 25 percent correct, since she has to point to one of 4 pictures as the correct answer. She had only 3 correct responses, rather than the 10 correct responses that would have been expected by chance. A person who is retarded will usually get 35 or so of these first 40 items correct, since they are so easy. She missed all but 3, so there was no question about the malingering. In the first 4 items on Form M, she had to point to pictures of a car, ball, money, and broom. She got every one wrong. On the initial items on Form L, she was asked to point to the pictures of a bus, bed, tractor, and snake, all of which she missed. This was all deliberate and she seemed to believe that it was in her best interest to act as if she were hallucinating.

Current Level Of Functioning
Present Daily Activities: I did not understand what she does all day, since she would not answer questions like this.

Ability to Relate: Her ability to relate is poor.

Current Medication
She is not taking any medication.

Diagnosis
Personality Disorder NOS (301.9), Malingering (V65.2). This is not a stable person. Three of her four children have been removed and she will be seen as odd and unusual by most people who observe her. However, her problems are longstanding and she has a personality disorder, rather than psychosis.

Prognosis
Her prognosis is guarded, given the length and chronicity of her behavior. She is not able to handle her own benefits. She was not honest and open and there was malingering.

Discussion
This claimant is an example of the most obvious and transparent malingering that a psychologist will ever see in clinical practice. She had a mental health history and had had various diagnoses, including depression and personality disorder. She was a terrible historian, so the information I could provide was limited. Even with the malingering, the report reflected that she was a disturbed and maladjusted person.

Because she continued her faking throughout the examination, this claim-ant could not be administered the intellectual/sensorium items. I therefore gave the first 20 items of each PPVT-R form, a total of 40 items. Even blindfolded, a person should get 25 percent of these items correct by chance. In reality, very young children and even the most retarded client should get the majority of these cor-rect, so it took intelligence to miss 37 of the 40. This left no doubt that she was malingering.

In addition to the PPVT-R, the Computerized Assessment of Response Bias, Revised Edition (CARB) could have been administered to assess faking or malinger-ing. The CARB is a computer-administered test designed to detect exaggeration of cognitive difficulties. It is introduced to the client as a test of memory and concen-tration and the norms suggest that even those with severe brain damage will score 96.8% correct. I have administered the CARB to ten mentally-retarded individuals with IQs ranging from 48 to 73 and their percentages were equivalent to the brain-damaged group. Thus, when a client obtains a score significantly less than 96.8% on the CARB, it can be assumed that there is malingering or faking involved.

I have no idea if this claimant got disability. The psychological consultant at DDS may have dismissed her application after reading that she was malinger-ing. On the other hand, disability benefits may have been awarded because she was so maladjusted, related so poorly, and had almost no work history. The CE report simply communicates what the claimant looks like. It is up to DDS to decide what happens from there.

Case 27

This is a typical case of an individual with medical complaints and secondary psy-chological problems.

Mental Status Examination Report

Name: Roy Nelson
(Required identifying information, date of testing, etc.)

General Observations
Mr. Nelson is a 38-year-old white male with a moustache and glasses. He walked with a cane and wore a hat. He recently had back surgery and walked with a great deal of pain. He is 6 feet, 6 inches tall and weighs 240 pounds. He said he lost about 50 pounds as a result of the surgery.

Present Illness
He said he hurt his back on the job in 1988 while trying to move a toolbox. After the injury he worked until 1991, when he stopped working. He had physical therapy from 1991 until 1994. He had two back surgeries to put steel rods and pins in his spinal column. He thinks he needs another surgery for continuing back pain. He said he has pain in his lower back and hip and he also has headaches. He said his back pain affects his hands. He said he tried to go to rehabilitation, but he could not sit or stand, so it was discontinued. He said he also has emphysema and asthma.

Mr. Nelson was hospitalized for depression at Baptist Medical Center in August 1994. He said he got depressed secondary to his back pain. He did not mention depression or mental illness as a disability and he focused on his back pain. When I asked him about the hospitalization, he acknowledged that he was depressed at the time and was thinking about suicide. He said his family took him to the hospital when they saw him with a .357 magnum. He said he still thinks about suicide, because he is depressed about his back pain.

Family, Social, and Environmental History
He and his wife have been married ten years and have two children. He has three children from a previous marriage, ages 19, 17, and 15, and his wife has a child from a previous marriage. He said his life is different because he cannot play with his kids or work. He said he feels depressed over the Social Security case. He has financial problems and he said the family is living on AFDC. His wife does not work and he said she "takes care of me." Last week he said he lost his balance, fell on a wood stove, and burned himself.

When asked about his work history, he said he worked as a mechanic at various car dealerships in Texas before coming to Arkansas ten years ago. He went to the twelfth grade. He denies any alcohol use.

Mental Status Examination
Attitude and Behavior: He was pleasant and cooperative. There was no noteworthy behavior other than his pain behavior.

Stream of Mental Activity: He was spontaneous, uninhibited, logical, and well-organized.

Thought Control: There are no hallucinations, delusions, thoughts of persecution, or homicidal ideation. He said he still thinks about hurting himself.

Affect: He seemed to be in a good mood today. He reports that he still feels depressed because of his back. He brought the x-rays and wanted me to see them.

Intellectual Functioning/Sensorium
Orientation: He was oriented to time, place, and person and in good contact with reality.

Memory: He repeated 5 digits forward and 4 digits backward. He knew his date of birth, but could not recall 3 objects after 5 minutes delay.

Information: He was able to say how many months are in a year, who Louis Armstrong was, and where the sun sets. He named 4 US Presidents and knew there are 52 weeks in a year. He was able to name 5 large cities.

Calculation: He subtracted 100 by 3's without a mistake. He knew 3 x 8 and 36 divided by 6, but he missed 25 + 17.

Abstract Thinking: For "Don't cry over spilled milk," he said, "it will get better in the long run." For "The grass is greener," he said, "you think things look better compared to somewhere."

Similarities and Differences: He said an apple and banana are both fruit, a dog and lion are animals, and north and west are directions.

Judgment: He would "tell someone" if he discovered fire in a movie theater and return a stamped addressed envelope if he found it.

Estimated IQ: His IQ is estimated to be about 85.
Organic Involvement: There is no organic involvement, but there was a great deal of pain behavior and he walked with a cane.

Current Level of Functioning
Present Daily Activities: He said he gets up in the morning and takes his medication. He watches television and sits on the deck. He said he goes to appointments, but he has no other meaningful activities.

Ability to Relate: He is a friendly man who seems to have good ability to relate to other people.

Current Medication
Relafen, amitriptyline, Propoxy–N/APAP, and cyclobenzaprine 10 mg.

Diagnosis
He continues to have some depression secondary to his back pain. At this point, he has an Adjustment Disorder with Depressed Mood (309.0). He acknowledges feeling depressed because of his pain and financial stress. He does not advance depression as his disability. His pain behavior appears to be legitimate and there was no exaggeration or malingering.

Prognosis
His prognosis is guarded, given his severe back pain. He does not feel he can be retrained as long as he has pain. He is competent to handle his own benefits. He seemed to be honest about his symptoms and daily activities.

He is able to understand, remember, and carry out simple instructions. He can get along with other people and respond to work pressure. The stress and pressure he reports is anything involving physical stamina or strenuous work.

Discussion
This mental status was ordered because the claimant apparently mentioned being depressed on his application for disability benefits. For claimants with medical claims, the mental status exam may influence the decision of the medical consultant at DDS regarding the patient's disability application. The information in this mental status exam was probably helpful to the medical consultant because it showed how this claimant functioned and coped with pain.

In the case of this claimant, the intellectual capacity items suggested his IQ was around 85, eliminating that as a significant factor. There was no impairment in his ability to understand, remember, carry out instructions, work with people, or respond to work pressure, except that which was related to his physical stamina. He was given a diagnosis of adjustment disorder with depressed mood, because the depression was secondary to back pain, there was no significant psychiatric history, and he never advanced depression as his disability.

Case 28

This was a typical mental status examination on an alcoholic.

Mental Status Examination Report

Name: Terry Floyd
(Required identifying information, date of testing, etc.)

General Observations
Mr. Floyd is a 44-year-old white male. He had shoulder-length hair and poor hygiene. He had an alcohol odor and I am sure he had been drinking prior to the evaluation. He is 6 feet tall and weighs 180 pounds. His posture and gait appeared to be normal.

Present Illness
Mr. Floyd said he is filing for disability because he has physical problems. He said he had a vehicle accident in 1965 in which he suffered many broken bones. His brother was killed in the accident. He said he worked after the accident, but his pain has progressively gotten worse. He said his left knee joint continues to be very unstable, going "sideways and backwards," and he has trouble supporting himself. He said his back and his right arm hurt. He cannot pick up anything or carry anything heavy. He said he has trouble bending or sitting. He said he has no other complaints other than the pain. He does not think he can get the medication he needs. He acknowledges a history of alcohol abuse, but said this does not keep him

from working. He has been at the Benton Detox Unit several times and at Freedom House. He obviously continues drinking at this time.

Family, Social, and Environmental History
He quit school during the twelfth grade and never got his GED. His mother is alive and his father is deceased. He has been married four times. He has four children, ages 24, 23, 12, and 11. He said he is not seeing his children, although they live within about fifty miles of him. He is living with an ex-wife now, who is not the mother of the children. They have been divorced about a year. In the past he worked at various salvage yards for about twelve years. He also drove trucks and did other labor. Now he said he does odd jobs for spending money. He said he had two DWI arrests, the last about a year ago. He denied any other arrest record.

Mental Status Examination
Attitude and Behavior: Mr. Floyd was cooperative and friendly. He did not have any noteworthy behaviors.

Stream of Mental Activity: He was spontaneous, logical, and well-organized.

Thought Control: There were no hallucinations, delusions, thoughts of persecution, suicidal or homicidal ideation.

Affect: His affect was normal and there was no indication of depression. He said he continues to drink, sometimes to excess. Although he does not acknowledge it, he continues to have alcohol addiction.

Intellectual Functioning/Sensorium
Orientation: He was oriented to time, place, and person, and in good contact with reality.

Memory: He repeated 6 digits forward and 4 digits backward. He knew his date of birth, 3 instead of 4 US Presidents, his social security number, and a couple of current events. He remembered 2 out of 3 objects after 5 minutes.

Information: He knew 5 large cities, how many months and weeks are in a year, and the direction the sun sets. He knew who Louis Armstrong and Amelia Earhart were.

Calculation: He counted backwards from 20 to 1 successfully and subtracted from 100 by 3's. He knew 36 divided by 6, but missed 3 x 8. He knew 42 + 9.

Abstract Thinking: For "Don't cry over spilled milk," he said, "there is nothing you can do." For "The grass is greener," he said, "it's not, it just looks better."

Similarities and Differences: He said an apple and banana are both fruit, a dog and lion are animals, and north and west are directions.

Judgment: He would ring the fire alarm if he discovered fire in a movie theater. He would take a stamped addressed envelope he found in the street to the post office.

Estimated IQ: His IQ is estimated to be in the high 80's, perhaps 88.

Organic Involvement: There are no organic symptoms. He did not demonstrate much pain behavior during the evaluation.

Current Level of Functioning

Present Daily Activities: He said he tinkers with his car, does some odd jobs for a man that has a truck, and cleans up this man's shop. He also drinks almost every day.

Ability to Relate: He seems to have good ability to relate.

Current Medication

He is not taking any medication.

Diagnosis

His only diagnosis is Alcohol Dependence, Continuous (303.90). He does not advance this as his disability and said he has back pain.

Prognosis

He will likely continue complaining about his back pain. I think his alcohol abuse is also going to continue and, in fact, he was drinking prior to the evaluation. He is not able to handle his own benefits if he is going to use his funds on alcohol. He was honest and open about his symptoms, but he seemed to minimize his alcohol abuse. He can understand, remember, and carry out simple instructions.

Discussion

Most alcoholics, such as this claimant, allege disability based on medical complaints. Sometimes they will not even mention that they have a history of alcohol abuse, but the accompanying papers sent by DDS will almost always include references to alcohol abuse.

The first paragraph of this report gives the reader a good picture of what he looks like, as well as indicating right away that he had probably been drinking prior to the evaluation. The report includes his history of substance abuse treatment, his DWIs, and his currently doing odd jobs for money, facts of interest to the DDS office.

It was hard to know what this claimant actually did all day and whether he worked more than he indicated. All the facts he stated were simply put in the report. If he had said that he had no gainful employment or ability to do physical labor, and yet appeared to be deeply suntanned, with grease and dirt under his fingernails, those physical descriptions would have been included in the report. The DDS consultant could then draw his or her own conclusions about whether the applicant was outside a lot and had his hands on tools or machines. This is neither fair nor unfair to the claimant. It is simply providing objective information. In fact, it would be irresponsible to omit such behavioral observations. The examining psychologist is neither trying to help the claimant get disability nor keep him from being awarded benefits. The psychologist's ethical responsibility is to simply report the facts.

This claimant's only symptom was his drinking. He had at least Low Average intelligence and there was no history of mental illness. After this report, he undoubtedly underwent another CE by a physician regarding his physical complaints.

ADULT INTELLECTUAL EVALUATIONS

Intelligence testing is the second most common CE ordered. Often, a purchase order will be received to perform both the mental status examination and a WAIS-R. In that case, there would be one report combining the mental status and IQ results.

The reporting requirements for intelligence testing are stated below. You will see that an IQ CE is in some way a mini-mental status examination. The following elements are included, at least briefly, in the narrative report.

1. Self-sufficiency of the claimant in coming to the examination.
2. History and background, including education, family and work history, and mental health treatment.
3. Verbal IQ, Performance IQ, and Full Scale IQ, including all of the subtest scores.
4. The reliability and validity of the scores in light of possible emotional concerns, sensory deficits, secondary gain, malingering, or other physical limitations. If the results are attenuated by any of these factors, estimate what the IQ is likely to be. Always state if the IQ is an underestimate or if the claimant did not try.
5. Adaptive functioning, at least in cases of sub-average intelligence, and comments on any significant inconsistencies with the test results. (For example, if an applicant had a 69 IQ, but had worked at a factory for 25 years, this would indicate very good adaptive functioning, in spite of mental retardation.)
6. Whether the claimant is capable of managing benefits to his or her own best interests, given the level of intellectual and emotional functioning.

As always, the reports should be hand signed and dated by the examiner.

Case 29

This case shows an intellectual evaluation of a mildly retarded individual.

Psychological Evaluation Report

Name: Tonya Hughes
(Required identifying information, date of testing, etc.)

Tests Administered
Wechsler Adult Intelligence Scale–Revised (WAIS-R).

Background Information
Ms. Hughes is a 38-year-old white female. She is 5 feet, 5 inches tall and weighs 200 pounds. Her posture and gait were good and her hygiene was fair. She has several teeth missing. She has an eighth-grade education.

When asked to describe her problems, she said she has asthma and trouble breathing. She said her legs bother her, she has high blood pressure, and she cannot read. She previously worked at two poultry plants. She was married once for fifteen years. She is divorced and is now a single mother. She recently had a baby and did not go back to work. She has five children, three who are grown and two who live at home. She denied alcohol and drug use and has no arrest record. She said she has not been able to get her driver's license because of her inability to read. She described her nerves as "shot." She does not have any mental health treatment history.

Test Results
The WAIS-R scaled scores were as follows:

Verbal Tests		Performance Tests	
Information	3	Picture Completion	4
Digit Span	2	Picture Arrangement	4
Vocabulary	3	Block Design	5
Arithmetic	3	Object Assembly	5
Comprehension	3	Digit Symbol	4
Similarities	3		
Verbal IQ	62		
Performance IQ	73		
Full Scale IQ	65		

Her IQ of 65 is in the mild range of mental retardation. This was reliable and valid and there was no reason to question the accuracy. She performed well and tried her best.

She was not able to say in what direction the sun rises, name 4 US Presidents, or say how many weeks are in a year. She knew what a thermometer is and how many months there are in a year. She identified only 6 missing details for Picture Completion. She repeated just 4 digits forward and 3 digits backward. She only did one Picture Arrangement item correctly. She could not give definitions of fabric, assemble, enormous, or conceal. She was able to define repair, breakfast, and winter.

On Block Design she did 2 designs correctly. She received full credit for 2 Object Assembly puzzles. She missed Arithmetic problems such as 4 + 5 and 6 x 25. For Comprehension she was not able to say why we cook food and what child labor laws are. She knew what to do with an envelope if she found it in the street and why we wash clothing. She said an orange and banana are both fruit, but she could not say how a dog and lion or a boat and automobile are alike.

Summary
Ms. Hughes has mild mental retardation. This is an accurate and valid measure of her intelligence. Even though she has a 65 IQ, her adaptive ability seems to be a little better than this. Her Performance IQ of 73 probably better reflects her level of adaptive ability. The illiteracy may account for the 62 Verbal IQ. If her problem-solving ability is more borderline in the low 70's, this accounts for her ability to work in the past and raise five children.

She is capable of handling her own benefits. She states that her nerves are "shot," but there is no evidence of mental illness or any diagnosis except mild mental retardation. She can understand, remember, and carry out simple instructions, as she did when she worked. She is able to get along well with others. Right now she has a number of physical complaints and a 1-year-old baby.

Discussion
This claimant had medical complaints, was obese, and stated that she could not read. She obtained a valid IQ of 65 on the testing. The reports should state a few examples of test performance, as this one did, to give some indication of what items were passed and failed. This claimant's adaptive behavior ability was found to be a little better than her 65 IQ, since she was able to raise five children. She had no history of mental illness or treatment, although she stated she was "nervous," which is a common complaint among Social Security applicants.

The CE in this case was very straightforward, reporting the results of the WAIS-R, the most commonly requested test. At times DDS will ask for a Stanford–Binet, Leiter, or an alternate intelligence test if the client had a recent Wechsler test and the IQ results were not clear, based on either malingering or practice effect. In such cases, the psychological consultants at DDS might also ask for an achievement test, neuropsychological testing, personality testing, or any combination of these.

The next section provides examples of complete psychological batteries ordered by administrative law judges. In addition to a comprehensive report, the psychologist will often be asked at this stage to complete the Medical Assessment form (see Tables 7–2 and 7–3). In evaluations done for administrative law judges, this form may be more important than the body of the report. In filling out this form, the psychologist is taking a much more active role than was done in CE reports. The psychologist rates the claimant's ability to make occupational adjustment, performance adjustment, and personal social adjustment, and states what other work-related activities are affected by the test results. As before, the psychologist is not actually stating whether the claimant is disabled or if the person should receive benefits. That decision is left to the administrative law judge. However, the form comes very close to asking for that information, since the law judge will probably award disability if several of the worst two categories are checked in the adjustment areas. The examining psychologist must read the "ability to perform" definitions very closely. "Poor or none" is an extreme category, indicating no useful ability to function in a particular area.

Case 30

In this case, the purchase order requested the following: "Complete battery of psychological testing with narrative report and subtest scores, MMPI with report, medical assessment form." The law judge knew he wanted an MMPI, but he did not specify the remainder of the battery.

Psychological Evaluation Report

Name: Matt Stroh
(Required identifying information, date of testing, etc.)

Tests Administered

> Wechsler Adult Intelligence Scale–Revised (WAIS-R)
> Incomplete Sentences Blank
> Minnesota Multiphasic Personality Inventory (MMPI)
> Millon Clinical Multiaxial Inventory (MCMI)
> Wide Range Achievement Test–Revision Three (WRAT-3)
> Beck Depression Inventory (BDI)
> Wonderlic Personnel Test

Clinical Interview
Mr. Stroh is a 36-year-old white male. He is 6 feet tall and weighs 220 pounds. He took two sessions to complete the tests, because he said he was too sore to finish the first session.

He said he has shoulder pain and he demonstrated a great amount of pain behavior during the evaluation. He also said that his back and his right hip hurt and he has problems with his right hand. He said he has "no kneecap" on the right side and "my back is messed up." He said he had a vehicle accident in 1980 in which he broke several bones. His jaw was broken in three places and he has sinus problems and headaches. He said he has hearing loss. His neck bothers him, but he is not taking any medication because he said he cannot afford it. He said he wakes up six to ten times every night. He said he is nervous, but he did not allege a mental impairment.

Mr. Stroh lives by himself in a rented house. He is supported by his parents, who lend him money, and he receives food stamps. He has never been married and has no children. He said he was 20 or 21 when he had the accident. He has a high school education. He said he cannot work because of the pain. He tried selling cars, but said he could not do it. His last job was two years ago. He said he has done odd jobs, such as mowing lawns, but he had to quit because of the pain. He said he would be better off in jail, because all of his needs would be met. At present he considers himself to be "just existing." He has no criminal record and he has never been in prison. He tried vocational rehabilitation, but said he could not stand, sit, push, or pull, so he could not continue or complete any rehab program.

Test Results
The WAIS-R scaled scores were as follows:

Verbal Tests		*Performance Tests*	
Information	9	Picture Completion	12
Digit Span	7	Picture Arrangement	10
Vocabulary	10	Block Design	13
Arithmetic	6	Object Assembly	9
Comprehension	7	Digit Symbol	6
Similarities	11		
Verbal IQ	91		
Performance IQ	105		
Full Scale IQ	96		

His IQ of 96 is in the Average range of ability at the 39th percentile. His lowest scores were for Arithmetic and Digit Span. On Arithmetic he missed problems as easy as 3 x 8. He seemed to have difficulty with arithmetic in a story problem format. His Comprehension subtest score was also a standard deviation below the mean. He did poorly on Digit Symbol, so there was a great deal of subtest scatter, although his overall IQ was average.

He was able to say how many senators there are in the United States Senate and whose name is associated with the theory of relativity. He knew why dark clothes are warmer than light colored clothes and he identified Amelia Earhart and Louis Armstrong. He was able to repeat 6 digits forward and 3 digits backward. He defined words such as encumber, fortitude, remorse, evasive, and compassion. He received credit for all of the Object Assembly puzzles. Although his Comprehension score was somewhat low, he understood why land in the city costs more than land in the country and he partially knew the meaning of "strike while the iron is hot," why prescriptions are needed for certain drugs, and how to get out of the forest if lost in the daytime. On Similarities he said a fly and tree are both living, work and play are both activities, and a poem and statue are both art.

The WRAT-3 scores were as follows:

	Standard Score	Percentile	Grade Equivalent
Reading	76	5	7
Spelling	85	16	8
Arithmetic	80	9	6

These scores indicate relatively poor academic ability compared to average intelligence. In spite of a 96 IQ, his academic scores are all less than the 20th percentile. He is able to read and write, but only on the seventh and eighth grade level, and his ability for advanced education is very limited. Any rehabilitation would have to involve on-the-job training or apprenticeship.

The Wonderlic Personnel Inventory was at the 45th percentile. This score is good enough to learn routines quickly. He can train with a combination of routine materials and actual on-the-job experience. He can read well enough to meet the literacy needs for most unskilled and semi-skilled jobs, but he could not benefit from education involving primarily book learning.

The MMPI scores were very extreme and were as follows: L = 54, F = 79, K = 34, HS = 94, D = 101, HY = 80, PD = 68, MF = 44, PA = 77, PT = 94, SC = 93, MA = 61, SI = 77. These scores are exaggerated. He reports a sense of emotional distress and feelings of worthlessness. He openly admits peculiarities of behavior, mood, and thought. There was a conscious desire to exaggerate his symptoms.

He did the same thing on the MCMI with following very extreme scores: Schizoid = 100, Avoidance = 105, Passive-aggressive = 107, Anxiety = 106, and Dysthymia = 95. He endorses numerous pathological items and his overall approach to the testing was to say, "I'm a nervous wreck." He lumps all of his physical and psychological problems into one category, so there is a great deal of somatic preoccupation. The amount of functional involvement is probably significant.

His Sentences suggested he is pessimistic and very preoccupied with pain. He said, he can't "do much anymore the way I used to," he feels "happy spending time with my dogs in the woods," and that people "are a pain most of the time." There is some secondary gain from his physical problems, because they seem to meet his avoidant tendencies. He said he does not think things will ever get better and he would like to live in Alaska. He said he hates crowded cities and he needs "to be away from crowded, populated areas." He said he suffers every day and he said his nerves are "so bad I can't stand to be around people much." His Beck Depression Inventory was 38, which is also extreme.

Summary
He reports so many psychological symptoms along with his physical complaints to justify a Pain Disorder Associated with both Psychological Factors and a General Medical Condition (307.89). This is a chronic pain disorder and the diagnosis means there is secondary gain, functional involvement, exaggeration, and amplification of whatever medical problems he actually does have. He derives secondary gain

from his pain disorder, because he is somewhat avoidant and socially uncomfortable. Despite treatment, he demonstrates a significant amount of pain behavior. He believes he cannot benefit from any rehabilitation. He is convinced that he will feel pain no matter what happens. He is strongly convinced that he is disabled under any circumstances, now and in the future. He reports an abundant amount of depression and anxiety, but this is part of the pain disorder and included in that diagnosis.

He can understand, remember, and carry out instructions, but he demonstrates little ability to handle stress due to his complaints of pain. He is capable of handling his own benefits. (See Table 7–2.)

Discussion
This report is very typical of applicants for SSI. (It is not necessarily typical of the occasional Title II evaluations that are performed). There were abundant medical complaints, a chronic history of unemployment, poor social adjustment, dependency, and wild exaggeration of "nervousness." He was bitter and resentful, which is also typical of disability applicants.

He had an average IQ of 96, but his academic ability was poor relative to his intelligence. Nevertheless, his WRAT-3 and Wonderlic scores were certainly sufficient to perform unskilled work. Despite that fact, he received a "fair" or "poor" rating for his ability to deal with the public, deal with stress, function independently, understand, remember and carry out complex job instructions, and demonstrate reliability. This man engaged in extreme pain behavior, although it was impossible to know what he experienced subjectively. In fact, he had so much pain behavior that he had to come back for a second session in order to complete the testing. As always, this behavior was noted in the report. If he acted this way on a job, whether or not he experienced the amount of pain alleged, his occupational adjustment would be affected. He demonstrated a great deal of secondary gain and avoidance of the workplace, which was mentioned in the report.

In this report, you see a typical Social Security MMPI. This is a non-psychiatric patient with elevated scores on Scales 1, 2, 3, 6, 7, 8, 9, and 0 of 77 or above. Are these patients faking or exaggerating? Are they inadequate? Are they genuinely disturbed? Or are they actually experiencing this much distress? Probably some of all of these. They are probably engaging in some exaggeration and malingering, as well as experiencing some emotional distress, subjective pain, and possibly depression and anxiety. They are intolerant of any physical discomfort related to their medical illness and they overstate symptoms.

The point is that the MMPI must be read in a special way for Social Security claimants. MMPIs this bad are not obtained by bona fide depressed or anxious psychiatric patients. A legitimate psychiatric patient who is depressed would be expected to have one or two spikes, such as on 2 and 7, while the other scales would be low. MMPIs on Social Security claimants, however, will indicate that everything is wrong. This is at least typical of MMPIs on medical claimants. This particular man had very extreme elevations on the schizoid, avoidant, passive/aggressive, anxiety, and dysthymia scales. He said he hated being around crowds,

Table 7–2. Medical Assessment of Ability to do Work-Related Activities (Mental)

NAME OF INDIVIDUAL	SOCIAL SECURITY NUMBER
Matt Stroh	

To determine this individual's ability to do <u>work-related activities on a day-to-day basis in a regular work setting</u>, please give us an assessment—BASED ON YOUR EXAMINATION—of how the individual's mental/emotional capabilities are affected <u>by the impairment(s)</u>. Consider the medical history, the chronicity of findings (or lack thereof), and the expected duration of any work-related limitations, but not the individual's age, sex, or work experience.

For each activity shown below:

    (1) <u>Describe the individual's ability to perform the activity according to the following terms:</u>
       <u>Unlimited or Very Good</u> – Ability to function in this area is more than satisfactory.
       <u>Good</u> – Ability to function in this area is limited but satisfactory.
       <u>Fair</u> – Ability to function in this area is seriously limited, but not precluded.
       <u>Poor or None</u> – No useful ability to function in this area.

    (2) <u>Identify the particular medical or clinical findings (i.e., mental status examination, behavior, intelligence test results, symptoms) which support your assessment of any limitations.</u>

       IT IS IMPORTANT THAT YOU RELATE PARTICULAR MEDICAL FINDINGS TO ANY ASSESSED LIMITATION IN CAPACITY: THE USEFULNESS OF YOUR ASSESSMENT DEPENDS ON THE EXTENT TO WHICH YOU DO THIS.

I. MAKING OCCUPATIONAL ADJUSTMENTS

Check the blocks representing the individual's ability to adjust to a job, and complete item 9.

	Unlimited/ Very Good	Good	Fair	Poor or None		Unlimited/ Very Good	Good	Fair	Poor or None
1. Follow Work Rules.	✓				5. Interact with Supervisor(s).	✓			
2. Relate to co-workers		✓			6. Deal with work stresses.				✓
3. Deal with the public.			✓		7. Function independently.			✓	
4. Use judgment		✓			8. Maintain attention/ concentration.		✓		

9. Describe any limitations and include the medical/clinical findings that support this assessment.

    He can understand, remember, and carry out work rules. His ability to relate to the public is quite poor because he has so much pain and is self-centered because of it. Right now he has no ability to deal with work stress because this individual demonstrates severe pain behavior. He was not able to make it through the first testing session and had to reschedule. Occupational adjustment is compromised because of his extreme pain behavior.

II. MAKING PERFORMANCE ADJUSTMENTS

Check the blocks representing the individual's ability to adjust to a job, and complete item #4.

	Unlimited/ Very Good	Good	Fair	Poor or None
1. Understand, remember and carry out complex job instructions.			✓	
2. Understand, remember and carry out detailed, but not complex job instructions.		✓		
3. Understand, remember and carry out simple job instructions.	✓			

Table 7–2. (continued)

4. Describe any limitations and include the medical/clinical findings that support this assessment; e.g., intellectual ability, thought organization, memory, comprehension, etc.

He can understand, remember and carry out simple and detailed instructions. Complex instructions would be difficult given his poor academic ability. He otherwise has average intelligence.

III. MAKING PERSONAL-SOCIAL ADJUSTMENTS

Check the blocks representing the individual's ability to adjust personally and socially:

	Unlimited/ Very Good	Good	Fair	Poor or None
1. Maintain personal appearance.	✓			
2. Behave in an emotionally stable manner.		✓		
3. Relate predictably in social situations.		✓		
4. Demonstrate reliability.			✓	

5. Describe any limitations and include the medical/clinical findings that support this assessment.

His personal and social adjustment tends to be avoidant. There is secondary gain for his medical condition because it reinforces his desire to avoid the work place.

IV. OTHER WORK-RELATED ACTIVITIES

State any other work-related activities which are affected by the impairment, and indicate how the activities are affected. What are the medical/clinical findings that support this assessment?

Work related activities are affected by a pain disorder. There is a great deal of exaggeration, secondary gain, and somatization. Whatever actual medical problem he has are amplified many times over due to psychological factors.

V. CAPABILITY TO MANAGE BENEFITS

Can the individual manage benefits in his or her own best interest?   Yes (✓)   No ( )

SIGNATURE/TITLE	DATE
	3/27/95

[Form SSA–1152 (4/85) Test]

which is also a typical statement made by these claimants. He was given a diagnosis of Pain Disorder from the *DSM-IV*, because there was so much psychogenic involvement and he did have problems with chronic pain. The law judge will still have to decide whether this claimant is markedly impaired in two of four functional areas. Otherwise, he would have to meet the criteria for a medical impairment, rather than the somatization disorder.

This examination showed a suggested battery for this type of evaluation. It included a number of tests and a great deal of work. Some psychologists may not feel there is adequate reimbursement for this amount of work. However, if you are going to excel in a forensic and assessment practice, I recommend always doing more than is asked. Administering the number of tests I did with this applicant results in a comprehensive battery with both intellectual and personality measures. The WAIS-R, WRAT-3, and Wonderlic provided the judge with information about his intellectual and academic functioning and potential. The personality testing was informative for his mental health state, attitude, and the presence of psychiatric symptoms. Judges are satisfied with reports such as this, because there was a lot of testing with relevant information in the report and a detailed description of the patient's behavior.

Case 31

The purchase order for the law judge in the following case read: "Neuropsychological battery (Halstead–Reitan or Luria-Nebraska), complete battery of psychological testing with narrative report and subtest scores, MMPI with report."

Psychological Evaluation Report

Name: Aaron Moss
(Required identifying information, date of testing, etc.)

Tests Administered

> Luria–Nebraska Neuropsychological Battery, Form II (LNNB II)
> Wechsler Adult Intelligence Scale–Revised (WAIS-R)
> Wechsler Memory Scale, Form I
> Wide Range Achievement Test–Revision 3 (WRAT-3)
> Incomplete Sentences Blank
> Minnesota Multiphasic Personality Inventory (MMPI)
> Millon Clinical Multiaxial Inventory (MCMI)
> Wonderlic Personnel Test
> Beck Depression Inventory

Clinical Interview
Mr. Moss is a 47-year-old white male who is 5 feet, 2 inches tall and weighs 138 pounds. His posture and gait were normal and his hygiene was fair.

He said he is blind in the right eye and has 15 percent paralysis in the right arm. He said he has numbness and pain in his right shoulder and arm. He had an odor of alcohol and he admitted drinking before he came to the appointment at 9:00 A.M. He said he has carpal tunnel pain in his left hand. He crushed his right foot and had a head injury in a motorcycle accident in 1966. He said he cannot work because of his left hand and right arm. He said he cannot stand very long because of his foot.

Mr. Moss said that he graduated from high school. His last job was at Tyson Foods in 1987. He also said he has worked at a body shop, as a mechanic, and as a machinist. He lives with his mother and father, who are in their mid-seventies. He was married twice to the same woman, but has been divorced from her for 25 years. He has a son and daughter. He said he spends his time visiting friends.

He said he does not have any mental health problems. He said he drinks some beer, but does not use drugs. He reports one DWI arrest five years ago. He is not taking any medication other than over-the-counter aspirin.

Test Results
The WAIS-R scaled scores were as follows:

Verbal Tests		Performance Tests	
Information	4	Picture Completion	9
Digit Span	6	Picture Arrangement	7
Vocabulary	8	Block Design	7
Arithmetic	11	Object Assembly	5
Comprehension	8	Digit Symbol	7
Similarities	10		

Verbal IQ	90
Performance IQ	89
Full Scale IQ	89

His IQ of 89 is in the Low Average range at the 23rd percentile. He knew where the sun rises, how many weeks are in a year, and who Louis Armstrong was. He knew whose name is associated with the theory of relativity, how yeast causes dough to rise, and at what temperature water boils. He repeated 4 digits forward and 4 digits backward. He was able to define words such as tangible, generate, and perimeter. He did well on arithmetic problems. He understood why a free press is necessary in a democracy, why land is more expensive in the city than the country, and why prescriptions are needed for certain drugs. He said a fly and tree are both nature, work and play are both something to do, and a poem and statue both have meaning. He knew that a table and chair are furniture and that an egg and seed are embryos.

The Wechsler Memory Scale was 87. This is in the Low Average range, commensurate with his intelligence. He was able to learn a pair of associated words. He drew 3 figures from memory and he recalled major portions of a paragraph that was read to him.

The Wonderlic score was at the 13th percentile. At this level he is able to operate simple processing equipment and, given time, he can learn a number of routine steps on a job. He needs to be explicitly taught most of what he learns on the job. Although he can read and write, he would probably not benefit much from academic training. His job skill is definitely at the unskilled (or semi-skilled) level.

The WRAT-3 scores were as follows:

	Standard Score	Percentile	Grade Equivalent
Reading	79	8	7
Spelling	63	1	4
Arithmetic	80	9	6

These scores indicate reading at the seventh grade level and spelling which is not as good as his reading ability. His arithmetic was adequate for adaptive functioning.
The Luria scores were as follows:

Motor Functions	42	Arithmetic	58
Rhythm	71	Memory	54
Tactile Functions	46	Intellectual Processes	63
Visual Functions	50	Intermediate Memory	62
Receptive Speech	70	Pathognomonic	49
Expressive Speech	58	Left Hemisphere	50
Writing	66	Right Hemisphere	43
Reading	49		

The critical level was 61. He had 5 scores above the critical level, which is significant. The deficits were for Rhythm, Receptive Speech, Writing, Intellectual Processes, and Intermediate Memory. The tactile examination was normal, but he had difficulty on Motor Functions with complex motor movements, such as tapping the right hand twice and the left hand once and vice versa. Simple concept recognition was not impaired, but he did have deficits with more complex areas. He had difficulty with sequential analysis, integration, and spatial verbal concepts. He probably has problems with complex behavior planning, novelty, and memory for complex material. He was easily confused with complex verbal and can only pay attention to simple material. For example, he was not able to follow sentences that were a little confusing, such as, "If I had dinner after I read a book, what did I do first?" and "Is the following sentence said by a neat or sloppy person: 'I am not accustomed to disregarding my appearance.'" He does not have aphasia or word finding problems, but he has reduced intellectual ability overall. The Reading scale was adequate and he is able to read most material. He did not have a significant problem on Arithmetic.

He is concrete in thinking and he had trouble with categories and classifications. For example, he could not say what a member of the group "insect" would be or name a member of the group "fruit." He did not understand those concepts. Most of the elevations were mild. He has retained overlearned material, so the 89 IQ represents long-term functioning. The Luria suggests that he will make mistakes on anything complex.

The MMPI scores were L = 66, F = 58, K = 60, HS = 90, D = 90, HY = 98, PD = 72, MF = 43, PA = 60, PT = 74, SC = 75, MA = 50, SI = 49. These scores indicate feelings of emotional distress and preoccupation with physical problems. He reports many more psychological problems indirectly than he does when asked if he has emotional problems. Emotional problems tend to be channeled physically. He is a dependent person and avoids conflict.

The MCMI was high for Dependency (75), Compulsive (75), Anxiety (80), Somatoform (82), and Dysthymia (80). This protocol also reflects some exaggeration of emotional problems and much somatic preoccupation.

On the Sentences he said he regrets what he cannot do, he is in pain, and his nerves are poor. He also said he suffers when he does anything and that it would be easy to give up.

He scored 10 on the BDI. He said he feels sad, he does not enjoy things he way he once did, and he gets tired from doing almost anything.

Summary

Mr. Moss has the following diagnoses: Alcohol Abuse (305.00), Psychological Factors Affecting Medical Condition (316), and Adjustment Disorder with Mixed Anxiety and Depressed Mood (309.28).

He has Low Average intelligence of 89 and an equivalent Memory Quotient of 87. His academic ability is at the seventh grade level. The neuropsychological testing and all of the other tests reveal concrete thinking and very little ability to do anything complex. He is confined to unskilled work which does not involve academic training or any dependence on book learning. He did well enough on the Luria–Nebraska to handle most simple material, but his performance deteriorates when anything is complex or involves abstract concepts. Although the neuropsychological evaluation was not normal, his adaptive functioning is still good for simple, concrete, and repetitive learning and work tasks. The problem is that he complains about physical limitations.

The personality testing indicated a history of nervousness and dependency. It also indicated some reliance on alcohol. He tends to be physically preoccupied and does not cope with adversity very well. Psychological symptoms seem to be a little exaggerated and he tried to emphasize his medical problems. He does not have a history of psychiatric treatment, so his psychological condition is within normal limits, other than to say that he is a "nervous man." Psychological factors alone would probably not affect his ability to engage in occupational functioning. His poor ability to cope, however, adversely affects and exacerbates his medical complaints. In other words, he will be a poor patient, focusing on his weakness, rather than on what he can do. There is definitely alcohol abuse, although he minimizes it.

He is capable of handling his own benefits. He can understand, remember and carry out simple instructions, but not anything complex. He is amiable enough and can get along with other people. The determination will have to rely primarily on his physical condition, since this is his claim, and there is no severe restriction in his ability to function based on intellectual or emotional factors. (See Table 7–3.)

Discussion

The test battery on this applicant is representative of those done when neuropsychological assessment is requested. As usual, it contains complete intellectual, academic, and personality measures, as well as the requested neuropsychological testing. In this case, as in many others, I was not sure why the law judge ordered a neuropsychological evaluation. Sometimes there is a history of head injury, cerebral vascular accident, alcoholism, or other neurological involvement. Other times there is no history of neurological impairment. Sometimes neuropsychological batteries are

Table 7–3. Medical Assessment of Ability to do Work-Related Activities (Mental)

NAME OF INDIVIDUAL   SOCIAL SECURITY NUMBER

Aaron Moss

To determine this individual's ability to do <u>work-related activities on a day-to-day basis in a regular work setting</u>, please give us an assessment—BASED ON YOUR EXAMINATION—of how the individual's mental/emotional capabilities are affected <u>by the impairment(s)</u>. Consider the medical history, the chronicity of findings (or lack thereof), and the expected duration of any work-related limitations, but not the individual's age, sex, or work experience.

For each activity shown below:

   (1)   <u>Describe the individual's ability to perform the activity according to the following terms:</u>

        <u>Unlimited or Very Good</u> – Ability to function in this area is more than satisfactory.
        <u>Good</u> – Ability to function in this area is limited but satisfactory.
        <u>Fair</u> – Ability to function in this area is seriously limited, but not precluded.
        <u>Poor or None</u> – No useful ability to function in this area.

   (2)   <u>Identify the particular medical or clinical findings (i.e., mental status examination, behavior, intelligence test results, symptoms) which support your assessment of any limitations.</u>
        IT IS IMPORTANT THAT YOU RELATE PARTICULAR MEDICAL FINDINGS TO ANY ASSESSED LIMITATION IN CAPACITY; THE USEFULNESS OF YOUR ASSESSMENT DEPENDS ON THE EXTENT TO WHICH YOU DO THIS.

I. MAKING OCCUPATIONAL ADJUSTMENTS

Check the blocks representing the individual's ability to adjust to a job, and complete item 9.

	Unlimited/ Very Good	Good	Fair	Poor or None		Unlimited/ Very Good	Good	Fair	Poor or None
1. Follow work Rules.	✓				5. Interact with supervisor(s).	✓			
2. Relate to co-workers	✓				6. Deal with work stresses.			✓	
3. Deal with the public.			✓		7. Function independently.				✓
4. Use judgment			✓		8. Maintain attention/ concentration.			✓	

   9.   Describe any limitations and include the medical/clinical findings that support this assessment.

      His occupational adjustment is adequate for unskilled work. He has the ability emotionally and intellectually to do such work, but from a medical standpoint, his occupational adjustment has been poor because he has so many complaints.

II. MAKING PERFORMANCE ADJUSTMENTS

Check the blocks representing the individual's ability to adjust to a job, and complete item 4.

	Unlimited/ Very Good	Good	Fair	Poor or None
1. Understand, remember, and carry out complex job instructions.				✓
2. Understand, remember, and carry out detailed, but not complex job instructions.				✓
3. Understand, remember, and carry out simple job instructions.	✓			

Table 7–3. (*continued*)

4. Describe any limitations and include the medical/clinical findings that support this assessment; e.g., intellectual ability, thought organization, memory, comprehension, etc.

Intellectual ability, thought organization, memory, and comprehension are all at the low average range in the high 80s. He has difficulty with complex material so he is concrete and literal.

III. MAKING PERSONAL-SOCIAL ADJUSTMENTS

Check the blocks representing the individual's ability to adjust personally and socially:

	Unlimited/ Very Good	Good	Fair	Poor or None
1. Maintain personal appearance.	✓			
2. Behave in an emotionally stable manner.		✓		
3. Relate predictably in social situations.		✓		
4. Demonstrate reliability.		✓		

5. Describe any limitations and include the medical/clinical findings that support this assessment.

Personal and social adjustment is somewhat marginal. He lives with his parents and is dependent.

IV. OTHER WORK-RELATED ACTIVITIES

State any other work-related activities which are affected by the impairment, and indicate how the activities are affected. What are the medical/clinical findings that support this assessment?

Occupational and work related activities are affected by his medical complaints which involve the left hand and right shoulder. These complaints are somewhat exacerbated by psychological factors because he may abuse alcohol and he underestimates his ability to cope with adversity. Those physical activities which he can probably objectively engage in are likely to be difficult for him because he focuses on medical complaints and seems very motivated to be disabled at this time. His report of physical symptoms is probably extreme at times even though there is little doubt that he does experience some degree of the symptoms he relates. This is someone with low average academic ability and a low average IQ who has a problem with anything complex. There is no history of psychiatric disturbance, but he can be described as someone who is nervous and prone to alcohol abuse. He has no retraining ability involving anything academic and could only do the type of unskilled work he has done in the past.

V. CAPABILITY TO MANAGE BENEFITS

Can the individual manage benefits in his or her own best interest?　Yes (✓)　No ( )

_____
Physicians Signature

3/11/95
Date

[Form SSA–1152 (4/85) Test]

ordered on claimants who have back pain or peripheral involvement with the extremities but no history of brain injury. It is possible that neuropsychological testing was ordered on this claimant to document possible damage from alcohol use.

The Luria indicated he had problems with complex planning, handling novel problems, and dealing with sequential analysis, integration, and spatial verbal concepts. He was usually confused by complex material, but he did fine with simple material. Receptive speech and rhythm were both elevated, suggesting he had relatively poor concentration. The report indicated that he was concrete in thinking, had trouble with categories and classifications, and had mild elevations on several of the scales. Basically, the Luria supported the other measures of academic and intellectual functioning, namely, that this applicant was not going to benefit from much academic retraining and that he was qualified for unskilled work not involving much literacy. Although by definition the Luria was abnormal, he still did well enough on the testing to handle most simple material in a job setting.

In this report, I did not have to say whether this applicant was or was not brain damaged. What was important for Social Security purposes was to report the neuropsychological test results relative to demonstrated skills or skill deficits. In reporting neuropsychological evaluations, it is a waste of time to focus on minor differences in left- and right-hand functioning, to theorize about what area of the brain is affected, or to focus on minor deterioration from premorbid ability. What is of interest is the claimant's functional ability and the neuropsychological examination should be approached as a measure of this. If the patient doesn't understand language because of severe aphasia, that is noteworthy. If finger-tapping is not what you would expect on the dominant hand, that should be mentioned, but the focus should be on whether this indicates impairment in the applicant's ability to perform unskilled work.

This applicant, like many Social Security applicants, was physically preoccupied and reported feelings of nervousness and anxiety, but denied mental health problems. The extremely elevated MMPI scores in this case were very typical of non-psychiatric claimants. The MCMI was also high on several scales, but the Beck did not show significant depression. It is often the case that physically preoccupied claimants can have very elevated MMPI scores, and yet score very low on the Beck Depression Inventory.

This claimant's personal and social adjustment were marginal. He was dependent, lived with his parents, and had lived this way most of his life. I gave him diagnoses of alcohol abuse, psychological factors affecting physical condition, and adjustment disorder. None of those are serious psychiatric disturbances and none would meet the criteria for disability. On the Medical Assessment form I did indicate that he had serious limitations functioning independently and rated him with poor to no ability to understand, remember, and carry out complex or detailed job instructions, a finding that was based primarily on the Luria test results.

I have no idea whether this claimant was found to be disabled or not, but I do believe this comprehensive evaluation was helpful to the law judge in making his decision.

When testifying as a medical expert for an administrative law judge, the psychologist may be asked to complete the Psychiatric Review Technique form (see Table 7–4), which addresses the paragraph A and B criteria.

Table 7–4. Psychiatric Review Technique

Name		SSN	

Assessment is For:	☐ Current Evaluation	☐ 12 Mo. After Onset:_____
☐ Date Last Insured: _____	☐ Other: _____ to _____	
Reviewer's Signature	Date	

PRIVACY ACT NOTICE: The information requested on this form is authorized by section 223 and section 1633 of the Social Security Act. The information provided will be used in making a decision on this claim. Completion of this form is mandatory in disability claims involving mental impairments. Failure to complete this form may result in a delay in processing the claim. Information furnished on this form may be disclosed by the Social Security Administration to another person or governmental agency only with respect to Social Security programs and to comply with federal laws requiring the exchange of information between Social Security and another agency.

1. **MEDICAL SUMMARY**

    A. **Medical Disposition(s):**

    1. ☐ No Medically Determinable Impairment

    2. ☐ Impairment(s) Not Severe

    3. ☐ Meets Listing _____ (Cite Listing and subsection)

    4. ☐ Equals Listing _____ (Cite Listing and subsection)

    5. ☐ Impairment Severe But Not Expected to Last 12 Months

    6. ☐ RFC Assessment Necessary (i.e., a severe impairment is present which does not meet or equal a listed impairment)

    7. ☐ Referral to Another Medical Specialty (necessary when there is a coexisting nonmental impairment) (Except for OHA reviewers)

    8. ☐ Insufficient Medical Evidence (i.e., a programmatic documentation deficiency is present) (Except for OHA reviewers)

    B. **Category(ies) Upon Which the Medical Disposition(s) is Based:**

    1. ☐ 12.02 Organic Mental Disorders

    2. ☐ 12.03 Schizophrenic, Paranoid and other Psychotic Disorders

    3. ☐ 12.04 Affective Disorders

    4. ☐ 12.05 Mental Retardation and Autism

    5. ☐ 12.06 Anxiety Related Disorders

    6. ☐ 12.07 Somatoform Disorders

    7. ☐ 12.08 Personality Disorder

    8. ☐ 12.09 Substance Addiction Disorders

II. **REVIEWER'S NOTES (Except OHA reviewers. OHA reviewers should record the subject information in the body and findings of their decision.):** A. Record below the pertinent signs, symptoms, findings, functional limitations, and the effects of treatment contained in the case, B. Remarks (any information the reviewer may wish to communicate which is not covered elsewhere in the form, e.g., duration situations).

III. DOCUMENTATION OF FACTORS THAT EVIDENCE THE DISORDER (COMMENT ON EACH BROAD CATEGORY OF DISORDER.)

A. 12.02 Organic Mental Disorders

☐ No evidence of a sign or symptom CLUSTER or SYNDROME which appropriately fits with this diagnostic category. (Some features appearing below may be present in the case but they are presumed to belong in another disorder and are rated in that category.)

☐ Psychological or behavioral abnormalities associated with a dysfunction of the brain. . . . as evidenced by at least one of the following:

PRESENT-ABSENT-INSUFFICIENT EVIDENCE

1. ☐ ☐ ☐   Disorientation to time and place

2. ☐ ☐ ☐   Memory impairment

3. ☐ ☐ ☐   Perceptual or thinking disturbances

4. ☐ ☐ ☐   Change in personality

5. ☐ ☐ ☐   Disturbance in mood

6. ☐ ☐ ☐   Emotional lability and impairment in impulse control

7. ☐ ☐ ☐   Loss of measured intellectual ability of at least 15 I.Q. points from premorbid levels or overall impairment index clearly within the severely impaired range on neuropsychological testing, e.g., the Luria-Nebraska, Halstead-Reitan, etc.

8. ☐ ☐ ☐   Other _____

B. 12.03 Schizophrenic, Paranoid and other Psychotic Disorders

☐ No evidence of a sign or symptom CLUSTER or SYNDROME which appropriately fits with this diagnostic category. (Some features appearing below may be present in the case but they are presumed to belong in another disorder and are rated in that category.)

☐ Psychotic features and deterioration that are persistent (continuous or intermittent), as evidenced by at least one of the following:

PRESENT-ABSENT-INSUFFICIENT EVIDENCE

1. ☐ ☐ ☐   Delusions or hallucinations

2. ☐ ☐ ☐   Catatonic or other grossly disorganized behavior

3. ☐ ☐ ☐   Incoherence, loosening of associations, illogical thinking, or poverty of content of speech if associated with one of the following:

    a. ☐ Blunt affect, or

    b. ☐ Flat affect, or

    c. ☐ Inappropriate affect

4. ☐ ☐ ☐   Emotional withdrawal and/or isolation

5. ☐ ☐ ☐   Other _____

C. 12.04 Affective Disorders

☐ No evidence of a sign or symptom CLUSTER or SYNDROME which appropriately fits with this diagnostic category. (Some features appearing below may be present

☐   in the case but they are presumed to belong in another disorder and are rated in that category.)

☐   Disturbance of mood, accompanied by a full or partial manic or depressive syndrome, as evidenced by at least one of the following:

PRESENT-ABSENT-INSUFFICIENT EVIDENCE

1. ☐ ☐ ☐   Depressive syndrome characterized by at least four of the following:

   a. ☐   Anhedonia or pervasive loss of interest in almost all activities, or

   b. ☐   Appetite disturbance with change in weight, or

   c. ☐   Sleep disturbance, or

   d. ☐   Psychomotor agitation or retardation, or

   e. ☐   Decreased energy, or

   f. ☐   Feelings of guilt or worthlessness, or

   g. ☐   Difficulty concentrating or thinking, or

   h. ☐   Thoughts of suicide, or

   I. ☐   Hallucinations, delusions or paranoid thinking.

2. ☐ ☐ ☐   Manic syndrome characterized by at least three of the following:

   a. ☐   Hyperactivity, or

   b. ☐   Pressures of speech, or

   c. ☐   Flight of ideas, or

   d. ☐   Inflated self-esteem, or

   e. ☐   Decreased need for sleep, or

   f. ☐   Easy distractability, or

   g. ☐   Involvement in activities that have a high probability of painful consequences which are not recognized, or

   h. ☐   Hallucinations, delusions or paranoid thinking

3. ☐ ☐ ☐   Bipolar syndrome with a history of episodic periods manifested by the full symptomatic picture of both manic and depressive syndromes (and currently characterized by either or both syndromes)

4. ☐ ☐ ☐   Other _____

D.12.05 Mental Retardation and Autism

☐   No evidence of a sign or symptom CLUSTER or SYNDROME which appropriately fits with this diagnostic category. (Some features appearing below may be present in the case but they are presumed to belong in another disorder and are rated in that category.)

☐   Significantly subaverage general intellectual functioning with deficits in adaptive behavior initially manifested during the developmental period (before age 22), or pervasive developmental disorder characterized by social and significant communicative deficits originating in the developmental period, as evidenced by at least one of the following:

PRESENT-ABSENCE-INSUFFICIENT EVIDENCE

1. ☐ ☐ ☐ Mental incapacity evidenced by dependence upon others for personal needs (e.g., toileting, eating, dressing or bathing) and inability to follow directions, such that the use of standardized measures of intellectual functioning is precluded*

2. ☐ ☐ ☐ A valid verbal, performance, or full scale I.Q. of 59 or less*

3. ☐ ☐ ☐ A valid verbal, performance, or full scale I.Q. of 60 to 69 inclusive and a physical or other mental impairment imposing additional and significant work-related limitation of function*

4. ☐ ☐ ☐ A valid verbal, performance, or full scale I.Q. of 60 to 69 inclusive or in the case of autism, gross deficits of social and communicative skills*

5. ☐ ☐ ☐ Other _____

*NOTE: Items 1, 2, 3, and 4 correspond to Listings 12.05A, 12.05B, 12.05C, and 12.04D, respectively.

E. 12.06 Anxiety Related Disorders

☐ No evidence of a sign or symptom CLUSTER or SYNDROME which appropriately fits with this diagnostic category. (Some features appearing below may be present in the case but they are presumed to belong in another disorder and are rated in that category.)

☐ Anxiety as the predominant disturbance or anxiety experienced in the attempt to master symptoms, as evidenced by at least one of the following:

PRESENT-ABSENT-INSUFFICIENT EVIDENCE

1. ☐ ☐ ☐ Generalized persistent anxiety accompanied by three of the following:

    a. ☐ Motor tension, or

    b. ☐ Autonomic hyperactivity, or

    c. ☐ Apprehensive expectation, or

    d. ☐ Vigilance and scanning

2. ☐ ☐ ☐ A persistent irrational fear of a specific object, activity or situation which results in a compelling desire to avoid the dreaded object, activity, or situation.

3. ☐ ☐ ☐ Recurrent severe panic attacks manifested by a sudden unpredictable onset of intense apprehension, fear, terror, and sense of impending doom occurring on the average of at least once a week

4. ☐ ☐ ☐ Recurrent obsessions or compulsions which are a source of marked distress

5. ☐ ☐ ☐ Recurrent and intrusive recollections of a traumatic experience, which are a source of marked distress

6. ☐ ☐ ☐ Other _____

F. 12.07 Somatoform Disorders

☐ No evidence of a sign or symptom CLUSTER or SYNDROME which appropriately fits with this diagnostic category. (Some features appearing below may be present in the case but they are presumed to belong in another disorder and are rated in that category.)

☐ Physical symptoms for which there are no demonstrable organic findings or known physiological mechanisms, as evidenced by at least one of the following:

PRESENT-ABSENT-INSUFFICIENT EVIDENCE

1. ☐ ☐ ☐   A history of multiple physical symptoms of several years duration beginning before age 30, that have caused the individual to take medicine frequently, see a physician often and alter life patterns significantly

2. ☐ ☐ ☐   Persistent nonorganic disturbance of one of the following:

    a. ☐ Vision, or

    b. ☐ Speech, or

    c. ☐ Hearing, or

    d. ☐ Use of a limb, or

    e. ☐ Movement and its control (e.g., coordination disturbances, psychogenic seizures, akinesia, dyskinesia), or

    f. ☐ Sensation (e.g., diminished or heightened)

3. ☐ ☐ ☐   Unrealistic interpretation of physical signs or sensations associated with the preoccupation or belief that one has a serious disease or injury

4. ☐ ☐ ☐   Other _____

G.12.08 Personality Disorders

☐ No evidence of a sign or symptom CLUSTER or SYNDROME which appropriately fits with this diagnostic category. (Some features appearing below may be present in the case but they are presumed to belong in another disorder and are rated in that category.)

☐ Inflexible and maladaptive personality traits which cause either significant impairment in social or occupational functioning or subjective distress, as evidenced by at least one of the following:

PRESENT-ABSENT-INSUFFICIENT EVIDENCE

1. ☐ ☐ ☐   Seclusiveness or autistic thinking

2. ☐ ☐ ☐   Pathologically inappropriate suspiciousness or hostility

3. ☐ ☐ ☐   Oddities of thought, perception, speech and behavior

4. ☐ ☐ ☐   Persistent disturbances of mood or affect

5. ☐ ☐ ☐   Pathological dependence, passivity, or aggressivity

6. ☐ ☐ ☐   Intense and unstable interpersonal relationships and impulsive and damaging behavior

7. ☐ ☐ ☐   Other _____

H.12.09 Substance Addiction Disorders: Behavioral changes or physical changes associated with the regular use of substances that affect the central nervous system.

Present   —   Absent   —   Insufficient Evidence

☐   ☐   ☐

If present, evaluate under one or more of the most closely applicable listings:

1. ☐   Listing 12.02—Organic mental disorders*

2. ☐   Listing 12.04—Affective disorders*

3. ☐   Listing 12.06—Anxiety disorders*

4. ☐   Listing 12.08—Personality disorders*

5. ☐   Listing 11.14—Peripheral neuropathies*

6. ☐   Listing 5.05—Liver damage*

7. ☐   Listing 5.04—Gastritis*

8. ☐   Listing 5.08—Pancreatitis*

9. ☐   Listing 11.02 or 11.03—Seizures*

10. ☐   Other _____

NOTE: Items, 1, 2, 3, 4, 5, 6, 7, 8, and 9 correspond to Listings 12.09A, 12.09B, 12.09C, 12.09D, 12.09E, 12.09F, 12.09G, 12.09H, and 12.09I, respectively. If items 1, 2, 3, or 4 are checked, only the numbered items in subsections IIIA, IIIC, IIIE, or IIIG of the form need be checked. The first two blocks under the disorder heading in those subsections need not be checked.

IV. RATING OF IMPAIRMENT SEVERITY

A. "B" Criteria of the Listings

Indicate to what degree the following functional limitations (which are found in paragraph B of listings 12.02–12.04 and 12.06–12.08 and paragraph D of 12.05) exist as a result of the individual's mental disorder(s).

NOTE: Items 3 and 4 below are more than measures of frequency. Describe in part II of this form (Reviewer's Notes) the duration and effects of the deficiencies (item 3) or episodes (item 4). Please read carefully the instructions for the completion of this section.

Specify the listing(s) (i.e., 12.02 through 12.09) under which the items below are being rated_____.

FUNCTIONAL
LIMITATION   DEGREE OF LIMITATION

					Insufficient Evidence
1. Restriction of Activities of Daily Living	None ☐	Slight ☐	Moderate ☐	Marked* ☐	Extreme ☐ / ☐
2. Difficulties in Maintaining Social Functioning	None ☐	Slight ☐	Moderate ☐	Marked* ☐	Extreme ☐ / ☐
3. Deficiencies of Concentration, Persistence or Pace Resulting in Failure to Complete Tasks in a Timely Manner (in work settings or elsewhere)	Never ☐	Seldom ☐	Often ☐	Frequent* ☐	Constant ☐ / ☐

	Never	Once or Twice	Repeated* (three or more)	Continual	Insufficient Evidence
4. Episodes of Deterioration or Decompensation in Work or Work-Like Settings Which Cause the Individual to Withdraw from that Situation or to Experience Exacerbation of Signs and Symptoms (which may Include Deterioration of Adaptive Behaviors)	☐	☐	☐	☐	☐

B. Summary of Functional Limitation Rating for "B" Criteria

Indicate the number of the above functional limitations manifested at the degree of limitation that satisfies the listings. ☐ (The number in the box must be at least 2 to satisfy the requirements of paragraph B in Listings 12.02, 12.03, 12.04, and 12.06 and paragraph D in 12.05; and at least 3 to satisfy the requirements in paragraph B in Listings 12.07 and 12.08.)

*Degree of limitation that satisfies the Listings; Extreme, Constant and Continual also satisfy that requirement.

C. "C" Criteria of the Listings

1. If 12.03 Disorder (Schizophrenic, etc.) and in Full or Partial Remission

NOTE: Item b. below is more than a measure of frequency. Describe in part II of this form (Reviewer's Notes) the duration and effects of the episodes. Please read carefully the instructions for the completion of this section.

Present	Absent	Insufficient Evidence	
a. ☐	☐	☐	Medically documented history of one or more episodes of acute symptoms, signs and functional limitations which at the time met the requirements in A and B of 12.03, although these symptoms or signs are currently attenuated by medication or psychosocial support.
b ☐	☐	☐	Repeated episodes of deterioration or decompensation in situations which cause the individual to withdraw from the situation or to experience exacerbation of signs or symptoms (which may include deterioration of adaptive behaviors).
c. ☐	☐	☐	Documented current history of two or more years of inability to function outside of a highly supportive living situation.

(For the requirement in paragraph C of 12.03 to be satisfied, either a. and b. or a. and c. must be checked as present.)

2. If 12.06 Disorder (Anxiety Related)

Present	Absent	Insufficient Evidence	
☐	☐	☐	Symptoms resulting in *complete* inability to function independently outside the area of one's home.

(If present is checked, the requirements in paragraph C of 12.06 are satisfied.)

[Form SSA-2506-BK (1/90)]

SSI DETERMINATION FOR CHILDREN

Children, as well as adults, are eligible for disability benefits under the SSI program. SSI benefits for children have been controversial and are sometimes referred to as "crazy checks." As always, it is important for consultative examiners not to get involved in any political, social, or moral arguments about SSI for children, but to focus on what they know best—IQ tests, developmental scores, mental status examinations, and behavioral assessments.

The qualifying mental disorders for children are: organic mental disorders (112.02), schizophrenia, delusional, paranoid, schizoaffective, and other psychotic disorders (112.03), mood disorders (112.04), mental retardation (112.05), anxiety disorders (112.06), somatoform, eating, and tic disorders (112.07), personality disorders (112.08), psychoactive substance abuse (112.09), autistic disorder and other pervasive developmental disorders (112.10), attention deficit–hyperactivity disorder (112.11), and developmental and emotional disorders of the newborn and younger infants (112.12). These listings are from the handbook entitled *Disability Evaluation under Social Security*, published by the U.S. Department of Health and Human Services.

To qualify for benefits, a child must first receive a diagnosis of one of these disorders, that is, meet the paragraph A criteria, similar to determinations in adult cases. After this is satisfied, the SSA medical professional or law judge must assess functional limitations, the paragraph B criteria. As in adult cases, the functional restrictions in paragraph B must be the result of the mental disorder in paragraph A. A child is found to be disabled when the criteria of paragraphs A and B are both satisfied. A child will not automatically get SSI benefits for attention deficit disorder (ADD), for example, unless the child is impaired in at least two functional areas. If a child is well-controlled for ADD, SSI will most likely not be awarded. The exception to this general requirement of fulfilling both A and B criteria is in cases of mental retardation and developmental and emotional disorders of the newborn and younger infants. In such cases, there are no paragraph B criteria to be satisfied. There are no paragraph C criteria for psychoses or anxiety disorders, as there are with adults.

Children ages 1–3 will meet the criteria of paragraph B if they have at least one of the following:

1. Gross or fine motor development at a level acquired by children no more than one-half the child's chronological age,
2. Cognitive and communicative functioning at a level acquired by children no more than one-half the child's chronological age,
3. Social functioning at a level no more than one-half the child's chronological age, or
4. Attainment of development or function generally acquired by children no more than two-thirds of the child's chronological age in two or more areas covered by 1, 2, or 3.

For children ages 3–18, two of the following paragraph B listings must be met:

1. Marked impairment in age-appropriate cognitive communication functions,
2. Marked impairment in age-appropriate social functioning,
3. Marked impairment in personal behavioral function, and
4. Deficiencies of concentration, persistence, or pace resulting in frequent failure to complete tasks in a timely manner.

The handbook *Disability Evaluation under Social Security* contains more detail on both A and B criteria for the determination of eligibility. Although it is useful to know these criteria, making the determination of disability is the job of either the DDS medical professional or the law judge, not the psychologist doing the CE. If the psychologist is serving as a medical expert to an administrative law judge in the appeal process, the judge may ask the psychologist to complete an Individual Functional Assessment form similar to the Medical Assessment form completed on adults. The Individual Functional Assessment form used by one DDS office is shown below (see Table 7–5). The form asks for ratings in the areas of cognitive development, communicative development, motor development, social development, and personal/behavioral development. The ratings are: no evidence of limitation, less than moderate, moderate, marked, and extreme limitation. These forms may vary from state to state, but all of them ask for similar ratings, so that the judge can make a determination of functional impairment under the criteria of paragraph B.

The CE for children will most often request a measure of intelligence or developmental ability. Tests that are commonly ordered include the Battelle Developmental Inventory, Bayley Scale of Infant Development–Second Edition, McCarthy Scales of Children's Abilities, Stanford–Binet, WISC-III. Mental status examinations are also ordered. What follow are typical consultative examinations performed on children.

Case 32

In this case the Bayley Scale of Infant Development was ordered on a child less than 2 years old. There was severe developmental delay in both motor and mental areas.

Psychological Evaluation Report

Name: Jennifer Irwin
(Required identifying information, date of testing, etc.)

Tests Administered
Bayley Scale of Infant Development–Second Edition (BSID-II)

Table 7–5. Individual Functional Assessment
Age 3 to Attainment of Age 16

Claimant: _____ Social Security Number: _____

Assessment is for: [   ] Current Evaluation   [   ] Date 12 Months After Onset _____

                  [   ] Other _____ to _____

A. Identify any medically determinable impairment(s): _____
_____
_____

B. Describe how the impairment(s) affects the child's development and performance of age-appropriate activities in the following domains and behaviors. Summarize the evidence that supports your descriptions of functional limitations. Indicate the level of severity of functional impairment in the developmental domains and behaviors.

   1. COGNITIVE DEVELOPMENT/FUNCTION: (Check One)
     [   ] No Evidence of Limitation   [   ] Less Than Moderate   [   ] Moderate
        [   ] Marked   [   ] Extreme

   2. COMMUNICATIVE DEVELOPMENT/FUNCTION: (Check One)
     [   ] No Evidence of Limitation   [   ] Less Than Moderate   [   ] Moderate
        [   ] Marked   [   ] Extreme

   3. MOTOR DEVELOPMENT/FUNCTION: (Check One)
     [   ] No Evidence of Limitation   [   ] Less Than Moderate   [   ] Moderate
        [   ] Marked   [   ] Extreme

   4. SOCIAL DEVELOPMENT/FUNCTION: (Check One)
     [   ] No Evidence of Limitation   [   ] Less Than Moderate   [   ] Moderate
        [   ] Marked   [   ] Extreme

   5. PERSONAL/BEHAVIORAL DEVELOPMENT/FUNCTION: (Check One)
     [   ] No Evidence of Limitation   [   ] Less Than Moderate   [   ] Moderate
        [   ] Marked   [   ] Extreme

   6. CONCENTRATION, PERSISTENCE AND PACE: (Check One)
     [   ] No Evidence of Limitation   [   ] Less Than Moderate   [   ] Moderate
        [   ] Marked   [   ] Extreme

Background Information

Jennifer is a 21-month-old white female who is a fraternal twin. She was born about one month premature. She has a seizure disorder and is taking phenobarbital and Dilantin. The seizures appear to her mother as a stiffening reaction. According to her mother, Jennifer is far behind her twin. She is not eating solid food. She has no language and is not yet walking by herself. She has frequent ear infections.

Test Results
The Motor Index was <50 at the 11-month level and the Mental Index was <50 at the 8-month level. This is a severe developmental delay in both areas. On the Motor scale, she is able to stand and she can walk with help. She takes one or two steps, at the most, before she stops and falls. She was not able to pass any items beyond walking on the Motor scale.

On the Mental scale she was also significantly delayed. She could not point to any pictures I identified in the booklet and she did not place the pegs in the board. She was unable to build a tower of cubes or place the circle piece in the pink board. She did not close a container and she was unable to put 9 cubes in a cup. She did not imitate any words or vocalize different vowel sounds. She did not scribble or place the blue block in the form board. She did not push the car in imitation and she never tried to secure 3 cubes when offered to her. She did not make gestures for her wants and needs. She never rang the bell purposely. She could not cooperate in a game, imitate verbalizations, attend to scribbling, or follow instructions. She was able to place one peg in the peg board. She put 3 cubes in a cup and she was able to play with the ring and suspend it by the string. She was able to lift the cup by the handle. She looks for a fallen spoon when it is dropped, transfers objects from hand to hand, and smiles and plays.

Summary
Jennifer had a Mental Developmental Index of <50, which is at the eight-month level, and a Motor Development Index of <50, at the 11-month level. She is significantly behind in both areas. She has a seizure disorder, which probably accounts for her developmental delay. She is behind her peers and cannot engage in age-appropriate behavior.

Discussion
On infant evaluations, the children are sometimes so grossly impaired and the impairments are so obvious that one may wonder why the children were referred for evaluation. CEs are ordered because the experts in the DDS office never see the claimants. They do not know these children except through the records. They must have an assessment by an independent source who is able to report test scores and report on each child's functioning.

In this case, medical evidence received from the DDS office indicated that Jennifer had a seizure disorder and was taking phenobarbital and Dilantin. Prescribed medications should always be included in the report, as well as the parents' concerns about the child. This 21-month-old was not using single words and was not walking. Both the motor and developmental index were less than 50.

Brief reports are sufficient in cases such as these. Age equivalencies are always reported, since the DDS office and the regulations rely on them to a great extent. While we may be more interested and accustomed to using standard scores to report results, age equivalencies are critical for the evaluation of developmental delays and determination of benefits under Social Security. If there is a motor or cognitive delay equal to or greater than one-half the child's chronological age, the child will qualify for benefits.

Case 33

This case is an example of a young child whose mental development was lagging behind her motor development.

Psychological Evaluation Report

Name: Tanesha Carpenter
(Required identifying information, date of testing, etc.)

Tests Administered
Bayley Scale of Infant Development–Second Edition (BSID-II)

Background Information
Tanesha is a 2-year-old black female brought to the office by her mother. She is not talking, except to say "mom." She has been walking since she was 14 months old. She is eating table food, but her mother has to feed her. She drinks from a cup with a cover on it. She is not very independent and is inseparable from her mother. At 2 years of age, she is not venturing out or exploring much. During the evaluation she was extremely shy and fearful. She did not utter a word and clung to her mother. She participated only reluctantly and slowly in the test as the items were presented to her.

Test Results
The Bayley Motor Scale Development Index was 73, which is an age equivalent of 19 months. (The raw score was 77.) She received a Mental Development Index of less than 50, which is a significant delay and is equivalent to the average 12-month-old child. (Her raw score was 90.)

On the Motor scale she began walking at 14 months and she is able to walk with good coordination. She can throw objects, squat while standing, walk sideways and backward, and grasp objects. She is able to walk up and down stairs with help and support. She did not have the ability to stand alone on the right and left foot. She does not walk on her tiptoes.

On the Mental Scale, Tanesha was able to lift the cup by the handle, look for objects that leave her visual field, attend to scribbling, and pull a string adaptively to get the ring. She did not verbalize any words. She retained 2 or 3 cubes when offered to her. She turned the pages of a book and put several cubes in a cup. She removed the lid from a box, patted the toy in imitation, removed the pellets from a bottle, and put the pegs in the form board. She was able to close a round container, put the forms in the pink form board, and build a tower of several cubes.

She did not point to 2 pictures when asked to point to objects that were named. She listens selectively to language, but does not say anything. She never used 2 words appropriately. She does not use language to make her wants known. She would not show her shoes or any body parts. She did not imitate crayon strokes. She did not retrieve the toy from the clear box.

Summary

Tanesha had a Mental Development Index of less than 50, which is significantly delayed. Her Motor Development Index was 73, which is also low at the 19-month level, since she is 2 years old. She is not engaging in age-appropriate behavior, because she is not speaking and she has less problem-solving ability than her 2-year-old peers.

Discussion

This 2-year-old female was delayed in walking and she had some symptoms of separation anxiety, since she would not leave her mother's side. The Motor Development Index of 77 was delayed, but with the motor age equivalency of 19 months, she would not be judged to be significantly delayed for DDS purposes. On the other hand, the Mental Development Index was 12 months, half her chronological age. This child probably qualified for benefits on that basis.

It is important to remember that infant developmental evaluation is an assessment at only one point in time. Children like Tanesha usually improve by the time they are 5 or 6 years old. Once language develops, scores improve dramatically. The challenge for DDS is to reevaluate these children, because they may look like entirely different children when they are in kindergarten or first grade. This is not something the consultant has to worry about, since his or her job is to measure the developmental progress at the time the child is referred.

At times evaluations are ordered on young children using the Battelle Developmental Inventory, which is different from the Bayley. The Bayley relies only on direct observation and performance of the infant. The Battelle relies on some performance items, but many of the items are dependent on the parents' interview, much like the Vineland. The problem is that a compensation-seeking parent can minimize the child's ability on the Battelle.

Another problem with the Battelle is that the norm groups are based on age and this can dramatically affect the child's percentile rank and standard scores. For example, a child who is 35 months and 25 days old will fall into one normative group. Let's say that child receives a score of 100, which is average performance for his normative group. After turning 36 months old in a couple days, the child would fall into another normative group. The same test scores could then result in a standard score 30–40 points lower, simply based on the new normative group. When this happens, I point it out in the report. Because of this problem, it is particularly important to report age equivalencies on the Battelle, since these are not affected by the various normative group categories used to determine standard scores and percentiles.

Case 34

This case shows the use of the Battelle on a 2-year, 10-month-old child.

Psychological Evaluation Report

Name: Joseph Pruitt
(Required identifying information, date of testing, etc.)

Tests Administered
Battelle Development Inventory (BDI)

Background Information
Joseph is a 2-year, 10-month-old black male brought to the office by his mother. She is concerned by Joseph's behavior, particularly his aggressiveness at daycare. Joseph was well-groomed, had good hygiene, and was a normal-appearing child. He was well-behaved during this particular evaluation. He is the youngest of three children; his siblings are 13 and 15. Ms. Pruitt is a single parent and is working. Joseph attends the Little Tykes daycare program.

Earlier this year Joseph hit another child at daycare with an object, causing him to have a couple of stitches. Ms. Pruitt said that when Joseph is frustrated, he can be aggressive and will try to fight her. Once he stabbed her with a pair of scissors, although he did not cause an injury. She said he does not sleep well and is up and down all night. In fact, she made his room safe and locks the room when he goes to bed so he does not wander around during the middle of the night.

Joseph's mother had no complaints about his development and indicated that he can say almost anything he wants to. I observed throughout the evaluation that Joseph had no problem with communication. He expresses himself without any difficulty and speaks in full sentences.

Test Results
The BDI scores were as follows:

	Percentile Rank	Standard Score	Age Equivalent
Personal–Social Total	64	105	32 months
Adaptive Total	65	106	34 months
Gross Motor Score	61	104	37 months
Fine Motor Score	51	100	30 months
Motor Total	52	101	31 months
Receptive Speech	19	87	23 months
Expressive Speech	26	90	27 months
Communication Total	21	88	24 months
Cognitive Total	22	88	24 months
BDI Total	44	98	30 months

The total BDI was at the 44th percentile rank; the standard score of 98 is average. His cognitive and communication ability were low average, but the scores for motor ability, adaptive, and personal social functioning were all average. There were no significant deficits on any of the BDI domains. Joseph is toilet trained, eats with utensils, participates in dressing himself, follows instructions, and is able to run, jump, and negotiate stairs. He speaks in sentences and understands most language. He had equally adequate fine motor and gross motor functions.

Summary

Joseph had BDI scores that were in the average range overall. He was low average for cognitive and communication ability, but there were no deficits and he is able to engage in all appropriate daily living activities and behaviors. Ms. Pruitt's report of his aggressive behavior was judged to be reliable and valid, so his diagnosis at this time is Disruptive Behavior Disorder NOS (312.9). Joseph is only 2 years, 10 months in age, and although he has aggressive behavior, I think it may be too early to diagnose him with Attention Deficit–Hyperactivity Disorder (ADHD). He may also be oppositional, but I think the most accurate diagnosis is Disruptive Behavior Disorder, which is primarily aggression. His mother may need some parent management assistance to manage Joseph more effectively.

Discussion

Evaluations of infants and children should always indicate whether the child is able to engage in age-appropriate daily living activities, behavior, and communication. Since this child had no deficits in these areas, he was probably denied disability, but as the evaluating psychologist, I do not know that for certain. Developmentally he was a normal child with good language skills.

    Many children who are seen for DDS evaluation have behavioral disorders and are either oppositional or conduct disorders. In this case, the mother had more complaints about her child's behavior than developmental functioning. Based on her report, he was diagnosed with a behavior problem and it was suggested that she needed parent management training.

    As always, it is important to take a realistic and moderate approach to evaluating these children. It is important not to overdiagnose them. There is some tendency among psychologists to diagnose every child that is seen, especially since the advent of private psychiatric hospitals. Some examiners might say this child had ADHD, a pervasive childhood development disorder, or some other more serious diagnosis. However, what I saw in this 2-year, 10-month-old child was disruptive behavior, primarily aggression.

    Some of the most common diagnoses for DDS evaluations are parent–child relationship problems (a V-code), oppositional defiant disorders, conduct disorders, or other disruptive behavior diagnoses. If a child is acting out, one of these diagnoses should be made. Diagnoses like these are more parsimonious than anxiety disorder, depressive disorder, or even ADHD, which is often overdiagnosed. If you can recognize and diagnose a simple behavior disorder, you will be recognized by the DDS office as someone who makes appropriate diagnoses rather than someone who has an agenda that all children are terribly sick and in need of treatment or not sick at all.

The most common type of CE for children is intellectual testing. Doing intelligence testing on children is a straightforward matter, as it is with adults.

Case 35

In this evaluation, the purchase order for the CE asked for a WISC-R and asked the examiner to "comment on his speech." Prior testing had not resulted in consistent, valid results that the DDS office could use to make its determination.

Psychological Evaluation Report

Name: Dillon Rader
(Required identifying information, date of testing, etc.)

Test Administered
Wechsler Intelligence Scale for Children–Revised Edition (WISC-R)

Identifying Information
Dillon Rader is a 6-year-old black male who arrived late for his scheduled appointment, accompanied by his mother and stepfather. His parents said they are applying for benefits for him because "the school told us he would need some help."

Background Information
Dillon is the middle of five children living with his mother and stepfather. His siblings are 9, 8, almost 5, and almost 4. He was in kindergarten last year, attending resource classes all day. Next school term he will be in "kindergarten and first grade." His parents say he is not a behavior problem, although he talks a lot.

A psychoeducational assessment was done on Dillon in October 1994, when he was 5 years, 6 months old. On the Stanford–Binet, he received a partial composite of 56, which falls in the mentally deficient range. The report states that "this score should be viewed with caution, as Dillon did not follow directions well and tended to answer impulsively." The Columbia Mental Maturity Scale was given on a second date. The Age Deviation score he received was 83. The report states, "This score also is of questionable validity. Dillon often pointed to answers impulsively and some correct responses were made which may have been lucky guesses." On the PPVT-R, he received a standard score of 46.

On the Burks' Behavior Rating Scale, the classroom teacher reported many deficits, including short attention span, poor vocabulary, use of inappropriate responses and unintelligible language, secretly laughing or talking to himself, and lack of interest in classwork of others. On the Vineland completed by the classroom teacher and parent, Dillon received a 69 in the Communication domain, 64 in Daily Living Skills, and 68 in Socialization. His Adaptive Behavior Composite was 64, which falls in the mentally deficient range.

Test Behavior and Results
Dillon presented in a very quiet, but cooperative manner for the testing. He talked somewhat more as the testing went on. He does have speech problems. Although I could understand most of his answers with difficulty, there were a couple of responses I simply could not understand, even after two or three repetitions. I had to give Dillon extra instructions throughout the testing and, even then, he often didn't seem to understand what was required. He sometimes gave strange verbal responses to questions or just repeated what I said.

On Picture Arrangement, he got one item correct on the first try and one correct on the second. However, as in the earlier testing mentioned above, I had the sense that these were probably just random answers which turned out to be right and he didn't actually know what he was rearranging. Thus, I consider his Scaled Score of 8 in Picture Arrangement an overestimation of his ability. With that in mind, his Performance IQ would actually be lower than that shown below. Verbal IQ and Full Scale IQ were not computed because Dillon did not receive above a raw score of 0 on at least 3 Verbal subtests.

The WISC-R scaled scores were as follows:

Verbal Scaled Scores:		*Performance Scaled Scores:*	
Information	2	Picture Completion	1*
Similarities	*	Coding	8
Arithmetic	*	Picture Arrangement	3*
Vocabulary	6	Block Design	6
Comprehension	*	Object Assembly	6
Digit Span	*		
Verbal IQ			
Performance IQ	67		
Full Scale IQ			

*Dillon received a raw score of 0 on these subtests.

These results suggest that Dillon is functioning in the Mentally Deficient range of intellectual functioning.

He showed deficits (SS 6, PR 9 or below) in all areas measured by the test. On Information, he correctly identified a thumb and said a dog had four legs. However, he said he had six ears, that a week has four days, and that "eighth" comes after March. When asked how to make water boil, he said, "the spray." When asked what a baby cow is called, he said, "a baby." When I asked for more information, he said, "a baby cow." On Arithmetic he counted randomly, "1, 2, 3, 8, 9, 10, 15," on the first item. On Vocabulary he knew the meaning of knife and umbrella and gave partially correct answers for bicycle and nail. For "hat," he said, "a hat to rain." For alphabet, he said, "at the store . . . go to the store, get some food." For donkey, he said, "to get some toys." When asked on the Comprehension subtest what to do if he cut his finger, he repeated, "cut your finger." When I asked him repeatedly what *he* would do if he cut his finger, he finally said, "I wouldn't do nothing." He could not repeat 3 digits forward. On Picture Completion he just kept naming the items on the pictures and didn't seem to understand that he was supposed to iden-tify what was missing. On Coding, I had to fold down the top of the form, because he seemed to be quite distracted by the other set of designs.

Adaptive Behavior
It was clear throughout this evaluation that Dillon has deficits in expressive, and probably receptive, communication. His parents say that he is behind his two younger siblings (who are almost 4 and almost 5) in everyday living skills. He can-not tie his shoes, dress himself right, or turn on the television. His parents say that sometimes he understands them at home and sometimes he doesn't. The Burks and the Vineland done on Dillon previously also show that he has significant defi-cits in adaptive behavior.

Summary
Dillon Rader, a 6-year-old student attending special education classes, functioned in the Mentally Deficient range in the current evaluation. He had deficits in adap-tive behavior.

Discussion
This report was somewhat atypical of intellectual assessments, since Verbal and Full Scale IQ scores were not computed on this child. The reasons for this, which are consistent with the testing manual, were quoted in the report.

It is often helpful to quote prior test scores that are available. The previous examiner questioned some of Dillon's scores because of the range they covered. When one score was similarly high in this evaluation, out of keeping with his other scores, it was concluded that this higher score was a chance occurrence. It is always appropriate, and necessary, to comment on the validity of the testing.

As mentioned earlier, the DDS psychological consultants never see the chil-dren that we evaluate. Thus, it is helpful to give them an actual picture of what the child looked and sounded like. In this report, Dillon's enunciation difficulties were commented on and many of his responses were quoted.

Mental status examinations are also occasionally ordered on children. Although they require an estimate of the child's intelligence, this is not the primary purpose of the testing. The purpose is to diagnose a mental disorder, if applicable, and to make comments about daily functioning. Claimants referred for mental status examination are usually alleging some type of behavioral disorder. In these cases, it is important to interview parents. Their statements will go in the reports under the heading of "present illness" or "presenting problem."

Case 36

This is an example of a mental status evaluation on a child whom the parents were stating was "hyper."

Mental Status Examination Report

Name: Ladonna Johnson
(Required identifying information, date of testing, etc.)

General Observations
Ladonna is a 14-year, 4-month-old black female brought to the office by her parents. Her posture and gait were good and she wears glasses. She had good hygiene. Ladonna was relaxed, unafraid, and appropriate.

Present Illness
Ladonna said she had a hole in her heart when she was born and she had surgery when she was a baby. She described herself as "hyper, I can't be still." She said her mother tells her to sit down, but "I can't, I have to move around." She said she talks a lot in school and sometimes acts up in class. The teacher tells her to be quiet, but she said, "I still talk." She is in the eighth grade at Williams Junior High School. She has not been suspended or put out of school this year. She has had some in-school discipline, such as alternative class. She said she is not in resource class and she gets a range of grades from A's to C's.

Mrs. Johnson confirmed Ladonna's congenital heart problem, saying it was repaired by surgery. She also said Ladonna is "hyper." She said her daughter has trouble calming down in school, often will not listen to the teacher, and sometimes skips class. She has never been placed in special education classes. She has no history of psychological treatment.

Ladonna had clear speech. She denied any physical problems or symptoms at this time. She is not taking medication. Mrs. Johnson said Ladonna was evaluated and did take some type of medication for hyperactivity at age 11 or 12, but it was discontinued.

Family, Social, and Environmental History
Ladonna lives with her biological mother and father; she is the only child. Her father works as a janitor and her mother is trying to get a job. Both of her parents appeared to be low functioning. They both agreed that Ladonna and her mother "are like sisters." They get along very well, so there are no behavior problems at home.

Ladonna likes to see friends, talk on the phone, and go to the mall. She has never had trouble with juvenile delinquency. There is essentially no treatment history.

Mental Status Examination
Attitude and Behavior: Ladonna had a very good attitude. She was positive, friendly, relaxed, and personable.

Stream of Mental Activity: She was spontaneous, uninhibited, logical, and well organized.

Thought Control: There were no hallucinations, delusions, suicidal or homicidal ideation. There was no evidence of psychosis or mental illness.

Affect: Her affect was bright and she had a full range of emotions. She was friendly and in no distress.

Intellectual Functioning/Sensorium
Memory: She was oriented to time, place, and person, and in good contact with reality. She repeated 6 digits forward and 3 digits backward.

Information: She was able to say who discovered America, what the stomach does, and what the four seasons are. She could not say in which direction the sun sets, what month has one extra day every four years, who invented the electric light bulb, or from what country America became independent.

Similarities and Differences: She gave partially correct answers to the similarity between beer and wine, cat and mouse, elbow and knee, and telephone and radio.

Calculation: She was unable to do arithmetic problems that were at all complicated. She was able to do single digit arithmetic, such as 3 x 8 and 8 + 6.

Vocabulary: She defined words such as nonsense, gamble, brave, diamond, and join. She understood the meaning of hazardous. She did not understand migrate, stanza, seclude, or mantis.

Comprehension: She knew what to do if she cut her finger and what to do if she found someone's wallet in the store. She understood not to fight if someone smaller than herself started to fight and she knew why a house of brick is better than a house of wood. She could not say why cars have license plates or why letters have stamps. She gave partially correct answers to why criminals are locked up, why the government should inspect meat, and why we have senators.

Estimated IQ: I think she has low intellectual functioning. I would estimate her IQ to be in the low 70's. She may be somewhat overactive, as her parents report, but this may be a symptom of the lower intellectual functioning.

Organic Involvement: There is no organic involvement, other than the probable low intellectual functioning.

Current Level of Functioning
Present Daily Activities: She is very close to her mother, she is well-behaved, and she enjoys talking on the phone and visiting with friends.

Ability to Relate: She has good ability to relate and is friendly and personable. I do not find her to be oppositional or a behavior problem.

Current Medication
None.

Diagnosis
Probably Borderline Intellectual Functioning. Her parents describe her as "hyper," but I do not think she has Attention Deficit–Hyperactivity Disorder, since the probable low intellectual functioning is a more parsimonious explanation.

Prognosis
Her prognosis is good. I think she is able to understand, remember, and carry out very simple, but unskilled instructions. She will eventually need to learn job skills, rather than plan on any higher education. As a minor she cannot handle her own benefits. She and her parents were honest and open about how they experienced this child's behavior. There was no exaggeration or malingering.

Discussion
Although Ladonna's parents alleged that she was "hyper," there was essentially no history of psychiatric or psychological treatment in this case. She was not oppositional or a behavioral problem. She had never been in trouble with the juvenile court system. I did not see her as hyperactive or as having ADD.

In evaluations of children for Social Security disability. I do not take at face value a parent's statement that a child is hyperactive. Various rating forms, such as Conners' Ratings Scales (filled out by both parents and teachers) and computer assessments, such as the Test of Variables of Attention (TOVA) and the Conners' Continuous Performance Test (CPT), are available to assess hyperactivity.

Low intellectual functioning was given as Ladonna's primary diagnosis. In cases such as this, when I have estimated the intelligence to be low, intelligence will need to be assessed further. In all likelihood, DDS will order intellectual testing on this child, possibly with another examiner. However, I did not recommend intellectual testing in my report, since DDS would then be obligated to perform the test, especially if the case went to appeal. The same guideline of not recommending additional testing would also apply if an intellectual assessment showed that the claimant had significant mental health problems. In those cases, the examining psychologist would simply state the full history or behavior that suggested emotional problems, but not recommend a mental status examination in the CE report.

In evaluations of children, DDS will usually limit the CE to a specific test or a mental status examination. An administrative law judge is more likely to order a complete battery for a total reevaluation.

Case 37

This is an example of a claimant who was turned down at the DDS level and was appealing to the law judge. A complete battery of tests was done in this case.

Psychological Evaluation Report

Name: Stacy Russell
(Required identifying information, date of testing, etc.)

Tests Administered

> Wechsler Intelligence Scale for Children–Third Edition (WISC-III)
> Wide Range Achievement Test–Revision 3 (WRAT-3)
> Bender Gestalt Drawings
> Peabody Picture Vocabulary Test–Revised (PPVT-R)
> Visual Aural Digit Span Test (VADS)
> Conners' Parent Rating Scale

Background Information
Stacy is an 8-year, 7-month-old white female brought to the office by her parents. She was a very personable child, well-behaved, and she concentrated well during the testing. When she and her sister were in the waiting room while I talked to her parents, they were both loud and very playful. This would not be unusual behavior for an 8-year-old child in an unsupervised setting with a sibling. When we were face to face and doing the testing for almost two hours, she behaved quite appropriately.

Stacy is taking the following medication: Aerobid, Intal, beclomethasone, methylphenidate (Ritalin) 5 mg BID, and Proventil.

Stacy's parents said she is hyperactive. They reported that she does not focus in school and that she is out of her seat a great deal. She went to summer school last summer to pass to the third grade. She attends special education for reading. Her parents said she plays appropriately for a while, then argues and fights with peers. They said she is uncontrollable at home and "does not mind." They said she whines and "throws fits." They report they have to grab her and sit her down.

Stacy has no history of head injury. Her father says the Ritalin helps. Perhaps it was because she had her medication prior to this evaluation that she was able to concentrate well on the testing.

Test Results
The WISC-III scaled scores were as follows:

Verbal Tests		Performance Tests	
Information	9	Picture Completion	7
Similarities	6	Coding	8
Arithmetic	5	Picture Arrangement	5

Vocabulary	9	Block Design	8
Comprehension	7	Object Assembly	8

Verbal IQ	84
Performance IQ	82
Full Scale IQ	82

According to the *DSM-IV*, her IQ of 82 is in the Borderline range of intellectual functioning at the 12th percentile. I think this is a valid and reliable measure of her ability, which is low average to borderline. She functioned at the 12th percentile overall, but had some subtests in the average range, such as Information and Vocabulary. She did poorly in Similarities, Arithmetic, and Picture Arrangement.

The WRAT-3 scores were good compared to her 82 IQ. For what intellectual ability she has, the academic scores are quite good. The scores were as follows:

	Standard Score	Percentile	Grade Equivalent
Reading	95	37	3
Spelling	87	19	1
Arithmetic	87	19	2

At the present time she is on grade level for reading, but at the 19th percentile for spelling and arithmetic. She may fall further behind as she climbs in grade level.

The PPVT-R score was 77, which is at the 6th percentile. This is roughly equivalent to her IQ score of 82. She had better recognition of vocabulary on the WISC-III than on the PPVT-R.

The Bender Drawings were poorly done. She had 11 errors, placing her at the 5-year level. She shows a deficit with problems in spatial relations.

The VADS percentile scores were as follows:

Aural-Oral	50
Visual-Oral	50
Aural-Written	10
Visual-Written	75
TOTAL VADS	25
Age equivalent: 7–0 to 7–5	

These scores are almost all average. She performed below average, especially when material was presented orally and expressed in written form. She did best when information was presented in a visual format and she could express herself through writing. She is slightly behind in the ability to repeat a series of digits in different modalities, indicating she has some difficulty with attention and memory.

The Conners' Rating Scale was filled out by the parents, so it has to be interpreted cautiously. Stacy was rated extreme in hyperactivity, conduct, learning problems, psychosomatic illness, anxiety, and hyperactivity. The parents also thought she was impulsive. The problem with rating scales is that the parents overendorsed items.

Summary
This is an 8-year-old child who has low intellectual functioning, with an IQ of 82. Her academic ability is a little better than her IQ would suggest. There is little doubt that she is low average to borderline and will struggle in school based on her intellectual ability. She will be at the lowest 10th percentile based on these scores. She has specific problems with visual motor coordination at this time, but this may improve with age. Her performance in this area was depressed because her intellectual ability is in the low average to borderline range. Her academic and intellectual deficits are not due to hyperactivity.

I have no problem with diagnosing her with Attention Deficit–Hyperactivity Disorder NOS (314.9), but I think this is under good control with the medication. The parents even acknowledge that she is much better with the medication and she will probably need to continue on the Ritalin for some time. Her parents seem to have a great deal of concern about her behavior and they probably need parent management training. There was little doubt that the parents were exaggerating her difficulties and much of her behavior was normal for an 8-year-old child. She will probably need some special education assistance.

This child is able to engage in age-appropriate behaviors. I do not think she is emotionally disturbed, but that she has a mild case of ADHD.

Discussion
A diagnosis of ADHD is made for Social Security purposes when all three of the following paragraph A criteria are met: marked inattention, marked impulsivity, and marked hyperactivity. To qualify for disability benefits, two of the paragraph B categories must be present to a "marked" degree of impairment. These are the same paragraph B requirements considered under every mental disorder: marked impairment in age-appropriate cognitive/communication functions, in age-appropriate social functions, in personal/behavioral function, or in concentration, persistence, and pace, resulting in frequent failure to complete tasks in a timely manner.

Stacy was a child who was low average overall. With an IQ of 82 and commensurate academic functioning, she would not necessarily be considered disabled for Social Security purposes. I diagnosed her with ADHD, but she was well-controlled on medication. In spite of the parents' claim that she was a behavior problem, she participated in a two-hour evaluation and did perfectly well. Thus, I did not see sufficient evidence of functional impairment for her to meet the paragraph B criteria.

As in all cases where medication is involved, we are required to pay attention to the effects of medication on the child's symptoms and functioning. Sometimes medication reduces or eliminates most of the symptoms and, therefore, functional capacity is improved. In cases where overt symptomatology is attenuated by psychoactive medications, we must focus on functional limitations which persist and other limitations which are caused by medication side effects. For example, if Stacy had drowsiness, apathy, or depression as a result of the medication, this would have been noted. These factors might have made her eligible for other paragraph

B listings. In her case, the medication seemed to be very positive overall and attenuated the very symptoms which would result in eligibility.

If this mental status examination had been ordered by the DDS office, the issue of functional impairment would have been addressed in the body of the report in narrative form, without the use of any specific ratings. However, when a case such as this is on appeal, the law judge will send an Individual Functional Assessment form on which you are to rate each of the paragraph B criteria. The Individual Functional Assessment form, filled out in this case, is shown below (see Table 7–6).

Stacy was judged to have only moderate limitation in cognitive functions, no evidence of limitation in communicative functions, moderate impairment of motor development and functioning, and no evidence of limitation in social functioning. She had a "less than moderate" impairment in personal/behavioral development and functioning. In this case, I did not state that she had a "marked" impairment in two or more functional areas, therefore my assessment was that she did not meet the paragraph B criteria.

This does not necessarily mean that the judge will deny benefits, since the judge is not bound by the expert's ratings. In this case, the law judge would take this report on Stacy, combine it with other information he has, including testimony which I would not participate in, and make a determination.

Table 7–6. Individual Functional Assessment
Age 3 to Attainment of Age 16

Claimant: _Stacy Russell_____   Social Security Number _____
Assessment is for: [   ] Current Evaluation   [   ] Date 12 Months After Onset _____
                       [   ] Other _____ to _____
A. Identify any medically determinable impairment(s):   _Attention Deficit Hyperactivity Disorder_
_(314.9)_

B. Describe how the impairment(s) affects the child's development and performance of age-appropriate activities in the following domains and behaviors. Summarize the evidence that supports your descriptions of functional limitations. Indicate the level of severity of functional impairment in the developmental domains and behaviors.
1. COGNITIVE DEVELOPMENT/FUNCTION: (Check One)
   [   ] No Evidence of Limitation   [   ] Less Than Moderate   [✓] Moderate
                       [   ] Marked   [   ] Extreme
   There was moderate delay in cognitive ability because she had an 82 IQ.

2. COMMUNICATIVE DEVELOPMENT/FUNCTION: (Check One)
   [✓] No Evidence of Limitation   [   ] Less Than Moderate   [   ] Moderate
                       [   ] Marked   [   ] Extreme
   Communication was excellent.

3. MOTOR DEVELOPMENT/FUNCTION: (Check One)
   [   ] No Evidence of Limitation   [   ] Less Than Moderate   [✓] Moderate
                       [   ] Marked   [   ] Extreme
   There was a moderate visual motor problem, mostly indicated on the Bender.

4. SOCIAL DEVELOPMENT/FUNCTION: (Check One)

   [✓] No Evidence of Limitation   [ ] Less Than Moderate   [ ] Moderate

              [ ] Marked   [ ] Extreme

      Her social development is good and she is a communicative, inquisitive, and appropriate child.

5. PERSONAL/BEHAVIORAL DEVELOPMENT/FUNCTION: (Check One)

   [ ] No Evidence of Limitation   [✓] Less Than Moderate   [ ] Moderate

              [ ] Marked   [ ] Extreme

She does have some behavior problems indicated at home and in school. Her parents likely over-emphasize the problems at home but her school behavior should be checked with the teacher.

Completed By: _____   Date: 3/22/95

8

EDUCATIONAL EVALUATION

Public Law 94–142 requires that children who have handicapping conditions be accommodated by the public school district in the least restrictive environment possible. All states have promulgated regulations to meet these federal requirements. Accommodations might range from indirect services within a regular classroom to partial or complete school days spent in a resource room to placement in a special day or residential school outside of the school district to homebound instruction. Many of these services are expensive and school districts may be reluctant to provide them. Parents and school districts constantly struggle in this area and will sometimes end up in court regarding what services are appropriate.

The handicapping conditions that require special services include autism, deafness and other hearing impairments, blindness and other visual impairments, mental retardation, multiple disabilities, orthopedic impairment, serious emotional disturbance, specific learning disabilities, speech or language impairment, traumatic brain injury, and other health problems. In order to qualify for special education services, the child must not only have a disability, but the disability must have an adverse effect on his or her educational performance. The three handicapping conditions relevant to the psychologist are mental retardation, specific learning disabilities, and serious emotional disturbance (SED).

Private practice psychologists will have opportunities to contract with school districts or regional educational cooperatives to perform these evaluations. Some of the evaluations can be performed by licensed master's-level personnel or technicians working under the supervision of a psychologist. Other evaluations, such as those for serious emotional disturbance, will generally be confined to Ph.D. psychologists or psychiatrists. Larger school districts may employ their own personnel to do evaluations of mentally retarded and learning disabled children, but even in those circumstances they do not usually employ doctoral-level psychologists and will rely on private practitioners to do the less frequent evaluations of SED students.

The role of the examiner in these cases is to do the assessment and submit it to the evaluation committee. This committee is typically made up of the teacher, parents, school counselor, speech therapist, and other appropriate school personnel. The psychologist's report will be just one part of the information that is considered by the committee making the decision about placement. Occasionally the psychologist may be asked to take part in the evaluation committee meeting, although that will be the exception, not the rule. The committee, not the psychologist, will make the determination about primary handicapping condition and will implement an Individual Education Program (IEP) for the student. If the parent does not agree with the findings and the proposal for remediation, the parent can appeal to the principal, then to the school district, and eventually to state and federal court.

THE EVALUATION

Hearing and vision screenings must be completed before any of these evaluations can be done. Certain data are required in each evaluation, whether for mental retardation, specific learning disability, or serious emotional disturbance. These are social history, an intelligence test, an achievement test, an adaptive behavior scale, and a comprehensive language screening measure to assess receptive and expressive language.

The social history required for these evaluations is not the type of detailed psychosocial history typical of mental health patients. It is just a brief background of the child and the child's circumstances.

The intelligence tests that are used in these assessments throughout the country, except perhaps in California, are the Wechsler scales. If a child is 16 or over, my recommendation is to use the WAIS-R, because the student has probably already been tested several times with the WISC-R or WISC-III. We know that the WISC-III is yielding low scores. There might be as much as a 20 point increase in IQ score from the WISC-III to the WAIS-R. For children from ages 4-0 to 6-6, the Wechsler Preschool and Primary Scale of Intelligence–Revised (WPPSI-R) can be used.

At times children with special needs will have to be tested with other tests. These might include the Leiter International Performance Scale (Arthur Adaptation), the McCarthy Scales of Children's Abilities, the Stanford–Binet Intelligence Scale–Fourth Edition, Test of Nonverbal Intelligence, and the Kaufman Assessment Battery for Children.

Although achievement tests will probably be administered by the school, you may be asked to administer additional achievement tests. Rather than giving separate tests for each subject area, it is probably better to administer an achievement battery, such as the Peabody Individual Achievement Test–Revised, the Wechsler Individual Achievement Test, Wide Range Achievement Test–Third Edition, Woodcock–Johnson Psychoeducational Battery–Revised, or Kaufman Test of Educational Achievement.

Adaptive behavior measures might include Adaptive Behavior Inventory, the Adaptive Behavior Inventory for Children, AAMR Adaptive Behavior Scale, Scales of Independent Behavior, the Burks' Behavior Rating Scales, or the Vineland Adaptive Behavior Scales. These will probably be administered by a person well-acquainted with the child, such as the teacher, and you may be simply asked to restate the results in your report.

Tests of receptive language might include the Clinical Evaluation of Language Fundamentals–Revised, the Detroit Test of Learning Aptitude–3, the Fullerton Language Test for Adolescents, the Language Processing Test, the Peabody Picture Vocabulary Test–Revised, the Reynell Developmental Language Scales, or the Test of Language Development, Primary and Intermediate.

MENTAL RETARDATION

The American Association of Mental Retardation (AAMR) defines mental retardation as substantial limitations in present functioning, characterized by subaverage intellectual functioning existing concurrently with related limitations in two or more adaptive skill areas. By their definition, mental retardation exists if the person's intellectual functioning is below an IQ of 70–75, the onset is age 18 or below, and there are adaptive skill deficits. The Wechsler definition of mental retardation begins at an IQ of 69 and the DSM-IV uses a cutoff of 70. Practically speaking, the evaluation committee can assign the label of mental retardation with an IQ as high as 75, if the other conditions are met.

The evaluation for mental retardation must include a functional skills assessment, evaluating the ability of the child to perform the activities required on a daily basis in his or her natural environment. The adaptive skills areas to be considered include communication, self-care, home living, social skills, community use, self-direction, health and safety, functional academics, leisure, and work. Functional skills assessment is based on information obtained from observations and interviews with family members, teachers, related service personnel, and/or the student.

Case 38

This report on a mentally retarded student was submitted in the format required by the regional educational cooperative contracting for the evaluation. Test results were listed in outline form at the beginning of the report and the results of school-administered testing were included in the report.

Comprehensive Evaluation

Name: Grayson Orwell
(Required identifying information, date of testing, etc.)

I. *Intellectual:*
   Wechsler Intelligence Scale for Children–Revised (WISC-R):

Verbal Scaled Scores		*Performance Scaled Scores*	
Information	3	Picture Completion	5
Similarities	4	Picture Arrangement	2
Arithmetic	3	Block Design	4
Vocabulary	3	Object Assembly	5
Comprehension	3	Coding	5
Digit Span	4		
Verbal IQ	58	Performance IQ	63
Full Scale IQ	56	Classification: Mentally Deficient	

II. *Achievement:*
   Woodcock–Johnson Psychoeducational Battery–Revised:

Letter–Word Identification:	GE	2.2	SS	60	PR 0.4
Passage Comprehension:	GE	2.7	SS	68	PR 2.0
BROAD READING CLUSTER:	GE	2.45	SS	59	PR 0.3
Calculation:	GE	3.0	SS	54	PR 0.1
Applied Problems:	GE	3.7	SS	78	PR 7.0
BROAD MATHEMATICS CLUSTER:	GE	3.35	SS	63	PR 1.0
Dictation:	GE	2.0	SS	52	PR 0.1
Writing Samples:	GE	1.4	SS	35	PR 0.1
BROAD WRITTEN LANGUAGE CLUSTER:	GE	1.7	SS	46	PR 0.1

Administered by the school:
Woodcock Reading Mastery Tests–Revised:

Word Identification:	GE	3.2	SS	61	PR <1
Word Attack:	GE	2.4	SS	77	PR 6

Word Comprehension: GE   3.7   SS   75   PR   5
Passage Comprehension: GE   3.0   SS   65   PR   1
TOTAL READING CLUSTER: GE   3.0   SS   66   PR   1

Test of Written Language (TOWL):
Written Language Quotient: 61

KeyMath Diagnostic Arithmetic Test—Revised:
Basic Concepts: GE   6.2   SS   88   PR   21
Operations: GE   4.7   SS   59   PR   <1
Applications: GE   5.8   SS   82   PR   12
Total Test Scores: GE   5.4   SS   74   PR   4

III. Receptive Language Assessment:
Peabody Picture Vocabulary Test—Revised, Form L (PPVT–R):

                                       AE   7–2   SS   52   PR   <1

IV. Adaptive Behavior:
Administered by the school:

Vineland Adaptive Behavior Scales:
Communication Domain: AE   4–6   SS   30   PR   <.01
Daily Living Skills Domain: AE   6–1   SS   36   PR   <.01
Socialization Domain: AE   5–8   SS   51   PR   <.01
Adaptive Behavior Composite: AE   5–5   SS   36   PR   <.01

V. Auditory Processing:
   Visual Aural Digit Span Test (percentile scores):

   Aural-Oral: 10
   Visual-Oral: 10
   Aural-Written: <10
   Visual-Written: <10
   Total VADS Score: <10
   AE of Total VADS Score: 7–0 to 7–5

VI. Visual-Motor Integration:
Bender Gestalt Test:

   Errors: 0
   PR: 70–95
   AE: 11–0 to 11–11

Reason For Referral
Grayson Orwell, a student aged 14–8 in Grade 8.3, was referred to the examiner for a comprehensive evaluation as part of his regular three year review. He was in a self-contained special education program at his previous school.

Social History
There were no significant findings in the student's social, developmental, or medical history, except that the parents report he seemed quicker than average in walking, talking, and coordination. He passed the hearing and vision screens last October.

Adaptive Behavior/Behavioral Observations
Grayson presented in a friendly and cooperative manner and rapport was easily established. He required no special instructions or directions and all test scores are considered valid.

On the Vineland Adaptive Behavior Scales, he scored equivalent to a child aged 4–6 in Communication skills, a child aged 6–1 in Daily Living Skills, and a child aged 5–8 in Socialization skills. Overall, his Adaptive Behavior Composite is equivalent to a child aged 5–5. Thus, he is functioning 9 years and 3 months below his chronological age in adaptive behavior skills.

During the classroom observation, Grayson seemed to be unorganized at the beginning of the task and it took him several minutes to get started. He was also easily distracted by other activity in the classroom. His lack of organization and distractibility were seen as possibly contributing to his low academic functioning. He did participate fairly well in the group discussion. If he gave an incorrect answer, however, his comment was, "I don't care."

Intellectual Ability
The Wechsler Intelligence Scale for Children–Revised (WISC-R) was administered to assess the student's intellectual ability. As measured by that test, Grayson has a Verbal IQ of 58, a Performance IQ of 63, and a Full Scale IQ of 56. This IQ score suggests he is in the Mentally Retarded range of intellectual functioning. On a theoretical normal curve, 2.2 percent of the population would be expected to fall in the Mentally Retarded range and below. He showed deficits (SS 6, PR 9 or below) in all Verbal and Performance areas measured by the test.

Academic Achievement
The Woodcock–Johnson Psychoeducational Battery–Revised was administered to determine progress in broad reading, mathematics, and written language skills. Compared to other students his age, the student scored as follows:

Broad Reading Cluster:	GE	2.45	SS	59	PR	0.3
Broad Mathematics Cluster:	GE	3.35	SS	63	PR	1.0
Broad Written Language Cluster:	GE	1.7	SS	46	PR	0.1

His scores on the Woodcock Reading Mastery Tests–Revised and the Test of Written Language (TOWL) were equally low. He scored somewhat higher on the KeyMath Diagnostic Arithmetic Test–Revised than he did on Broad Mathematics on the Woodcock-Johnson.

Receptive Language
The Peabody Picture Vocabulary Test–Revised (PPVT-R) was administered to assess the student's receptive vocabulary. He scored below the 1st percentile, equivalent to an age of 7–2. In receptive vocabulary he is functioning in the Extremely Low range. His receptive verbal abilities are underdeveloped for his chronological age.

Learning Processes
The Visual Aural Digit Span Test (VADS) was administered to assess intersensory integration, sequencing and recall. Significant weaknesses are indicated in scores which fall at the 10th percentile or below. Using the highest norms available (those for students aged 12), he scored below the 10th percentile. Based on the total VADS score, his intersensory integration, sequencing and recall skills are equivalent to those of a person aged 7–0 to 7–5. As shown by his scores, Grayson has significant difficulty processing and recalling all information.

Visual-Motor Integration
The Bender Gestalt Test was administered to determine the developmental level of the student's visual-motor integration skills. After the age of 10, only children with marked immaturity or malfunction in visual-motor perception will show any significant scores on the Bender. Using the Koppitz scoring method, Grayson obtained no errors. This places him in the 70–95th percentile using the highest norms available (those for students aged 11). In terms of perceptual-motor skills, he functions in the 11–0 to 11–11 age range.

Summary and Recommendations
Grayson Orwell, a student aged 14–8 in Grade 8.3, is functioning in the Mentally Retarded range of intelligence, as evidenced by his Full Scale IQ of 56 on the WISC-R. He shows significant deficits in adaptive behavior, as measured by the Vineland. His receptive vocabulary skills, as measured by the Peabody, are equivalent to a person aged 7–2. He is functioning at the 2.45 grade level in Broad Reading, the 3.35 grade level in Broad Mathematics, and the 1.7 grade level in Broad Written Language skills, as measured by the Woodcock–Johnson. His visual-motor integration skills, as measured by the Bender, are at the 70–95th percentile. His auditory processing skills, as measured by the VADS, are below the tenth percentile.

It is recommended that the Evaluation/Programming committee assign this student to the least restrictive environment to meet his educational needs.

Discussion

All handicapped students are reevaluated every three years to see if their placement is appropriate. This was a straightforward evaluation done on a student who had undoubtedly been in special classes for many years and who would probably continue receiving services at his local school. When students are so mentally handicapped that they cannot attend regular schools, the district usually contracts with an exceptional school for full-time placement.

SPECIFIC LEARNING DISABILITY

A specific learning disability is a disorder of the basic psychological processes involved in understanding or using spoken or written language that may manifest itself in an imperfect ability to listen, think, speak, read, write, spell, or do mathematical calculations. It includes such conditions as perceptual disabilities, brain injury, minimal brain dysfunction, dyslexia, and developmental aphasia. The term does not apply to children who have learning problems that are primarily the result of visual, hearing, or motor disabilities, mental retardation, emotional disturbance, or environmental, cultural, or economic disadvantage.

The definition of learning disability is a vague one. The definition that a particular school district or educational cooperative uses may be supplied to the examiner. This definition, which may change from time to time, usually entails functioning a certain number of grade levels or standard deviations below the norm.

In many students with learning disabilities, intelligence is within the average range, but academic ability is inconsistent, with great variability between expected ability and actual performance. There may also be associated problems with short attention span, inability to concentrate, distraction, disorganization, or inability to follow instructions. Students diagnosed with attention deficit–hyperactivity disorder (ADHD) may be classified as learning disabled for educational purposes.

In addition to the five required areas to be covered in each report, visual and auditory learning processes must be assessed, a written observation must be included, and oral expression, listening comprehension, written expression, basic reading skill, reading comprehension, mathematics calculation, and mathematics reasoning must be assessed. The simplest test for assessing visual perceptual skills is the Bender Visual-Motor Gestalt Test. A measure of auditory perception is the Goldman–Fristoe–Woodcock Test of Auditory Discrimination. A comprehensive evaluation for learning disabilities would include a measure of neuropsychological functioning. This would mean adding the Halstead–Reiten to the test battery, since it is the most comprehensive measure to evaluate problems in receptive ability, processing, and expressive ability. However, this is not likely in the testing done for school districts.

Case 39

This student had both ADHD and learning disabilities. Testing administered by the school was incorporated into the report.

Comprehensive Evaluation

Name: Cody Lawton
(Required identifying information, date of testing, etc.)

Reason For Referral
Cody Lawton, a student aged 8–1 in Grade 2.4, was referred to the examiner for a comprehensive evaluation because his reading level is equivalent to the "end of kindergarten year." It is very difficult for him to distinguish sounds and put them together to form words. The referral information also noted that he is very creative, but that he has a hard time expressing himself in writing.

Social History
There were no significant findings in the student's social or developmental history, except that his parents note that he was "very quick" to talk and walk and had "very developed" coordination. His medical history indicates that he is on Ritalin, 10 mg twice daily, for attention deficit–hyperactivity disorder. He passed the hearing and vision screens last November. He wears glasses.

Adaptive Behavior/Behavioral Observations
Cody was friendly and cooperative during the evaluation and rapport was easily established. He required no special instructions or directions and all test scores are considered valid.

On the Burks' Behavior Rating Scales, he shows the following weaknesses in adaptive behavior: Poor Ego Strength, Poor Intellectuality, Poor Academics, Poor Attention, and Poor Impulse Control.

Intellectual Ability
The Wechsler Intelligence Scale for Children–Revised (WISC-R) was administered. He obtained the following scaled scores:

Verbal Scaled Scores		*Performance Scaled Scores*	
Information	11	Picture Completion	16
Similarities	9	Picture Arrangement	13
Arithmetic	7	Block Design	12
Vocabulary	13	Object Assembly	8
Comprehension	12	Coding	6
Digit Span	6		

| Verbal IQ | 102 | Performance IQ | 106 |
| Full Scale IQ | 104 | Classification: Average | |

This Full Scale IQ of 104 places him in the Average range of intellectual function-ing. There was considerable scatter in his subtest scores. He showed deficits (SS 6, PR 9 or below) in Digit Span (attention, concentration, rote and immediate memory, sequencing) and Coding (speed and accuracy of learning meaningless symbols, immediate visual memory, motor coordination.)

He showed strength (SS 12–13, PR 75–84) in Vocabulary (word knowledge, verbal fluency, receptive and expressive vocabulary), Comprehension (practical knowledge and social judgment, reasoning, logical solutions), Picture Arrangement (interpretation of social situations, sequencing, visual alertness), and Block De-sign (ability to reproduce a design from a pattern, visual perception). He showed superior ability (SS 16, PR 98) in Picture Completion (visual memory, alertness to details).

Academic Achievement
The Woodcock–Johnson Psychoeducational Battery–Revised was administered to determine his progress in broad reading, mathematics, and written language skills. Compared to other students his age, he scored as follows:

Broad Reading Cluster:	GE	1.65	SS	86	PR	18
Broad Mathematics Cluster:	GE	1.9	SS	88	PR	21
Broad Written Language Cluster:	GE	1.5	SS	86	PR	17

In Broad Reading, Broad Written Language, and Calculation, he is function-ing below the level that would be expected of a student of his intellectual level.

He was also administered the Woodcock Reading Mastery Tests–Revised. Total reading cluster scores were as follows: GE 1.4 SS 78 PR 7.

On the KeyMath Diagnostic Arithmetic Test–Revised, he obtained the fol-lowing total test scores: AE 6–11 SS 83 PR 13.

These tests confirm the difficulties that he had in reading and mathematical skills on the Woodcock–Johnson.

Receptive Language
The Peabody Picture Vocabulary Test–Revised (PPVT-R) was administered to assess receptive vocabulary. His scores were:

Standard Score: 112
Percentile Rank: 79
Age Equivalent: 9–5

In receptive vocabulary he is functioning in the High Average range.

Learning Processes
The Visual Aural Digit Span Test (VADS) was administered to assess intersensory integration, sequencing, and recall. Significant weaknesses are indicated in scores which fall at the 10th percentile or below. His percentile scores were as follows:

Aural-Oral:	10–25	Aural Input:	10
Visual-Oral:	25–50	Visual Input:	25
Aural-Written:	10–25	Oral Expression:	10–25
Visual-Written:	25	Written Expression:	25

Total VADS Score: 10–25

Based on the total VADS score, his intersensory integration, sequencing and recall skills are equivalent to those of a child aged 6–9 to 6–11. As shown by his scores, Cody has difficulty processing and recalling information. He does somewhat better when he can see the information presented, rather than just hearing it.

Auditory Discrimination
On the Wepman Auditory Discrimination Test, he showed adequate development.

Visual-Motor Integration
The Bender Gestalt Test was administered to determine the developmental level of Cody's visual-motor integration skills. After the age of 10, only children with marked immaturity or malfunction in visual-motor perception will show any significant scores on the Bender. Using the Koppitz scoring method, he obtained 5 errors. This places him in the 40th percentile for his chronological age. In terms of perceptual-motor skills, he functions in the 7–6 to 7–11 age range.

Summary and Recommendations
Cody Lawton, a student aged 8–1 in Grade 2.4, is functioning in the Average range of intelligence, as evidenced by his Full Scale IQ of 104 on the WISC-R. His receptive vocabulary skills, as measured by the Peabody, are in the High Average range. He is functioning at the 1.65 grade level in Broad Reading, the 1.9 grade level in Broad Mathematics, and the 1.5 grade level in Broad Written Language skills, as measured by the Woodcock–Johnson. In Broad Reading, Broad Written Language, and Calculation, he is functioning below the level that would be expected of a student of his intellectual level. His visual-motor integration skills, as measured by the Bender, are at the 40th percentile. His auditory processing skills, as measured by the VADS, are at the 10–25th percentile. On the Burks', he shows weaknesses in several areas of adaptive behavior, including attention.

   It is recommended that the Evaluation/Programming committee assign this student to the least restrictive environment to meet his educational needs. Cody still shows deficits in attention, despite being on medication. Consequently, the committee may wish to recommend that he receive further medical evaluation to make sure his dosage is adequate and/or that Cody be taught cognitive methods to help him focus his attention better.

Discussion
This student showed a tremendous amount of scatter in his WISC-R subtest scores, which is not uncommon in students with learning disabilities. The school district requesting this examination furnished a list of standard scores that students of each IQ level would be expected to obtain on academic tests, as well as the standard score at which the student would be considered to have a learning disability. That listing was used to determine in which areas this student was functioning "below the level that would be expected of a student of his intellectual level." With other school districts, the psychologist might have been able to use more independent judgment in deciding whether this student had specific learning disabilities.

Other recommendations were made in the report regarding Cody's ADHD and medication levels. Since school districts are bound by what is put in reports, this report did not state that the committee had to send Cody for a follow-up medical exam or send him to counseling to learn cognitive skills, but simply stated that the committee might wish to consider those measures.

SERIOUS EMOTIONAL DISTURBANCE

A serious emotional disturbance is defined as:

1. An inability to learn that cannot be explained by intellectual, sensory, or health factors,
2. An inability to build or maintain satisfactory interpersonal relationships with peers and teachers,
3. Inappropriate types of behavior or feelings under normal circumstances,
4. A general pervasive mood of unhappiness or depression, or
5. A tendency to develop physical symptoms or fears associated with personal or school problems.

The behavior must be exhibited over a long period of time and to a marked degree that adversely affects the child's educational performance. This does not include children who are socially maladjusted, unless it is determined that they have a Serious Emotional Disturbance (SED).

In diagnosing SED, there must be a failure to achieve academically that cannot be attributed to one of the other handicapping conditions, truancy, or lack of motivation. There must be a disturbance in mood, inappropriate behavior related to the mental disorder or neurotic complaints, deficits in interpersonal ability, and deficiencies in self-concept and self-esteem. Communication is impaired and there may be somatic preoccupation.

Although a label of SED is not a psychiatric diagnosis, SED students are children who have genuine emotional disturbances and are therefore not able to learn. An example might be a child who is so depressed and despondent that he cannot go to school, or, if he does attend, cannot concentrate or do his work. Another example might be a child with a serious anxiety disorder or one who has a schizotypal or schizoid personality. Children who are schizophrenic would certainly qualify for SED. Autism is a separate handicapping condition from SED.

In practice, very few children will be diagnosed with SED, since behavior disorders, oppositional defiant disorder, conduct disorder, antisocial behavior, truancy, and delinquency are all excluded. Some school districts may fight labeling students as Seriously Emotionally Disturbed, because the schools do not have adequate placements for SED students. If a child is determined to be SED, the Individual Education Program could require almost anything, from outpatient psychotherapy to education in an institutional setting. If the student is placed in a residential psychiatric treatment facility, the local school district is responsible for the educational portion of the inpatient placement.

The evaluation for SED must include the same elements found in the earlier evaluations, with the addition of the clinical diagnosis of Serious Emotional Disturbance by a licensed psychologist or psychiatrist. (The definition of the mental health professional providing the diagnosis may vary from state to state.) Behavioral observation of the student in a variety of settings is also required.

When you perform an SED evaluation, the basic testing will probably already have been completed. Therefore, you will have access to the intelligence testing, academic measurements, and other required assessment instruments. Your evaluation can use any combination of tests or no tests at all. The psychologist's diagnosis of SED or the suggestion of SED as a handicapping condition is what the committee needs. There is no formula for this. In making this diagnosis, you need to make sure that the child is truly SED and cannot achieve in school because of the emotional disturbance. The goal is to find a way to accommodate the disability so that the child can learn, as it is with any handicapping condition.

Case 40

This evaluation was requested by a school district on a child who was already diagnosed as learning disabled. This student had been diagnosed as SED three years prior to this report.

Psychological Evaluation

Name: Leonard Walker
(Required identifying information, date of testing, etc.)

Tests Administered

Minnesota Multiphasic Personality Inventory (MMPI)
House–Tree–Person Drawings
Incomplete Sentences Blank
Beck Depression Inventory
Carlson Psychological Survey (CPS)
Thematic Apperception Test (TAT)
Hand Test
Clinical Interview

Clinical Interview
Leonard is a 16-year, 9-month-old white male who was reevaluated for Special Education. When I evaluated him three years ago, I found him to have a Schizotypal Personality Disorder, in addition to his already diagnosed learning disability. He has average intelligence, but severe deficits in academic ability. He is now in the tenth grade and has remediation for math and English and mainstream instruction in other classes. He is continuing to see the school counselor and, according to the records, his adjustment is about the same as it was in junior high school.

Leonard was cooperative during the testing. He has very long hair and this appeared to be very important to him. He is living with his mother and 18-year-old brother. His parents have been divorced all of his life and his mother is working. He does not seem to get along with his brother and wishes his brother were out of the home. When I asked Leonard about his academic problems, he blamed the teachers and said he gets discouraged easily. He said he is slow, referring to his learning disability. He said his behavior has been good and that he has had no suspensions or discipline. In the eleventh and twelfth grades he hopes to take drafting, more science, and possibly vocational education.

Leonard is an avoidant person, as he was three years ago. He is very careful to avoid anything he considers stressful. He said he did not want to take a job or work at a fast-food restaurant because he is learning disabled. He also said he hoped to be a pilot, as well as an engineer designing and building airplanes. Thus, on one hand, he uses his learning problems as an reason not to do things and, on the other hand, he considers himself to be very capable and able to be a pilot or engineer. When I confronted him about this, he said he will somehow get around his reading difficulty. Given both his learning disability and his emotional problems, this is extremely unrealistic and shows that he is narcissistic and uninsightful. His counselor and teachers, who have been dealing with his unrealistic self-appraisal, say it is very difficult to lower his expectations about his ability. Leonard said he gets along with friends, but he gave few details about his relationships. He said he dates girls, but again he could not give many details. I believe his social activity is actually very limited and that he has almost no social activity away from school. He does not drive, does not attend any activities, and finally admitted, "What they find exciting is boring to me," referring to social activities. He denied feeling depressed or uncomfortable with himself. He is a very well defended and insulated young man who does not acknowledge some of the problems so obvious to others.

Test Results
Leonard reported feelings of well-being and denied depression on the Beck Depression Inventory. His MMPI scores were high on Scales F and 8. He has unusual thoughts and attitudes, very poor judgment, and beliefs which are unrealistic. He has a schizoid lifestyle, feels he is not part of his social environment, and is alienated, isolated, and misunderstood. He is withdrawn, seclusive, secretive, and inaccessible. He avoids dealing with people and with new situations. He is described by others as shy, aloof, and uninvolved. He misrepresents his accomplishments and, at some level, he believes his fantasies. (For example, he said he was a black belt, but gave no verifying details about this.) He is difficult to redirect, is resistant, and does not have much respect for authority. He has little responsibility and very low motivation. He blames others for his problems and avoids any discussion of his problems or limitations. His typical response to stress is to withdraw into daydreams and fantasies. He has a hard time separating reality from fantasy. He is plagued by feelings of inferiority, incompetence, and dissatisfaction, but he rarely faces this. He is nonconforming, unusual, unconventional, stubborn, moody, and opinionated. His prognosis for therapy is poor, because he is reluctant to relate in any meaningful way to a therapist.

On the CPS he endorsed several antisocial items. He does not trust anyone and he believes other people are against him. On the House–Tree–Person Drawings, he drew a stick figure for a person. He has low self-esteem and strong feelings of insecurity. His spelling on the Sentences was extremely poor. He has a difficult time writing a coherent sentence. He said he wanted to know more about space, that he regrets nothing, and that he is annoyed by gun control. He mentioned gun control several times on the test.

On the TAT he was very uncomfortable with interpersonal themes, especially anything denoting heterosexual relationships. He had several aggressive responses on the TAT, indicating that he probably has a lot of violent mentation.

Summary And Recommendations
Leonard has a Learning Disorder NOS (315.90) for all academic areas and he continues to have a Schizotypal Personality Disorder (301.22). His educational performance is adversely affected by his learning disability and secondarily affected by his emotional disturbance. He has almost no ability to build and maintain satisfactory interpersonal relationships with peers and teachers. He is fearful and avoidant of any pressure and resorts to his "disability" to avoid stress. He is unrealistic, has very poor judgment, and is somewhat narcissistic and delusional about his own ability. He does not have a pervasive mood of unhappiness or depression and, in fact, has an elevated sense of well-being. It is likely that Leonard will need continued services for the remaining high-school years. I certainly recommend that he receive some vocational training and practical on-the-job experience in the elev-

enth and twelfth grades. He has a severe personality disorder and, in my opinion, continues to be Seriously Emotionally Disturbed.

Discussion
In this case, both the *DSM-IV* diagnoses and the educational diagnosis of Seriously Emotionally Disturbed were given in the report. It is doubtful that this student would receive any extraordinary educational measures. He was already receiving resource education for his learning disability, which provided smaller classes and individual attention. Often the same measures taken for a learning-disabled child are effective for an SED child. It is not unusual for a self-contained classroom to include one or two SED students and students with other learning or behavioral problems. In some districts, there might even be mentally retarded children in the self-contained classroom. That is not an ideal situation, but, as psychologists, our job is to do the assessments, identify the children who need services, and leave the rest to the school.

Psychologists in the community have a certain amount of power that comes with the written report and it is important that this power not be abused. It is not uncommon for psychologists treating children to write uninvited reports to the school districts saying that the children have learning disabilities or are SED and require special education services. These psychologists do not understand the process that is required to determine a handicapping condition. Because of the procedures a school district must go through to meet legal requirements, it is only appropriate to write these reports when a school or educational cooperative has contracted with you to do such assessments.

9

FINAL DOS AND DON'TS

The practice of forensic psychology is perhaps the most open and public specialty of the mental health specialties. Since the work of the forensic psychologist is to produce a report that is by its very nature public, everything a forensic psychologist does is subject to evaluation. This can work to your benefit. If you are doing objective work for a finder of facts and your conclusions are reasonable and rational, your reputation will be enhanced. You will be able to build a successful practice doing work that is immensely gratifying.

What follows are fifty "dos and don'ts" of forensic practice:

1. Don't accept work from one side, whether it is a defense lawyer, the lawyer for a parent in a custody case, a claimant for Social Security, or any other litigant.
2. Do accept forensic referrals from finders of fact, including judges, state departments of mental health and human services, school districts, and adversarial parties who agree on one psychologist and one evaluation.
3. Do use technicians and psychological assistants. It is almost impossible to be a forensic psychologist if you are administering one IQ test after another.
4. Do complete reports in a timely fashion and meet all the requirements for court dates. The report is worthless if it arrives after a court disposition.
5. Don't charge unreasonable fees.
6. Don't allow clients to owe money after an evaluation has been completed. You won't appear to be unbiased if one of the litigants owes money that you have to collect after you render an opinion.

7. Do ask for background information, especially police reports in criminal cases.

8. Do ask for access to any person who is needed to complete the evaluation, such as children, grandparents, or other important persons in custody cases.

9. Do make specific recommendations and, in most cases, answer the ultimate question in the evaluation.

10. Don't try to please everyone when you prepare your report or testify in court. In most cases there will be a winner and a loser, and your report and testimony will support one side or the other.

11. Do dress conservatively when you testify in court.

12. Don't wait outside a courtroom all day. Have the attorneys call your office when they are ready for your testimony.

13. Don't exaggerate or mislead the judge about your qualifications as an expert. Don't testify about matters in which you have no expertise.

14. Do answer specific questions you are asked on the stand. If you wish to elaborate on an answer, ask if you may explain.

15. Don't refuse to answer a question in court because of confidentiality or privilege. If you have concerns about privilege and the lawyers don't object to the question, address your concerns to the judge and let him/her decide.

16. Don't get angry, argumentative, sarcastic, contentious, or arrogant on the stand. Be professional and ready to defer to the legal process.

17. Do present yourself as confident and knowledgeable on the stand. Don't back down on your findings. Defend your results confidently, knowing that your procedures are accepted standards of psychological practice.

18. Do state that your conclusion took into account all the facts of the case and was based on your overall clinical judgment, not on the results of one assessment tool.

19. Don't be intimidated by questions about things you didn't do in the evaluation. Be as thorough as you can be, realizing that there will always be more you could have done.

20. Don't allow a lawyer to undermine your conclusions by presenting factual information that is new to you. If the information is significant and you did not know about it, you will need to reexamine the parties to reassess the information.

21. Don't worry about what other professionals may testify to in a particular case. Give your testimony and go back to your office. The lawyers and finders of fact will appreciate your findings if you have a reputation for doing competent, objective work.

22. Do make specific recommendations for dispositions of juveniles. Reports with long discussions of psychodynamics and no referral recommendations are worthless to the court.

23. Do interview the parents of a juvenile, even if it has to be by telephone.

24. Don't think that juvenile delinquents are all victims of circumstances or have underlying mental illness to explain their crimes.

25. Do realize that juvenile delinquents can and do have psychopathic and antisocial character disorders, just as adults do. Antisocial adults were once adolescents.

26. Do try to separate juvenile delinquents into appropriate categories: those with psychiatric and emotional problems, those who are mentally retarded, or those with character disorders.

27. Don't automatically think that a juvenile committed the offense because of substance abuse. Almost every delinquent uses alcohol or other drugs and you must separate the juveniles with legitimate substance abuse problems from those whose substance usage is one component of a conduct disorder.

28. Don't classify a juvenile offender as one who needs sex offender treatment if the sexual offense is symptomatic of an antisocial personality, if the offense was particularly vicious, or if it was one among many other offenses.

29. Do recommend sex offender treatment if the overall personality appears to be inadequate, the victim is young, there are no other criminal behaviors, and there is a history of victimization of the offender.

30. Don't be persuaded by exotic claims of mental illness in competency and responsibility evaluations. Posttraumatic stress disorder, blackouts, ingestion of alcohol or drugs, sleepwalking, multiple personalities, and endless other excuses are not the legal standard for determining competency or responsibility.

31. Do remember that in the absence of psychosis, moderate to severe mental retardation, or dementia, most defendants will be judged competent and responsible.

32. Don't state that a defendant is competent or responsible when testifying in court. State whether the defendant is capable of cooperating with an attorney in his defense (competency) and if the defendant had the capacity to appreciate the criminality of his conduct and to conform his conduct to the requirements of the law (responsibility).

33. Do state that a defendant is competent or responsible in your written report.

34. Do make specific recommendations for custody and visitation in custody cases.

35. Don't accept at face value what one side alleges about the other side in a custody dispute. Always see both parents.

36. Don't have a bias toward the mother or father in custody cases. Draw your conclusions based only on the best interest of the child, realizing that in some cases both parents will be inadequate and in other cases both will be excellent parents.

37. Don't feel guilty about your decisions in custody cases. You are not responsible for the parents' decision to divorce.

38. Don't expect to get much useful information from an interview with a child under the age of 6 in a custody dispute. These children have often been programmed and pulled back and forth between parents.

39. Do give great weight to the test data (such as high MMPI scores) in custody disputes.

40. Don't mix therapy with custody evaluations. Perform the custody evaluation and let someone else do the therapy and treatment. There will almost certainly be additional court involvement.

41. Do be extremely suspicious when sexual allegations are raised in the middle of a custody battle. There will be no shortage of cases in which this allegation is made right at the time of the custody dispute.

42. Do be suspicious of reports of sexual abuse when the child is very young and the case is vigorously pursued by a neurotic, histrionic mother.

43. Do include projective testing in difficult sexual abuse evaluations. Some clients can look fairly normal on objective testing, yet very pathological on projective testing.

44. Don't answer the ultimate question of whether claimants are disabled in Social Security disability cases. Do answer the questions posed to you, such as whether a claimant is able to understand, remember, and follow simple, detailed, or complex instructions.

45. Do review previous mental health and medical records of Social Security claimants.

46. Do suspect that every client for a Social Security disability determination evaluation is amplifying, exaggerating, or even faking symptoms. As you proceed through the evaluation and analyze the data, the hypothesis of faking or exaggerating can be disproved.

47. Do use the Computerized Assessment of Response Bias, Revised Edition (CARB), the PPVT–R, or other instruments to detect malingering when IQ or neuropsychological test results are extremely impaired. This will ensure that your results are valid.

48. Don't interpret MMPIs and other objective instruments for Social Security claimants at face value. Social Security claimants with no history of mental health treatment often produce MMPIs that exceed the disturbance level of documented psychiatric patients.

49. Don't accept at face value that a minor child for a Social Security disability evaluation is hyperactive because the parent says so. Administer tests and rating forms to assess hyperactivity.

50. Don't be discouraged by the very difficult questions with which you will be confronted every day in forensic practice. Forensic psychology provides services that psychologists are uniquely qualified to perform. If you choose to work in this specialty, you will be making a valuable contribution to family and criminal law.

ORDERING INFORMATION

THE PSYCHOLOGICAL CORPORATION
Harcourt Brace and Co.
555 Academic Court
San Antonio, TX 78204–2498
1-800-228-0752

Adaptive Behavior Inventory for Children
Bayley Infant Neurodevelopment Screener
Bayley Scale of Infant Development–Second Edition
Beck Depression Inventory
Children's Depression Inventory
Children's Personality Questionnaire
Clinical Evaluation of Language Fundamentals–Revised
Incomplete Sentences Blank–Adult Form
Incomplete Sentences Blank–High School Form
McCarthy Scales of Children's Abilities
Mooney Problem Check List–Adult Form
Mooney Problem Check List–High School Form
Thematic Apperception Test (TAT)
Visual Aural Digit Span Test (VADS)
Wechsler Adult Intelligence Scale–Revised (WAIS-R)
Wechsler Individual Achievement Test (WAIT)
Wechsler Intelligence Scale for Children–Revised (WAIS-R)

Wechsler Intelligence Scale for Children–Third Edition (WISC-III)
Wechsler Memory Scale

WESTERN PSYCHOLOGICAL SERVICES
12031 Wilshire Blvd.
Los Angeles, CA 90025–1251
1-800-648-8857 or 1-310-478-7838 FAX

Adaptive Behavior Scale
Burks' Behavior Rating Scale
Competency to Stand Trial Evaluations
Hand Test
House–Tree–Person Drawings
Luria-Nebraska Neuropsychological Battery
Reynell Developmental Language Scale
Test of Language Development–Primary and Intermediate
Wide Range Achievement Test–Revised
Wide Range Achievement Test–Third Edition

PSYCHOLOGICAL ASSESSMENT RESOURCES, INC.
P. O. Box 998
Odessa, FL 33556
1-800-331-8378

AAMR Adaptive Behavior Scale
Bender Gestalt Drawings
Carlson Psychological Survey
Detroit Test of Learning Aptitude–Third Edition
Leiter International Performance Scale (Arthur Adaptation)
Rorschach Ink Blots
Test of Nonverbal Intelligence
Wide Range Achievement Test–Third Edition
Wonderlic Personnel Test

AMERICAN GUIDANCE SERVICE
4201 Woodland Road
P. O. Box 99
Circle Pines, MN 55014-1796
1-800-328-2560

Goldman–Fristoe–Woodcock Test of Auditory Discrimination
Kaufman Assessment Battery for Children (K-ABC)

Kaufman Test of Educational Achievement (K-TEA)
Peabody Individual Achievement Test–Revised (PIAT-R)
Peabody Picture Vocabulary Test–Revised (PPVT-R)
Vineland Adaptive Behavior Scale

NCS ASSESSMENTS
P. O. Box 1416
Minneapolis, MN 55440
1-800-627-7271

Millon Adolescent Clinical Inventory (MACI)
Millon Adolescent Personality Inventory (MAPI)
Millon Clinical Multiaxial Inventory (MCMI, MCMI-II, MCMI-III)
Minnesota Multiphasic Personality Inventory (MMPI, MMPI-2)
Minnesota Multiphasic Personality Inventory–Adolescent Form (MMPI-A)

RIVERSIDE PUBLISHING CO.
8420 Bryn Mawr Ave.
Chicago, IL 60631
1-800-767-8378

Battelle Developmental Inventory
Scales of Independent Behavior
Stanford-Binet Intelligence Scale–Fourth Edition
Woodcock–Johnson Psycho-Educational Battery–Revised

REITAN NEUROPSYCHOLOGICAL LABORATORY
2920 South 4th Avenue
Tucson, AZ 85713-4819
1-520-882-2022

Aphasia Screening Test
Halstead Category Test
Halstead–Reitan Neuropsychological Test Battery

A.D.D. WAREHOUSE
300 Northwest 70th Ave., Suite 102
Plantation, FL 33317
1-800-233-9273

Conners' Ratings Scales
Conners' Continuous Performance Test (CPT)
Test of Variables of Attention (TOVA)

MULTI-HEALTH SYSTEMS, INC.
908 Niagara Falls Blvd.
North Tonawanda, NY 14120-2060
1-800-456-3003 or 1-416-424-1700

Conners' Rating Scales
Jesness Inventory

PRO ED
8700 Shoal Creek Blvd.
Austin, TX 78757-6897
1-512-451-3246 or 1-512-451-8542 FAX

Children's Apperception Test (CAT)
Fullerton Language Test for Adolescents

LINGUISYSTEMS, INC.
716 17th St.
Moline, IL 61265
1-800-776-4332 or 1-309-755-2300

Language Processing Test

COGNISYST, INC.
3937 Nottaway Rd.
Durham, NC 27707
1-800-799-4654

Computerized Assessment of Response Bias, Revised Edition (CARB)

SOCIAL SECURITY DISABILITY
OFFICE OF PUBLIC INQUIRIES
4100 Annex Building
6401 Security Blvd.
Baltimore, MD 21235
1-410-965-7700

Disability Evaluation under Social Security (SSA Publication No. 64–039)

SUGGESTED READING

Applebaum, G. (1992). Identification of perpetrators of child sexual abuse by nonleading techniques used with the alleged victim. *American Journal of Forensic Psychology* 10:49–56.

Blau, T. (1984). *The Psychologist as Expert Witness*. New York: Wiley.

Brodsky, S. (1991). *Testifying in Court*. Washington, DC: American Psychological Association.

Campbell, T. (1992a). False allegations of sexual abuse II: case example of a criminal defense. *American Journal of Forensic Psychology* 10(4):37–48.

———— (1992b). False allegations of sexual abuse and the persuasiveness of play therapy. *Issues in Child Abuse Accusations* 4:118–124.

———— (1992c). False allegations of sexual abuse and their apparent credibility. *American Journal of Forensic Psychology* 10:21–35.

———— (1992d). The "highest level of psychological certainty": betraying standards of practice in forensic psychology. *American Journal of Forensic Psychology* 10(2):35–48.

———— (1992e). Promoting play therapy: marketing dream or empirical nightmare. *Issues in Child Abuse Accusations* 4:111–117.

Curran, W., McGarry, A., and Shah, S., eds. (1986). *Forensic Psychiatry and Psychology*. Philadelphia: F.A. Davis.

Doris, J., ed. (1991). *The Suggestibility of Children's Recollections*. Washington, DC: American Psychological Association.

Erving, C., ed. (1985). *Psychology, Psychiatry and the Law*. Sarasota, FL: Professional Resume Exchange.

Faust, D., and Ziskin, J. (1988). The expert witness in psychology and psychiatry. *Science* 241:31–35.

Freedman, M., Rosenberg, S., Gettman-Felzien, D., and Van Scoyk, S. (1993). Evaluator countertransference in child custody evaluations. *American Journal of Forensic Psychology* 11(3):61–73.

Grisso, T. (1988). *Competence to Stand Trial Evaluations: A Manual for Practice*. Sarasota, FL.: Professional Resource Exchange.

Hambacher, W. (1994). Expert witnessing: guidelines and practical suggestions. *American Journal of Forensic Psychology* 12:17–35.

Happel, R., and Auffrey, J. (1995). Sex offender assessment: interrupting the dance of denial. *American Journal of Forensic Psychology* 13(2):5–22.

Lanyon, R. (1993). Assessment of truthfulness in accusations of child molestations. *American Journal of Forensic Psychology* 11:29–44.

Loftus, E. (1993). The reality of repressed memories. *American Psychologist* 48:518–537.

Long, D., and DeVault, S. (1992). Juvenile offenders: case studies and issues in the process of waiver. *American Journal of Forensic Psychology* 10:5–18.

Maloney, M. (1985). *A Clinician's Guide to Forensic Psychological Assessment*. New York: Free Press.

Melton, G., Petrilu, J., Paythress, N., and Slobogin, C. (1987). *Psychological Evaluations for the Courts*. New York: Guilford.

Meyer, R., Landis, E., and Hays, J. (1988). *Law for the Psychotherapist*. New York: Norton.

Monahan, J. (1981). *Predicting Violent Behavior*. Beverly Hills, CA: Sage.

Morrison, M. (1994). The use of psychological tests to detect malingered intellectual impairment. *American Journal of Forensic Psychology* 12:47–64.

Pinkerton, J., Haynes, J., and Keiser, T. (1993). Characteristics of psychological practice in juvenile court clinics. *American Journal of Forensic Psychology* 11:3–12.

Pope, K., Butcher, J., and Seele, J. (1993). *The MMPI, MMPI-2, and MMPI-A in Court: A Practical Guide for Expert Witnesses and Attorneys*. Washington, DC: American Psychological Association.

Rogers, R., Bagley, R., and Perera, C. (1993). Can Ziskin withstand his own criticisms? Problems with his model of cross-examination. *Behavior Sciences and the Law* 11:223–233.

Weiner, J., and Wettstein, R. (1993). *Legal Issues in Mental Health Care*. New York: Plenum.

Williams, L., and Finkelhor, D. (1990). The characteristics of incestuous fathers: a review of recent studies. In *Handbook of Sexual Assault*, ed. W. Marshall, D. Laws, and H. Barbaree, pp. 231–256. New York: Plenum.

Ziskin, J. (1981). *Coping with Psychiatric and Psychological Testimony*, 3rd ed. Venice, CA: Law and Psychology Press.

——— (1993). Ziskin can withstand his own criticisms: a response to Rogers, Bagley, and Perera. *American Journal of Forensic Psychology* 11:17–34.

LANDMARK LEGAL DECISIONS

COMPETENCY TO STAND TRIAL:

Drope v. Missouri, 420 U.S. 162 (1975).
Dusky v. U.S., 362 U.S. 402 (1960).
Jackson v. Indiana, 406 U.S. 715 (1972).
Wilson v. U.S., 391 F. 2d 460 (D.C. Cir. 1968).

CRIMINAL RESPONSIBILITY:

Durham v. U.S., 214 F. 2d 862 (1954).
Insanity Defense Reform Act, 18 U.S.C. 402 (1984).
McNaughten's Rule, 8 Eng. Rep. 718 (1843).
U.S. v. Browner, 471 F. 2d 969 (D.C. Cir. 1972).
U.S. v. Currens, 290 F. 2d 751 (3rd Cir. 1961).

JUVENILE CASES:

In re Gault, 387 U.S. 1 (1967).
Kent v. U.S., 383 U.S. 541 (1966).
Painter v. Bannister, 258 Iowa 1390, 140 NW 2d 152 (1966).

EXPERT TESTIMONY:

Frye v. U.S., 293 F. 1013 (D.C. Cir. 1923).
Jenkins v. U.S., 307 F. 2d 637 (D.C. Cir. 1961).

INDEX